Robert Weatherley · Qiang Zhang

History and Nationalist Legitimacy in Contemporary China

A Double-Edged Sword

palgrave
macmillan

Robert Weatherley
University of Cambridge
Cambridge, UK

Qiang Zhang
University of Oxford
Oxford, UK

ꜝ

ISBN 978-1-137-47946-4   ISBN 978-1-137-47947-1   (eBook)
DOI 10.1057/978-1-137-47947-1

Library of Congress Control Number: 2017939328

Cover illustration: © Fatima Jamadar

Printed on acid-free paper

This Palgrave Macmillan imprint is published by Springer Nature
The registered company is Macmillan Publishers Ltd.
The registered company address is: The Campus, 4 Crinan Street, London, N1 9XW, United Kingdom

To Douglas Weatherley and Zhang Baoxin

ACKNOWLEDGEMENTS

Many thanks to Shaun Breslin (Warwick University) for his excellent feedback on the various drafts of this book. Thanks also to the families of the two authors for their support and patience.

CONTENTS

CHAPTER 1

Introduction

Visitors to China will find it hard to avoid the level of patriotism that permeates just about every aspect of Chinese society. Chinese national flags are ubiquitous, whether on street corners, in apartment or shop windows or for sale in popular tourist destinations. Every morning at sunrise, hundreds of hardy Chinese tourists and locals gather in Beijing's Tiananmen Square for the daily flag raising ceremony under the auspices of the People's Liberation Army (PLA) elite honour guard. Seemingly apolitical government campaigns are often linked to the welfare of the nation, particularly patriotic health campaigns propagated on public notice boards or in public lavatories. Museums and other patriotic education bases commemorating Chinese wars of liberation or the revolutionary struggle of the ruling Chinese Communist Party (CCP) can be found throughout the country.

But even for those people who have never visited China, the extent of Chinese nationalism is demonstrable. International media coverage of anti-Japanese protestors marching angrily down Chinese streets or vandalising Japanese cars and restaurants has featured prominently in the last 20 years or so, usually after a flashpoint incident in and around the disputed Diaoyu (or Senkaku) Islands on the South China Sea. Chinese people living overseas can often be seen expressing their fervent nationalism during, for example, a visit by a high-level Chinese dignitary. Nyiri, Zhang and Varrall (2010) have noted the high level of support that existed amongst Chinese nationals studying abroad for China's controversial policy towards Tibet, as well as the fury directed towards

© The Author(s) 2017
R. Weatherley and Q. Zhang, *History and Nationalist Legitimacy in Contemporary China*, DOI 10.1057/978-1-137-47947-1_1

pro-Tibetan demonstrators and the seemingly pro-Tibetan international media in the prelude to the 2008 Beijing Olympics.

So why are Chinese people so nationalistic? How do we account for this? One reason can be traced back to China's entrenched legacy of suffering at the hands of foreign imperialist powers during the Century of Humiliation. This began with Britain's invasion of southern China during the First Opium War in 1839, continued into the 1800s and 1900s when China was forced to sign a number of unequal treaties with overseas aggressors, peaked in the 1930s when the Japanese committed atrocities in Manchuria and further south and ended with the liberation of China from foreign occupation in 1949 and the establishment of the People's Republic of China (PRC). The deep-rooted public feelings of shame, anger and perhaps even inferiority deriving from this period (China as "victim"), combined with an impassioned pride at the recent rapid growth of the Chinese economy and China's (re)emergence as an international force (China as "victor"), serve as the engine room of an often combustible and volatile Chinese nationalism.

Leading on from this, some scholars have suggested that the ultra-nationalism of the Chinese public is exclusively attributable to the far-reaching propaganda campaigns implemented by the CCP since the early 1990s which serve as constant reminders of the Century of Humiliation. In other words, the party has "brainwashed" the people so that they will never forget the traumas of the past (Wang 2012) and will react en masse every time the CCP wants to mobilise them against a former imperialist power that is still deemed to be acting aggressively towards China (Leonard 2008).

This book is not about why the Chinese people are so palpably nationalistic. That would probably require a separate (and no doubt very interesting) volume of its own. We do, however, focus on the close inter-relationship between history and nationalism in China. In particular, we examine the methods deployed by the CCP in coupling history to nationalism, the political rationale for doing so which is mainly linked to the legitimation of CCP rule and the response from the public, which is increasingly critical of the regime's claims to be the sole defender of Chinese national interests. In short, we will show how nationalism has become something of a double-edged sword for the CCP.

HISTORY AND NATIONALISM

The use of history and historical memory to stimulate popular nationalism is second nature to the CCP. The harrowing and often bitter memories associated with, for example, the First Opium War (Lovell 2011), the Second Sino-Japanese War (Mitter 2000) and the Korean War (Hays Gries et al. 2009) are comprehensively documented in the annals of CCP history and frequently articulated by the state-controlled media. Sometimes the trigger for an official reminder is to commemorate the anniversary of an event epitomising China's subjugation by foreign powers (e.g. the Nanjing Massacre or the Mukden incident) or to mark the end of a war against an imperialist power (e.g. Japan or the USA in Korea). Sometimes the reminder is precipitated by a perceived act of foreign aggression or a diplomatic slight against China. On other occasions, there is no obvious trigger. The aim is just to keep the legacy of foreign imperialism fresh in the Chinese memory.

This book identifies two different modes of nationalism generated by the CCP through its utilisation of Chinese history. The first is an aggressive, sometimes xenophobic form of nationalism which dwells on China's Century of Humiliation. This type of nationalism is deliberately designed to incite popular resentment towards prominent foreign powers (e.g. America, Japan and Britain) for the wrongs that they committed against China during that traumatic period of Chinese history. By contrast, the second mode of nationalism is more positive and conciliatory, emphasising common historical ties between the CCP and Taiwan's nationalist party, the Guomindang (KMT), against whom the CCP fought a bitter civil war from 1945 to 1949. This type of nationalism seeks to portray the CCP as flexible and tolerant on issues of recent historical significance, with the furtherance of China's wider national interests as its overriding objective. The long-term objective is ultimately peaceful reunification with Taiwan.

In developing our concepts of aggressive and consensual nationalism, we use four case studies (for want of a better term). For aggressive nationalism, we examine the official portrayal of the 1860 Anglo-French destruction of the Old Summer Palace (or Yuanmingyuan) in Beijing (Chap. 3) and the brutal legacy of Japanese imperialism in China during the nineteenth and twentieth centuries (Chap. 4). For consensual nationalism, we analyse the party's sympathetic reassessment of the KMT's participation in the 1937–1945 Sino-Japanese War, a role which was either ignored or denigrated during the Mao era (Chap. 5) and the toleration of a more open public debate on China's Republican era (1912–1949), again in contrast to what was allowed during the Mao era (Chap. 6).

Aggressive Nationalism
Yuanmingyuan

The annihilation of Yuanmingyuan was the final act of the Second Opium War (1856–1860) between China and an Anglo-French alliance. This vast complex of residential palaces, temples, ancestral shrines, libraries and art galleries situated in north-west Beijing was incinerated at the instruction of Britain's High Commissioner to China Lord James Elgin in retaliation for the kidnap and torture of a small delegation of Anglo-French emissaries (some of whom died) who had arrived in Beijing to insist on the enactment of the terms of the 1858 Treaty of Tianjin. Prior to igniting the palaces, British and French troops stole thousands of valuable antiques, many of which are now displayed in museums around the world.

Perhaps surprisingly given the often vehement nationalist rhetoric of the regime, there were very few references to the destruction of Yuanmingyuan under Mao. Indeed, it was not really until the early 1990s that the incident began to feature more prominently on the Chinese political agenda. This was initially as part of a nationwide movement known as the Patriotic Education Campaign which sought to remind the Chinese public about the suffering endured by foreign imperialism. One aspect of this campaign was the publication of a Circular on Fully Using Cultural Relics to Conduct Education in Patriotism and Revolutionary Traditions which made direct reference to the destruction of the palaces and stressed the importance of retrieving the stolen antiques. As the campaign spread into the education sector, students of all ages were taught in detail about the indignity of Yuanmingyuan within the wider context of the Century of Humiliation. The site was officially designated as one of a number of patriotic education bases (established throughout China during the early 1990s) where visitors are encouraged to contemplate the misery of China's imperialist subjugation.

There are a number of other ways in which the CCP has exploited the memory of Yuanmingyuan. One method is to remind the Chinese public of the incident whenever certain foreign nations are perceived as still acting aggressively towards China. For example, after the 1999 US bombing of the Chinese Embassy in Belgrade which killed three Chinese employees, dozens of Chinese newspaper articles drew angry parallels with the Yuanmingyuan incident, suggesting that some foreign countries were still intent on violating China's national sovereignty. On other occasions, high-profile events hosted in Beijing have provided an opportunity to resurrect the ghost of Yuanmingyuan. In the prelude to the Beijing Olympics, the state media drew symbolic and somewhat exaggerated comparisons between the ruins of Yuanmingyuan and the ruins of Olympia and between the Olympic torch flame and the flames that engulfed Yuanmingyuan. The tone became particularly abrasive when overseas demonstrators began disrupting the international Olympic torch relay in protest at China's human rights record. Particular venom was directed towards the French government for supporting the activities of pro-Tibetan French protestors including accusations of gross hypocrisy in the context of what France did to Yuanmingyuan in 1860.

Japanese Imperialism

The history of Japanese imperialism in China is well-documented. Encroachments into Chinese territory began during the early 1890s as the Meiji government looked to construct an extensive territorial empire in Asia which included parts of northern China and Taiwan. Japan's occupation of Manchuria in 1931 and invasion of Nanjing in 1937 led to millions of Chinese deaths, including over 300,000 during the Nanjing Massacre in December 1937 and January 1938. In addition to mass killings (including "competition killings" carried out by Japanese officers), Japanese war crimes included human experimentation (such as vivisection and amputations without anaesthesia), biological warfare causing thousands of cases of bubonic plague, cholera and anthrax, and the mass sexual enslavement of Chinese girls and women (known as comfort women) by the Japanese military.

Like the Yuanmingyuan incident, Japanese atrocities in China are intermittently recalled by the CCP and official media outlets. During the Patriotic Education Campaign, a total of 20 patriotic education bases were established to commemorate the Second Sino-Japanese War. This included the Memorial for Compatriots Killed in the Nanjing Massacre by Japanese Forces of Aggression (known otherwise as the Nanjing Massacre Memorial Hall) built in 1985 and the Memorial Hall of the War of Resistance Against Japan which opened in Beijing in 1987 (to mark 50 years since the war began) and was rebuilt in 1995. As with the ruins of Yuanmingyuan, the Chinese public are encouraged to visit these bases so that they can contemplate the tragedy of China's recent past as carefully depicted by the written word and highly graphic pictorial illustrations. Reminders of Japanese imperialism are also made following diplomatic spats between China and Japan. As we will see in Chap. 4, this includes flashpoint incidents in and around the Diaoyu Islands, revisions to Japanese history textbooks which are seen as whitewashing Japan's brutality in China (including denials about the Nanjing Massacre and the use of comfort women) and periodic visits by high-level Japanese politicians to the controversial Yasukuni Shrine in Tokyo which commemorates those who died in the service of the Japanese empire, including those responsible for thousands of Chinese deaths during the Second Sino-Japanese War

The rationale behind these often inflammatory references to Yuanmingyuan and Japanese imperialism is directly linked to the CCP's quest for nationalist legitimacy. The economic crisis of the 1980s leading up to the mass demonstrations of 1989, forced the party to diversify the foundations of its legitimacy to include, amongst other things, nationalism. This seamlessly evolved into a confrontational form of nationalism in response to the international criticism directed towards the CCP over its human rights practises, particularly the violent military crackdown in Tiananmen Square that brought the demonstrations to a shuddering halt. By reminding the Chinese public of the misery of Yuanmingyuan and Japanese aggression, the intention is to simultaneously remind them that it was the CCP who freed China from that terrible era and the CCP who has since restored China to its rightful place in the world as a major international power, so ensuring that the nation will never again return to an era of foreign domination. In other words, the party is juxtaposing the weakness of China's recent past against the self-proclaimed nation-building achievements of the modern era.

Consensual Nationalism
The Second Sino-Japanese War

But aggressive nationalism is not the only mode of nationalism that has been propagated by the CCP in recent times. In an effort to promote itself as the party of national unity—part of a broader policy on reunification with Taiwan—the CCP has loosened political controls to allow for

greater public discussion of China's Republican era, tolerating and sometimes even articulating perspectives that acknowledge the successes of
the period. This has included recognition of the KMT's key contribution
to winning the Second Sino-Japanese War, the first real sign of which
emerged in the early 1980s when KMT generals such as Zhang Zizhong
and Li Zongren were posthumously honoured as national heroes for
their role in defeating Japan. This was followed later in the decade by
the screening of anti-Japanese war films such as the Great Battle of
Taierzhuang which portrayed the KMT in a much more favourable light
than was acceptable under Mao.

Although this positivity diminished during the 1990s as the Taiwan
Straits missile crisis caused a deterioration in CCP–KMT relations, the
two political parties were thrust back together in 2000 by the election
as Taiwan's president of Chen Shuibian. As leader of the Democratic
Progressive Party (DPP), Chen championed independence from mainland China, so in an effort to isolate him, the CCP initiated a charm
offensive towards the KMT, itself an opponent of formal independence. Part of this initiative included inviting KMT politicians to the
PRC, including the KMT Chairman Lian Zhan who went to Beijing in
July 2005 to commemorate the 60th anniversary of the end of the war.
During Lian's visit, Hu Jintao publicly acknowledged the KMT's participation in the war, and this freed up the political breathing space for
a wider public debate on the war period. Following this, the Chinese
media began scouring the country for surviving KMT veterans with a
story to tell. Several of those who were found became overnight heroes,
as millions of people learned about their unsung bravery during the war.
In addition to this, innovative individuals initiated (and often paid for)
their own projects to commemorate the war by filming documentaries or
by funding the construction of war museums. Some people even organised a commemorative tour of the memorial sites in Burma where their
long-lost KMT relatives fought and died.

The Republican Era

At about the same time as the party began honouring KMT generals such as Zhang Zizhong and Li Zongren, it also began to relax the
parameters of permissible debate regarding the legacy of the Republican
era. This was initially apparent within academic circles as archival materials from Taiwan and further abroad became increasingly available to

PRC historians, who for years had been starved of anything meaningful to research and write about the Republic. Then in 1984 the party authorised the screening of The Bund, a Hong Kong television drama about the criminal activities of the 1920s Shanghai triads, which quickly became a hit with the viewing Chinese public. Coinciding with this was the publication of a number of books on the Republic in what became known as Republican exposé. These were cheaply produced, low-quality books about the criminal underworld in which the Republic was characterised by corruption, internecine gangland warfare and high-level assassinations.

Just as the 2005 visit of Lian Zhan precipitated greater public discussion of the war against Japan, so it served to intensify a Chinese interest in the Republican era generally and by 2006 references to a new phenomenon called Republican fever began to appear in the PRC media. This followed the launch a series of scholarly and non-specialist books on the Republic which moved away from the negative portrayal of the period as shady, dangerous and corrupt, towards an era characterised by diversity, sophistication and unrealised potential. An increasing number of Republican-based dramas have since been screened on Chinese TV to massive popular appeal, including 'The Grand Mansion Gate' based on the real life experience of the family who owned the renowned Chinese pharmaceutical company Tongrentang. Some of these dramas still follow the model set out in The Bund by focusing on the darker aspects of the era, but, as a whole, the televisual image of Republican society represented in these dramas has become more diverse, colourful and modern. Public interest has also extended to political issues, as the constitutionalist and democratic ideals of Republican revolutionaries became hot topics for discussion in the media and online.

THE DOUBLE-EDGED SWORD

But if the party was seeking to enhance its nationalist legitimacy through a diverse utilisation of history, this has not always materialised because in each of our four case studies the emerging public debate has sometimes been critical rather than supportive of the CCP. On the Yuanmingyuan incident, critics have argued that, despite its outraged anti-imperialist rhetoric, the party has consistently shown that it is not prepared to match its strong words with affirmative actions. This has led some people to conclude that the party is no more willing (or able) to stand up to foreign aggression now than the Qing government was in 1860 when Anglo-French forces marched effortlessly into Beijing and incinerated the ancient palaces. This claim is usually made when the CCP is seen as reacting too passively to a foreign infringement of Chinese national sovereignty such as US incursions into the South China Sea or Japanese assertions of sovereignty over Diaoyu. Others have used the Yuanmingyuan debate to broaden the focus of their criticism beyond the CCP's apparent inability to defend the nation. One critic accuses the party of shamelessly rewriting the history of the incident to serve its own nationalists ends. Another has questioned the appropriateness of using Yuanmingyuan as a symbol of national suffering given the era of elitism and inequality that the palaces symbolised. Doubts have also been raised about the wisdom of spending public money on partially restoring the ruined site or sending expensive delegations overseas in an attempt to retrieve the stolen antiques when this money would have been better spent on much-needed domestic projects such as repairing China's schools and hospitals.

A similar backlash (if we can call it that) has emerged over Japan, usually in relation to the disputed Diaoyu Islands. For example, anti-Japanese public demonstrations (often encouraged by the CCP) have sometimes turned against the party with some protestors carrying banners of Mao Zedong, perceived (rightly or wrongly) as being much firmer with Japan than the incumbent administration. Online activists (known as netizens) have been more direct in their criticism, drawing unfavourable comparisons between the CCP and the ineffectual late Qing regime or imploring the party to follow the lead of international strongmen such as Russia's Vladimir Putin. Aside from concerns about national assertiveness, critics have accused the party of being as culpable as Japan of atrocities against the Chinese people and of whitewashing Chinese history in the same way that Japan has allegedly whitewashed its own history. Others have used the Japan debate as an opportunity to accuse the CCP of failing to deal with widespread domestic grievances about housing, unemployment and public security.

The party's conciliatory approach to the KMT's role in the Second Sino-Japanese War has also resulted in censure from some quarters. As the Chinese media began to unearth surviving KMT veterans living in the PRC who had fought alongside the CCP during the war, popular sympathy for their plight turned to anger towards the CCP following stories of their mistreatment and persecution after 1949. As with

Yuanmingyuan and Japan, the party is accused of rewriting history, in this case by generously bolstering the CCP's contribution to the war effort, whilst negating the role played by the KMT. Some critics have insisted that the CCP actually betrayed the Chinese nation by deliberating avoiding direct combat with Japan, leaving the KMT to shoulder the burden of fighting and winning the war as part of a ploy to reserve CCP energies in preparation for the inevitable oncoming civil war. Others have even claimed that the CCP turned its guns on the KMT during the war rather than fighting alongside them against a common enemy.

Nor has the Republican era debate always worked in the party's favour, with many people expressing a deep nostalgia for that period of China's history. For example, some critics claim that successive Republican governments were much more liberal and tolerant than the CCP, allowing for much greater freedom of expression in education, the media and in society as a whole. Conversely, the CCP is accused of steadfastly withholding basic civil rights and freedoms after 1949. The party is also accused, particularly during the Mao era, of negating some of the economic advancements made during the Republic, whilst post-Mao economic reforms are derided as little more than making up for lost time. Other critics insist that the KMT was much more successful in its diplomatic achievements than previously recognised, ending China's Century of Humiliation several years before the CCP came to power. Official claims that the CCP unified and liberated China are rejected as a fabrication.

PARTICIPANTS IN THE DEBATE

Turning now to the participants in the four debates covered by this book, a number of them are from the scholarly community, covering a broad range of academic disciplines. They include Xie Yong, a professor of Chinese literature at Xiamen University, Zhang Ming, a political scientist at Beijing's Renmin University and Yuan Weishi, a historian at the Sun Yat-sen University in Guangzhou, each of whom has expressed views on the Republican era which are supportive of the Republican legacy and critical of the PRC. Issues of political sensitivity and government censorship usually prevent these scholars from publishing the full extent of their controversial perspectives in academic books or journals. As such, their views are usually articulated in the liberal-oriented written media such as the Guangzhou-based Southern Metropolis Daily and Southern

Weekend which are distributed nationally and renowned for their investigative reporting and contributions to debates on democracy, civil society and social injustices.

Journalists have also contributed to some of the debates referred to in this book, particularly regarding the Second Sino-Japanese War. Those journalists who located surviving KMT veterans at around the time of Lian Zhan's 2005 visit to Beijing worked for newspapers in Chongqing and Shanghai, regions where the KMT was popular during the Republican era and where there is a keen appetite to learn more about the KMT's true role in the war (although this appetite is spreading throughout China). One newspaper even paid for a nonagenarian veteran, Yang Yangzheng, to travel from his hometown in Chongqing to Shanghai so that he could visit the scene of the 1937 Defence of the Sihang Warehouse, a historic seven-day battle between the KMT and a vastly superior Japanese military division. Many of the articles published at around this time were sympathetic towards Yang and the KMT and impliedly critical of the CCP.

Television channels have participated in the discussions. During 2007, the Hong Kong-based (and Beijing-backed) Phoenix TV screened a documentary about Wu Dehou, one of several KMT officers who helped defeat Japan during the landmark Battle of Taierzhuang in 1938, the first major Chinese victory of the Second Sino-Japanese War. The documentary shows how after 1949, Wu was ruthlessly persecuted for his earlier membership of the KMT, sparking fury across the Chinese netizen community. Phoenix TV has also published online special reports praising certain aspects of the Republican era. A 2010 report applauded the independence and openness of university education during the Republic, drawing a stark contrast to the grim post-49 situation. In addition, the channel has authorised the publication of blogs whose authors are critical of the CCP on issues of historical national importance.

Other participants include pioneering individuals such as the high-profile TV personality Cui Yongyuan, who spent over 8 years and more than 130 million RMB compiling what he called a 'verbal history project' of the Second Sino-Japanese War. After carrying out interviews with over 3500 people who had lived through the war, Cui released a highly popular 35-part documentary series called My Resistance War, containing sympathetic perspectives on the KMT's military contribution. Another innovative (and self-funded) individual is Fan Jianchuan, a real estate developer and private collector from Sichuan. In 2006,

Fan founded the Jianchuan Museum near Chengdu, a significant section of which commemorates the Second Sino-Japanese War. Fan has also established several smaller museums dedicated to the war and other significant historical events in China such as the Cultural Revolution (1966–1969).

Of course, as is the way of the modern world, many participants articulate their views online. As an alternative to using the written press, some Chinese scholars have published their opinions on the Sina Blog website or on their own personal blog sites. However, the majority of online perspectives are written by less identifiable netizens using barely decipherable titles such as PLANavy, Carp in Sea 111 and the Philosopher is Dead. They often publish on the microblogging platform Weibo (similar to Twitter) or in response to articles on points of national sensitivity published by the Global Times or the People's Daily. Many netizens are part of subject-specific internet groups. Douban.com, one of China's largest social networking sites, hosts a number of Republican era interest groups, with topics of discussion ranging from history and politics to art and literature. Supporters of the Republican era are also active on Weibo and Renren.com (China's equivalent to Facebook). A number of Diaoyu-related internet groups have been set up, referred to generically as Bao Diao (Defend Diaoyu) groups. They include the China Federation for Defending the Diaoyu Islands, the Patriots Alliance Network and the (mainly Hong Kong-based) Action Committee for Defending the Diaoyu Islands. As well as expressing strong opinions online, these groups help organise sailing expeditions to land on the islands and spearhead anti-Japanese public demonstrations throughout China.

So who are these netizens? Where do they come from? Peter Hays Gries et al. (2016, p. 5) suggest they tend to be at the younger, more urban and educated end of the Chinese demographic spectrum. Feng and Yuan (2014) agree with this view but go into more detail, identifying the netizens as part of what Philip Huang (2008) refers to as a middle social stratum. This stratum acts as an unofficial mouthpiece for the disillusioned and disenfranchised members of Chinese society with strong socio-economic grievances. As Feng and Yuan (2014, p. 120) explain:

> Subject to the volatility brought about by the country's ongoing market reforms in employment, housing and health care, members of this particular social stratum face a precarious socioeconomic future. They are

vulnerable to the drawbacks of the party-state's authoritarian regime such as corruption, ineffective public services, and arbitrary government administrative power. Most are thus sensitive to social justice and motivated to speak out on behalf of less privileged social groups.

As we will see throughout this book, netizen dissatisfaction with the CCP's position on national issues, particularly in relation to Japan, often spills over into a wider dissatisfaction with the party's inability to resolve some of the socio-economic dislocations caused by the reforms it has implemented over the last three decades or so.

What Is Nationalism?

As with any political concept, it is difficult to find a consensus definition of nationalism despite (or perhaps because of) the abundance of scholarly literature on the subject. At the more esoteric end of the scale, Richard Handler (1988, p. 6) defines nationalism as 'an ideology about individuated being. It is an ideology concerned with boundedness, continuity and homogeneity encompassing diversity. It is an ideology in which social reality, conceived in terms of nationhood, is endowed with the reality of natural things'. John Breuilly (1985, p. 3) adopts a more intelligible perspective, categorising nationalists as people who hold three basic convictions. The first conviction is that there 'exists a nation with an explicit and peculiar character'. The second is that the 'interests and values of this nation take priority over all other interests and values'. The third is that the nation must be 'as independent as possible. This usually requires the attainment of political sovereignty'.

Adrian Hastings believes that nationalism arises from a perceived internal or external threat to a particular ethnicity or nation. This draws close parallels to the circumstances under which Chinese nationalism emerged during the nineteenth and twentieth centuries as we will see shortly. In his volume entitled 'The Construction of Nationhood' Hastings (1997, p. 4) writes that:

> As something which can empower large numbers of ordinary people, nationalism is a movement which seeks to provide a state for a given 'nation' or further to advance the supposed interests of its own 'nation-state' regardless of other considerations. It arises chiefly where and when

a particular ethnicity or nation feels itself threatened in regard to its own proper character, extent or importance, either by external attack or by the state system of which it has hitherto formed part.

Just as there are different definitions of nationalism so there are different types of nationalism. Hall (1993) distinguishes between the liberal, culturally inclusive nationalism which is prominent in Western Europe from the illiberal, culturally exclusive nationalism found in other parts of the world. However, Michael Hechter (2000, p. 15) rejects what he calls 'these normative differences between nationalist movements' in preference for a typology 'derived from analytical considerations'. This leads him to identify four different types of nationalism: state-building nationalism, peripheral nationalism, irredentist nationalism and unification nationalism, each explained as follows.

State-building nationalism is characterised by the assimilation of culturally distinctive territories into a given state. This is often the result of a centralised attempt 'to make a multicultural population culturally homogeneous'. Hechter provides as an example intermittent attempts by British and French rulers to integrate Celtic regions into their own culture between the sixteenth and twentieth centuries. Such attempts often result in peripheral nationalism which occurs when a 'culturally distinctive territory resists incorporation into an expanding state, or attempts to secede and set up its own government'. Hechter cites Quebec, Scotland and Catalonia as examples of this type of nationalism. Irredentist nationalism describes efforts to 'extend the existing boundaries of a state by incorporating territories of an adjacent state occupied principally by co-nationals'. The Sudeten Germans is an example given by Hechter. Unification nationalism takes place with the merger of a 'politically divided but culturally homogenous territory into one state'. Nineteenth-century France and Germany are two examples of this. Hechter suggests that in contrast to state-building nationalism which is usually culturally inclusive, unification nationalism is usually culturally exclusive as new states seek to unify the nation under a single culture.

Perhaps the most lucid interpretation of nationalism is provided by Anthony Smith who locates common academic themes which he then incorporates into his own definition. First and foremost, there is an overriding concern with the nation: 'nationalism is an ideology that places the nation at the centre of its concerns and seeks to promote the nation's well-being' (Smith 2001, p. 9). From this, Smith identifies three primary objectives that fall within the promotion of the nation's well-being. These are national autonomy, national unity and national identity. For nationalists, Smith argues, a nation cannot subsist unless it possesses a significant degree of all three. This leads him to the following definition of nationalism as 'an ideological movement for attaining and maintaining autonomy, unity and identity for a population which some of its members deem to constitute an actual or potential "nation"' (Smith 2001, p. 9) .

So what do we mean by nation? Again, scholarly definitions are innumerable (Tilly 1975, p. 6; Miller 1995, p. 27; Brubaker 1996, p. 21) but Smith (2001, p. 13) provides a clear response. A nation is 'a named human community occupying a homeland and having common myths and a shared history, a common public culture, a single economy and common rights and duties for all members'. Picking up on three of the characteristics in Smith's definition—common myths, shared history and common public culture—we might usefully define nationalists as a group of people who identify with the common myths, shared history and common public culture of their nation.

Chinese Nationalism

Turning now to Chinese nationalism, these three core characteristics of what constitutes a nation are especially pertinent to the Chinese experience. Common myths might plausibly refer to the widespread belief in China's once greatness as a nation, formerly the Middle Kingdom, the centre of all civilisation to whom all other nations and cultures were subordinate and were required to pay tribute (if fortunate enough to be invited). Many contemporary Chinese nationalists express a strong desire to return to the halcyon days of China's imperialist past. For example, in his study of a phenomenon known as Ming fever, Michael Szonyi (2010) has identified a growing popular nostalgia in China for the Ming Dynasty (1368–1644), a period greatly admired by the Chinese public for its economic vibrancy and global engagement.

Continuing with the theme of historical nostalgia, the idea of a common public culture might apply to what it is that makes China great. This could include a common language and writing system which dates all the way back to the Shang dynasty (1766–1122 BC) and was passed down to Japan and Korea. There is also Confucianism, China's state ideology for over two millennia which was based on the principles of harmony and hierarchy, again handed down to certain neighbouring tributary states. In addition, there are the Four Great Inventions—the compass, paper, printing and gunpowder—all of which are cited with great admiration by modern-day Chinese nationalists. These examples of China's common public culture then feed into Smith's concept of a shared history in that they embody a shared history of achievement and success that spans several centuries.

So when did nationalism first emerge in China? We cannot be certain, but probably the first Chinese thinkers to allude to nationalism were late Qing political reformers including Kang Youwei, Liang Qichao and his mentor Yan Fu. The context for this was the threat that China faced from foreign imperialism. The humiliating defeats suffered by China during the two Opium Wars and the subsequent ease with which China was opened up by imperialist powers exposed the alarming fragility of the Chinese nation. For Kang, Liang and Yan, a system of constitutional monarchy provided a potential answer to China's weakness through its perceived capacity to generate popular loyalty and obedience to the Qing regime. The logic was as follows: if the people were allowed to participate in politics for the very first time by voting, standing for election and exercising their basic civil freedoms of speech and association, then they would come to respect and support those in authority who had invested them with these new-found democratic rights and freedoms. This loyalty could then be channelled by the Qing court into its broader nation-saving objectives so that China would not perish in the international struggle amongst nations.

However, these thinkers comprised a small minority of intellectuals and their views were far from representative of those held by the broader Chinese public. Instead, there was a very weak public perception of nationhood at this time, primarily because ordinary Chinese people had, for thousands of years, aligned themselves much more closely to their immediate family in keeping with the strictures of Confucianism. This was a point made by Yan Fu in his narrative on why the Chinese people had no real sense of national consciousness (Schwartz 1964, pp. 70–71). Confucianism required strict obedience to family members in accordance with the Five Relationships and the Rules of Propriety (Baker 1979), and as James Sheridan (1975, p. 17) has concluded 'the primacy of family relations inhibited the development of truly national loyalties'. Outside of the immediate family, personal loyalty was owed to the clan and the village, but the nation as a single entity was scarcely perceptible.

If any feelings of personal loyalty did exist outside of the family, clan or village during the imperial period, they were more likely to be directed towards the incumbent dynasty or sometimes even the preceding dynasty.

One of the key points made by Paul Cohen (1984) in his analysis of domestic rebellions in China during the nineteenth century is that they were not a manifestation of xenophobic anti-Westernism as the consensus view would have us believe. Rather, they constituted a racial statement against the Qing Dynasty Manchus and a desire to restore the perceived glory days of the Ming Dynasty Han. This was exemplified by the slogan "destroy the Qing, restore the Ming" which was prominent during the early stages of the Boxer Rebellion (1898–1901).

The Republican era brought with it a greater focus on nationalism under the banner of Sun Yat-sen's Three Principles of the People, one of which was nationalism (the other two being democracy and people's livelihood). Sun (1972) interpreted nationalism as comprising a popular desire to rid the nation of foreign imperialism (drawing parallels with Hechter's state-building nationalism) something which could only be achieved if each of China's five major ethnicities united behind a single, centralised state. The five ethnicities were the Han, Mongols, Tibetans, Manchus and Muslims, as represented by the five colour flag of the new Chinese Republic. But Sun did not succeed in instilling his brand of anti-imperialist nationalism into the consciousness of the Chinese masses. Despite the projected symbolism of the Chinese Republican flag, many Chinese people could not accurately describe the flag when asked or even recognise it when they were shown it. Although the Confucian system had been dismantled, it was a case of old habits die hard as individual loyalty was still largely confined to the family or village unit rather than to the nation. In general, Chinese nationalism remained at a more esoteric level. It had relevance and meaning for politicians, scholars and a growing number of students, particularly during the period of Chinese scholarly enlightenment known as the May Fourth era (1915–1921) but was of little real significance to the broader Chinese public.

The watershed event of the twentieth century that served to unite the Chinese people behind the nation was the invasion by Japan in 1931, followed by the Second Sino-Japanese War. The explosion of nationalist sentiment sparked by these Japanese incursions derived from a widespread feeling of shame and humiliation that this once great imperial power had been plundered and colonised by a much smaller and "culturally inferior" neighbour. Japan provided a common focal point of hatred for the mass cruelty inflicted on the Chinese people during the occupation and a common objective of removing the Japanese from Chinese soil featured very strongly after 1931 (Shum 1988). In effect, the Japanese invasion gave rise to a sharp distinction in China between "us" and "them", an integral feature of what Allen Whiting (1983) has termed assertive nationalism.

As has been said many times before, the victory of the CCP in 1949 was as much a victory for Chinese nationalism as it was for communism, finally ending the Century of Humiliation and uniting China behind a single, centralised state (Gillin 1964; Johnston 1962). When Mao proclaimed the establishment of the PRC on the Gates of Heavenly Peace on 1 October 1949, he did not refer to Marxist dialectics or to the superiority of the socialist system. China's majority peasant population did not understand these concepts and probably did not much care for them either. Instead Mao famously couched his victory speech in nationalist tones, claiming that, 'ours will no longer be a nation subject to insult and humiliation. We have stood up' (Mao 1949).

A desire to remain free from imperialist subjugation continued to inform Chinese nationalism after 1949. Hundreds of anti-foreign rallies took place with the support of the Mao regime. Many of these targeted America for its military presence in Taiwan and Japan, and of course, for its direct intervention in the Korean War (1950–1953). In 1950, the CCP launched the Resist America Assist Korea Campaign which, as well as encouraging strong anti-US sentiments amongst the public, called on millions of people throughout the country to participate in supporting activities such as collecting funds for the families of Chinese soldiers, signing patriotic pacts for increased production and cutting links between Chinese Christian churches and their Western counterparts (Dietrich 1998, p. 70). In 1960, the People's Daily reported that no fewer than 283 anti-American protests took place during the course of that year, along with 99 anti-Soviet demonstrations and 54 rallies against other hostile nations (Weiss 2014, p. 8). Anti-foreignism reached its zenith during the Cultural Revolution when Red Guard groups attacked foreign embassies and consulates in Beijing (including incinerating the British Embassy in August 1967) and assaulted embassy staff from the Soviet Union and other embassies.

Some of the other patriotic campaigns that took place during the Mao era were less focused on anti-foreignism, but no less patriotic. For example, the Campaign to Eliminate the Four Pests launched in 1958 was heavily shrouded in patriotic language and oriented exclusively towards nation-building goals such as improving the personal hygiene of the all-important workforce by eliminating rats, flies and mosquitoes and increasing the nation's grain production by eliminating sparrows. The sparrows campaign is particularly renowned, involving scores of peasants hitting pots and pans together or banging drums so that any nearby sparrows would be too frightened to perch and eventually die of exhaustion (Shapiro 2001). The aim in trying to wipe out this notorious crop-eating menace was to enable China's national grain output to accelerate and catch-up with Western output levels. The outcome, however, was the exact opposite. Although the campaign successfully decimated the unfortunate sparrow population, there was no natural predator left to prevent plagues of insects from taking up where the sparrows had left off. This precipitated a substantial reduction in grain yields and epitomised the eccentricity and tragedy of the Great Leap Forward (1958–1960) which caused millions to die from starvation.

ASSESSING THE LITERATURE

There is, of course, no shortage of literature on the topic of Chinese nationalism, and it is not our intention to trawl through all of it. Some of the key works covering the pre-liberation and Mao eras have already been noted in the previous section. Useful sources on the CCP's rationale for the Patriotic Education Campaign and the deliberate linking of post-Tiananmen nationalism to historical trauma are provided in articles by Zhao Suisheng (1998), Xu Guangqiu (2001, 2012) and Wang Zheng (2008). Wang (2012) has since furthered this area of research in his volume (Never Forget National Humiliation) which examines the party's cultivation of a patriotic support base founded on the Century of Humiliation, particularly during the Beijing Olympics and throughout the relief effort following the 2008 Sichuan earthquake. There is, however, no clear discussion of any adverse public reaction to the CCP's efforts, almost as though the public has simply swallowed the official line.

Wu Zeying (2012) has examined the impact of the Patriotic Education Campaign on Chinese public perceptions of foreign countries, specifically what Chinese young people think about Japan. Based on empirical data, together with comparative and content analyses of relevant official documents and secondary school history textbooks, Wu argues that the official narrative of Japan has remained consistently negative since the campaign was conceived back in the early 1990s.

Notwithstanding this, many young people perceive Japan in a multifaceted and rational way, often resisting the political and ideological indoctrination inherent in the campaign. This is mainly because of a diverse range of stronger influences, particularly from the internet.

The role of the internet in the articulation of Chinese nationalist sentiments—referred to as online Chinese nationalism—is another important and relevant area covered in the scholarly literature. Xu Wu's (2007) book (Chinese Cyber Nationalism) contains an extensive account of the historical development of this phenomenon, including a detailed empirical survey of the key websites and online participants. Breslin and Shen (2010) have examined the pressures that the netizens have exerted on the CCP's ability to conduct bilateral relations with, for example, Japan and the US. Shen (2007) has also written a sole-authored volume assessing the impact of online nationalist sentiments on Sino-US relations. Zhao's (2014) edited volume (Construction of Chinese Nationalism in the Early 21st Century) contains a more contemporary and broader overview of online nationalism.

The work of Peter Hays Gries (2004, 2009, 2016) on Chinese nationalism is extensive and helpful. Hays Gries (2004) is one of the first China specialists to identify the advent of a vociferous grassroots nationalist movement in the wake of high-profile bilateral clashes such as the 1996 landing on the Diaoyu Islands by the right-wing Japan Youth Federation (see Chap. 4) and the US bombing of the Chinese embassy in Belgrade in May 1999 (see this chapter). In both cases, participants in this movement derided the CCP for failing to act with due force for fear of disrupting hard-earned economic ties with Japan and the USA, respectively. Hays Gries also argues that a strong public reaction on issues of national sensitivity has forced the party to modify its approach to dealing with this reaction. This has seen a movement away from the rapid state suppression of public protest in 1996 towards the accommodation of such protest in 1999 when the authorities in Beijing provided transport for the protestors to come in from the outskirts of the city to the embassy district so that they could hurl abuse and objects at the US embassy building. In other words, Hays Gries suggests that the party is not only losing control of the debate over nationalism and but is also losing control of the actions of the nationalist participants.

Jessica Chen Weiss (2014) questions this last point. She argues that the CCP still retains the capacity to rein in the protesters if things start to get out of hand, as it did following the sporadically violent public demonstrations in 2005 in reaction to a proposal by the so-called G4 (Japan, Germany, Brazil and India) that Japan should be granted permanent membership of the United Nations Security Council (UNSC). Sometimes, when it is politically convenient to do so, the party has been able to nullify public ill feeling towards other nations before it has the opportunity to fully materialise. This was apparent in the period after 2005 when the CCP was keen to repair Sino-Japanese relations. In addition to this, the party has been able to incite public protest to suit its own political purposes. The anti-Japanese demonstrations in 2005 came about because the CCP deliberately relaxed political controls over freedom of speech and assembly, as well as stepping up news reports on Japan's imperialist history and anti-China demonstrations that were taking place in Tokyo. The party then used the level of public outrage that broke out across the country as the reason why it could not possibly support the G4 proposal. Weiss (2014, p. 3) concludes from this that whilst the party 'is worried about grassroots nationalism it is not uniformly paralysed'.

CHAPTER OUTLINE

The remainder of this book is divided into five substantive chapters. Chapter 2 sets the scene for the rest of the book by suggesting that regime legitimacy was at the very core of why the CCP turned its focus so obviously towards nationalism in the early post-Tiananmen era. The mass rallies in Tiananmen Square and across China during spring 1989 were as much a protest about the failings of the CCP's economic reform programme as they were about the party's unwillingness to countenance comprehensive political reform. As the party's economic legitimacy waned alarmingly with the onset of spiralling and unprecedented rates of inflation, growing unemployment and a rise in official corruption, so it was forced to diversify the basis of its legitimacy by embracing nationalism. The aggressive anti-foreign tone and content of the early 1990s Patriotic Education Campaign was carefully linked to the international condemnation and sanctions imposed on China in response to the infamous military crackdown at Tiananmen that abruptly ended the protests. In effect, the outraged (albeit moderate) foreign response to Tiananmen was used as evidence that the USA and other Western nations were still acting like imperialist powers, still determined to hold China down and prevent it from resuming its rightful place in the world. However, as we will see towards the end of the chapter, not everyone rallied obediently behind the party's nationalist line, particularly after the 1996 Diaoyu incident and the US bombing of the US embassy in Belgrade.

Chapter 3 provides the first of our two cases studies on aggressive nationalism, focusing on the official propagation of the Anglo-French destruction of Yuanmingyuan. Here we will trace the different ways in which the party has reminded the Chinese public about this traumatic incident, including the drawing of analogies with more recent diplomatic humiliations such as the Belgrade bombing and the French disruption of the 2008 Olympic torch relay in protest at China's treatment of Tibetans. But if the underlying objective has been to enhance the CCP's status as the party which liberated China from the Century of Humiliation and established the PRC as a major international power, this has not always materialised. Instead, some members of the public have been critical of the CCP, levelling accusations of diplomatic weakness and historical whitewashing as well as criticising the apparent diversion of state money away from domestic socio-economic necessities and towards the funding of unnecessary and expensive trips overseas to locate the stolen Yuanmingyuan artefacts.

In Chapter 4 we will see how the party also draws analogies between past and present on the subject of Japanese imperialism, usually as a means of expressing its outrage and indignity after a bilateral spat over the disputed Diaoyu Islands, state-approved revisions to Japanese history textbooks or a visit by a high-level Japanese politician to the Yasukuni Shrine. Here again we will explain how the objective is to bolster the CCP's position as the sole voice of Chinese national interests. But the effect has been limited, with critics expressing a preference for the strongman approach of Mao Zedong or Vladimir Putin and accusing the CCP of being no stronger than the late Qing administration. The party also stands accused of abusing the human rights of its own people, whitewashing Chinese history and failing to deal with widespread domestic grievances over housing, unemployment and public security.

Chapter 5 turns to consensual nationalism by examining the party's recognition of the KMT's key role in the Second Sino-Japanese War. This intensified after the election in Taiwan of President Chen Shuibian in 2000, precipitating a palpable warming of CCP–KMT relations. Previously stringent political restrictions were noticeably relaxed during 2005 (to mark the 50th anniversary of the end of the war) and this gave rise to an upsurge in investigative journalism and internet activity which highlighted the true role of the KMT during the war. The CCP's under-lying objective has been to promote itself as the party of national unity, looking to build bridges with the KMT as part of a broader policy on reunification with Taiwan. But as we will see and as alluded to already, the public response has not always been supportive of the CCP, includ-ing anger over CCP mistreatment of KMT veterans after the war and accusations of a cover-up over the KMT's key contribution in defeating Japan and the CCP's lack thereof.

Chapter 6 examines how the party has also loosened political con-trols in relation to the Republican era, allowing academics and the media greater freedom to explore and discuss this era. Here we will analyse how this has since developed into a Republican fever amongst some sec-tors of the Chinese public, but with a familiar backlash against the party. For example, exponents of the fever have expressed a preference for the superior educational, democratic and diplomatic achievements of the Republic compared to the People's Republic and dismissed the CCP's economic reforms as simply making up for the time lost under the calam-itous Mao regime.

Our concluding chapter suggests that the pattern of political relaxa-tion followed by public censure against the party as identified in this book is far from unprecedented in the PRC, with reference to the 1957 Hundred Flowers Campaign and the late 1970s scar literature and Democracy Wall movements. In both cases, the party backlash against its critics was much more virulent than anything experienced by the mod-ern-day nationalist dissenters, although some pro-Republican era activists have been harassed, arrested and sometimes incarcerated. We then assess the extent to which nationalist dissent is representative of public opin-ion in China and examine the challenges that such dissent poses for CCP decision-making.

REFERENCES

Baker, H. (1979). *Chinese family and kinship*. New York: Columbia University Press.

Breslin, S., & Shen, S. (Eds.). (2010). *Online Chinese nationalism and Chinese bilateral relations*. Lanham: Rowman and Littlefield.

Breuilly, J. (1985). *Nationalism and the state*. Chicago: University of Chicago Press.

Brubaker, R. (1996). *Nationalism reframed: Nationhood and the national ques-tion in new Europe*. Cambridge: Cambridge University Press.

Cohen, P. (1984). The problem with China's response to the west. In P. Cohen (Ed.), *Discovering history in China: American historical writing on the recent Chinese past.* New York: Columbia University Press.

Dietrich, C. (1998). *People's China: A brief history.* New York: Oxford University Press.

Feng, M., & Yuan, E. (2014). Public opinion on Weibo: The case of the Diaoyu islands dispute. In T. Hollihan (Ed.), *The dispute over the Diaoyu/Senkaku islands: How media narratives shape public opinion and challenge the global order* (pp. 119–140). New York: Palgrave.

Gillin, D. (1964). Peasant nationalism in the history of Chinese communism. *Journal of Asian Studies, 23*(2), 269–289.

Hall, J. (1993). Nationalisms: Classified and explained. *Daedalus, 122*(3), 1–28.

Handler, R. (1988). *Nationalism and the politics of culture in Quebec.* Madison: University of Wisconsin Press.

Hastings, A. (1997). *The construction of nationhood: Ethnicity, religion and nationalism.* Cambridge: Cambridge University Press.

Hays Gries, P. (2004). *China's new nationalism: Pride, politics and diplomacy.* California: University of California Press.

Hays Gries, P., Prewitt-Freilino, J., Cox-Fuenzalida, L.-E., & Qingmin, Z. (2009). Contentious histories and the perception of threat: China, the United States, and the Korean war—An experimental analysis. *Journal of East Asian Studies, 9,* 433–465.

Hays Gries, P., Steiger, D., & Wang, T. (2016). Popular nationalism and China's Japan policy: The Diaoyu islands protests, 2012–2013. *Journal of Contemporary China, 98*(25), 264–276.Hechter, M. (2000). *Containing nationalism.* Oxford: Oxford University Press.

Huang, P. (2008). *Zhongguo de Xiao Zichanjieji he Zhongjian Jieceng: Beilun de Shehui Xingtai* [Petty-Bourgeoisie and middle social stratum in China: The paradox of social formation], *Leaders,* 22, Retrieved from http://www.21ccom.net/articles/rwcq/article_20100120381.html.

Johnson, C. (1962). *Peasant nationalism and communist power: The emergence of revolutionary China, 1937–1945.* Stanford: Stanford University Press.

Kwong, S. K. (1988). *The Chinese communists' road to power: The anti-Japanese national united front.* Oxford: Oxford University Press.

Leonard, M. (2008). *What does China think?* London: Fourth Estate.

Lovell, J. (2011). *The opium war: Drugs, dreams and the making of China.* London: Picador.

Mao, Z. (1949). *The Chinese people have stood up!* Retrieved from https://www.marxists.org/reference/archive/mao/selected-works/volume-5/mswv5_01.htm.

Miller, D. (1995). *On nationality.* Oxford: Oxford University Press.

Mitter, R. (2000). Behind the scenes at the museum: Nationalism, history and memory in the Beijing war of resistance museum, 1987–1997. *China Quarterly, 161,* 279–293.

Nyiri, P., Zhang, J., & Varrall, M. (2010). China's cosmopolitan nationalists: Heroes and traitors of the 2008 olympics. *China Journal, 63*, 25–55.

Schwartz, B. (1964). *In search of wealth and power: Yen Fu and the West.* Cambridge, MA: Harvard University Press.

Shapiro, J. R. (2001). *Mao's war against nature: Politics and the environment in revolutionary China.* New York: Cambridge University Press.

Shen, S. (2007). *Redefining nationalism in modern China: Sino-American relations and the emergence of public opinion in the 21st century.* Basingstoke: Palgrave.

Sheridan, J. (1975). *China in disintegration: The republican era in Chinese history, 1912–1949.* New York: Free Press.

Smith, A. (2001). *Nationalism.* Cambridge: Polity Press.

Szonyi, M. (2010). Ming fever: The present's past as the people's republic turns sixty. *China Heritage Quarterly, 21*, Retrieved from http://www.chinaheritagequarterly.org/articles.php?searchterm=021_mingfever.inc&issue=021.

Tilly, C. (1975). *The formation of national states in Western Europe.* Princeton: Princeton University Press.

Wang, Z. (2008). National humiliation history education, and the politics of historical memory: Patriotic education campaign in China. *International Studies Quarterly, 52*(4), 783–806.

Wang, Z. (2012). *Never forget national humiliation: Historical memory in Chinese politics and foreign relations.* New York: Columbia University Press.

Weiss, J. (2014). *Powerful patriots: Nationalist protest in China's foreign relations.* New York: Oxford University Press.

Whiting, A. (1983). Assertive nationalism in Chinese foreign policy. *Asian Survey, 23*, 913–933.

Wu, Z. (2012). *The effects of patriotic education on Chinese youths' perceptions of Japan.* Mphil Thesis, Lingnan University.

Xu, G. (2001). Anti-western nationalism: 1989–1999. *World Affairs, 163*(4), 151–162.

Xu, W. (2007). *Chinese cyber nationalism: Evolution, characteristics, and implications.* Lanham: Rowman and Littlefield.

Xu, G. (2012). Chinese anti-westernism, 2000–2010. *Asian and African Studies, XVI, 2*, 109–134.

Yat-sen, S. (1972). *San Min Chu I: The three principles of the people.* Taibei: China Publishing Company.

Zhao, S. (1998). A state-led nationalism: The patriotic education campaign in post-Tiananmen China. *Communist and Post-Communist Studies, 31*(3), 287–302.

Zhao, S. (Ed.). (2014). *Construction of Chinese nationalism in the early 21st century: Domestic sources and international implications.* London: Routledge.

CHAPTER 2

Turning to Nationalism: Another Crisis of Regime Legitimacy for the CCP

As established, this book will examine the efforts made by the CCP, mainly during the post-Tiananmen era, to bolster its nationalist legitimacy through history and historical memory. However, before we can explore this topic any further, we need to provide some background. Firstly, we need to understand why the CCP turned (or arguably returned) to nationalism shortly after 1989. Secondly, we need to understand why it drew on history, specifically recent historical trauma, as part of this process.

To be clear, the CCP has always presented itself as a nationalist party. We noted in the introductory chapter how the victory of the 1949 revolution was as much a victory for nationalism as it was for communism. This strong nation-building perspective continued into the post-revolutionary era, not just through the wave of anti-foreign mass campaigns that took place during the Mao era, but also as manifested by China's early post-revolutionary rural and industrial reforms which focussed on building a strong socio-economic infrastructure as quickly as possible all under the patriotic leadership of the CCP. Many of China's borders remained unstable when the CCP came to power, under threat to differing degrees from the Soviet Union to the north, the USA in the east (from its bases in Japan, Taiwan and South Korea), France in the south and India in the west. CCP leaders knew that, in the short term, the military was ill-equipped to defend China from foreign encroachments, so it was deemed imperative to strengthen China's economy and infrastructure rapidly in order to be able to resist potential attacks from foreign enemies.

© The Author(s) 2017
R. Weatherley and Q. Zhang, *History and Nationalist Legitimacy in Contemporary China*, DOI 10.1057/978-1-137-47947-1_2

As national security concerns intensified following a sharp decline in Sino-Soviet relations, the party implemented the Great Leap Forward, directing, or in many cases coercing millions of Chinese workers towards projects ill-conceivably designed to help China surpass US and UK steel and grain outputs in just a few years and with the long-term objective of further fortifying China's borders. Later, during the Cultural Revolution, Red Guards were required to demonstrate their commitment to Mao specifically, and to the nation more generally by, amongst other things, eradicating the "four olds" (ideas, customs, traditions and habits), all of which were thought to make China vulnerable to foreign aggression and attack.

The 1980s saw a distinct softening in anti-foreign nationalism as the CCP under Deng Xiaoping sought to improve relations with Western nations in the context of a rapid domestic shift in emphasis towards open market economic reform. From a legitimacy perspective, the CCP was looking to reinvent itself as the party of economic prosperity rather than political revolution which was the failed legacy of the Mao era. Scholarly portrayals of the West became much more positive, with support expressed for Western culture and criticism directed at traditional Chinese culture which was blamed for China's previously slow rate of development (Zhao 1997; Guo 1998). But as this chapter will show, a series of reform-related dislocations emerged during the decade which began to erode the party's economic legitimacy, culminating in the mass national demonstrations of spring 1989. It was this growing unpopularity and disenchantment with the reforms that forced the party to move towards nationalism in an attempt to resuscitate its waning popular appeal.

The decline of the party's Marxist legitimacy also explains the transition towards a more nationalistic platform after Tiananmen. Whilst the calamity of the Mao era had done much to damage the credibility of Chinese Marxism, the party tried to retain its status as a Marxist party during the 1980s by attempting to align the practice of market economic reform with the principles of Marxism. This led to the formulation of scarcely believable concepts such as the Socialist Commodity Economy and the Primary Stage of Socialism, neither of which successfully achieved what was, in any event, a seemingly impossible and contradictory objective.

The key event which accounts for the aggressive tone and history-based content of the party's nationalist agenda was the international condemnation and sanctions that China faced following the military crackdown in Tiananmen Square in June 1989. This presented the CCP with the ideal opportunity to propagate an anti-foreign, specifically anti-Western line by arguing that, despite the unification of China under the CCP in 1949 and the ousting of the foreign imperialists from Chinese soil, the West remained intent on trying to subjugate China as evidenced through its unwarranted criticism and interference in Chinese affairs post-Tiananmen. Intrinsic to this aggressive nationalistic approach was a sharp rise in reminders of the past sufferings inflicted on China by the West during the Century of Humiliation, all of which formed part of the Patriotic Education Campaign. The aim was not only to create public hostility to the West, but to simultaneously garner support for a beleaguered and "internationally persecuted" CCP, looking to safeguard China's interests from a hostile external environment. As we will see, however, whilst there was a growth in expressions of nationalism from the general public, some of these expressions proved to be critical of the CCP rather than supportive of it.

THE EROSION OF ECONOMIC LEGITIMACY

The Mao era had a catastrophic impact on the legitimacy of the CCP. Mao's unrelenting faith in the masses to carry out his radical objectives and realise his utopian vision of socialism was completely shattered by the chaos and unprecedented human suffering caused during the Great Leap Forward. Similarly, Mao's charismatic authority as manufactured by his nationwide cult of personality served only to destroy the institutions of party and state during the equally calamitous Cultural Revolution, pushing the country towards civil war and international disrepute albeit temporarily. Sociopolitical turmoil, economic stagnation and elite intra-party warfare came to define the Mao epoch, casting a huge shadow of the credibility and durability of Marxism, the CCP's ruling ideology (Weatherley 2006).

With the CCP facing an acute crisis of legitimacy as evidenced by widespread labour unrest, industrial sabotage and attacks on government buildings (Domes 1985, pp. 140–141), the Deng Xiaoping regime moved towards what Stephen White (1986) would define as a performance-based mode of legitimacy based on the principles of market economic reform. Put simply, Deng calculated that the party's popularity would increase if it satisfied the base material needs of the Chinese people, following years of neglect and abuse. In the rural sector, the state reduced the amount of grain and cotton under compulsory purchase, increased its procurement prices and allowed farmers to sell any excess produce and "cash crops" (e.g. tomatoes or bananas) in the local marketplace. In industry, managers were given limited rights to produce and sell products in the market once all central quotas were fulfilled and to promote employees without the obstacle of prior government approval. Any profit was put into separate funds, including a workers' bonus fund to be distributed according to individual performance. Small-scale entrepreneurialism was encouraged especially in the consumer market as outdoor stalls began to line Chinese streets selling anything from cigarettes to basic household appliances. Deng also encouraged foreign investment through the special economic zones (SEZs) as China strived to create an export-based market primarily from its light industrial sector.

But as the Chinese economy began to thrive and as China began to recover from the tumult of previous decades, a number of reform-related challenges emerged. One of the main challenges was official corruption. Although corruption was not unprecedented during the Mao era—cases often involved securing "favours" rather than embezzling money (Meany 1991)—the post-Mao embrace of the market made a rise in corruption almost inevitable. Ironically, one of the underlying reasons for corruption during the early stages of the reforms was the piecemeal nature of those reforms, particularly in the industrial sector. Whilst the majority of the small and medium state-owned enterprises (SOEs) were required to operate on the open market following a government directive in October 1984 (Wong 1985), large SOEs remained firmly under the control of the central plan. This meant that large SOEs were prioritised when it came to the central allocation of scarce energy and mineral resources such as coal, iron ore and oil, creating acute demand amongst small and medium SOEs which then led to bribes being offered in order to gain access to these resources. Most large SOEs were run by senior party cadres and given the modest salaries they received (especially in comparison with the amounts managers of smaller SOEs were earning), the temptation to supplement their income by accepting (or in some cases demanding) bribes often proved irresistible (Baum 1997, pp. 368–369).

The children and relatives of high-level cadres also became embroiled in corruption. Referred to disparagingly as "princelings," the political contacts enjoyed by this privileged elite allowed them to make money through legitimate means by, for example, securing bank loans with which to set up small businesses or establish lucrative networks for marketing or supply purposes. If this was not infuriating enough for the Chinese public, tensions escalated during the mid-1980s as reports began to surface that the princelings were also making money illegally, especially those living in the SEZs and open coastal cities where economic activity was frenetic. One of the main profiteering activities was the smuggling into China of luxury foreign items which could then be sold on the black market at inflated prices. The most high-profile case took place on the duty-free island of Hainan in August 1985 where military cadres and their offspring spent over US$1 billion on illegally importing cars, television sets and video recorders. These were then sold on the black market for two or three times the purchase price (Chang 1985).

During its formative years in Yanan, the CCP enjoyed a reputation founded on honesty and integrity in its dealings with local people. One of the defining characteristics of a party member was willingness to subordinate personal interests to the good of the party and society (Gong 1989). But by the 1980s, this public image had evaporated as illustrated by a spate of officially sponsored opinion polls, the first ever to be held in the PRC (Rosen 1990). For example, in a nationwide poll conducted in 1988, 1700 people were presented with a list of over 20 occupations and asked to rank them in order of desirability and public perception. Government, local party and national party cadres all came in the bottom third of the list, below manual workers and only just above the universally despised tax collector. In another poll conducted in 1988, over 600,000 workers were asked whether they thought the party was winning the fight against corruption within its own ranks. Only 7% of interviewees answered in the affirmative.

Perhaps of most concern to the party leadership was the decline in the party's image amongst young people in response to increasing corruption scandals. In a poll carried out in Gansu province in 1988, 2000 educated rural youths were asked whether they were interested in joining the CCP. Less than 6% said they were. In a survey of Chinese university students conducted just after the national demonstrations which took place in 1986, 92% of graduates and 62% of undergraduates said that the protests arose as a result of official corruption and less than 10% expressed any optimism that corruption would decrease in the future (Rosen 1990, pp. 82–83). Despite official efforts to stamp out corruption, this negative impression of the party continued to escalate throughout the decade and as millions gathered in protest during 1989, official corruption was at or very near the top of their list of grievances.

Another reform-oriented problem for the CCP was rising inflation (Naughton 1989). Unprecedented during the Mao era, by 1987 inflation had spiralled to around 35% in some urban areas, despite official estimates which put the figure at 21%. One contributory factor was the increased purchasing power (at least theoretically) of the urban workforce. Enjoying greater autonomy than ever before, partly as a result of Deng's regional decentralisation policy (Goodman 1989), SOE managers began to grant large salary increases to employees. Flush with money, employees began spending increasing amounts on consumer goods, causing a sudden influx of money to flood an economy that was already overheating. Inevitably, as consumer demand increased so did retail prices despite attempts by the state to control prices. Initially, only luxury household items were affected such as colour televisions, fridges and automatic washing machines. But when the price of essential items such as meat, fresh fruit and vegetables began to spiral (in some areas by a reported 50%), the CCP leadership was confronted with a genuine economic crisis as people throughout the country complained that despite having more money than ever before, their purchasing power was actually falling. For example, in a 1987 survey of residents from 33 Chinese cities, more than 65% of those sampled said that their real income was in decline, whilst over 70% identified rising prices as their principal source of concern (Baum 1997, pp. 416–417).

This dire economic situation was accentuated by the ill-timed implementation of price reform by then General Secretary Zhao Ziyang. In April 1988, controls were officially lifted on 14 categories of foodstuffs and when the leadership announced shortly afterwards that price controls were to be relaxed on all consumer goods, a spate of panic buying swept the country. In anticipation of further price rises (which duly came), the urban population purchased anything they could get their hands on ranging from basic foodstuffs to expensive electronic household goods. As shop shelves emptied so too did bank accounts, causing unprecedented problems for the banking system as the national money supply began to dry up. The problem was particularly acute in Fujian province where savings plummeted by RMB 57.8 million (£4.1 million) in 7 days during July 1988. Similarly, the Shenyang (Liaoning province) branch of the Industrial and Commercial Bank saw a RMB 52 million (£3.7 million) fall in reserves between 25 July and 5 August (Breslin 1996, pp. 70–71). In an effort to lure investors back, many banks put up their interest rates on long-term deposits, but with inflation already eating away at savings, the public concluded that it was wiser to spend than to save.

Other socio-economic dislocations triggered by the reforms included an increase in rents. After decades of state subsidised accommodation as part of the "iron rice bowl," rents began to go up as the party gradually removed housing price controls with a view to eventually selling off state-owned accommodation (which it did 10 years later) (Saich 1991). The timing could not have been worse. Already faced with rises in food prices, urban dwellers were now being asked to pay a larger share of their household income on rent.

Unemployment was also fast becoming an issue. Following the implementation of the 1987 Enterprise Reform Law which placed greater emphasis on cost cutting and profit margins in the industrial sector, nervous employers began to lay off large numbers of employees, primarily those on temporary contracts who could be made redundant immediately and without the expense of redundancy pay. By mid-1988, party officials claimed that over four million people from urban areas were out of work, although the real figure was thought to be somewhere between 20 and 30 million. Many of those still in work found that their salaries were frozen and in some areas even reduced. Confronted with the very real prospect of redundancy, this led to a sharp rise in walkouts and other forms of labour unrest.

A combination of these (and other) socio-economic hardships compelled millions of people to take to the streets during spring 1989, most infamously in Tiananmen Square (Naughton 1990). Whilst the international media focused on the student protestors' demands for political reform and the striking image of the Goddess of Democracy erected opposite the portrait of Mao that hangs below the Gates of Heavenly Peace, many of the demonstrators were ordinary urban dwellers protesting about the decline in living and working standards and rises in prices. Having directed its efforts almost exclusively towards economic reform and remoulded the basis of its legitimacy accordingly, the party discovered just how fragile its support base could be if the reforms were not perceived to be working all of the time. Put simply, all the while that the economy was growing, so too was support for the party, but when the economy flagged in the late 1980s, the party's popularity flagged with it. As White (1993, pp. 205–206) concludes, the rise in popular expectations induced by the reforms put the leadership on a kind of treadmill:

To the extent that their own popularity and the credibility of the political system they represent depends on their ability to deliver ever higher amounts of welfare, even temporary reverses, often prompted by the dictates of sound economic policy (such as the austerity programme beginning in 1988), bring popular discontent which is translated by opposition activists into a challenge to the regime itself (as in early 1989).

Manufacturing Marxism

If the implementation of economic reform was intended to resurrect the CCP's waning legitimacy, it simultaneously (and ironically) created another legitimacy-related quandary for the party, that of how to reconcile its erstwhile adherence to Marxist ideology with the introduction of markets in the economic sphere, something that was, of course, anathema to Marxist doctrine. During the first few years of the reforms, the party managed to avoid confronting this problem by relying on the theory of Seek Truth from Facts, first developed by the young Mao Zedong and then shamelessly reinterpreted by Deng in the late 1970s in his bid to oust Mao's hapless successor, Hua Guofeng (Weatherley 2010, pp. 150–152; Teiwes and Sun 2011). The principles of Seek Truth emphasised the importance of linking theory (i.e. ideology) with practice so that if a particular theory did not prove consonant with the practical realities of the day, it would be necessary to take a more flexible and pragmatic approach to the application of that theory and possibly even to revise it. In this way, policy issues were to be governed less by rigid adherence to dogma and more by practical considerations. This provided Deng with the political space he required to experiment with market reforms to the economy (White 1993, pp. 151–152). Also, simply not being the old and failed Maoist CCP or the Gang of Four gave Deng some political room for manoeuvre. However, as the reforms gathered pace and the use of markets become more and more entrenched, the pressure increased on Deng to authorise an official reformulation of Chinese Marxism.

Socialist Commodity Economy

The first attempt came in 1984 following the implementation of a document known as the October Directive (Wong 1985). The October Directive represented a significant intensification of the economic reform process by, amongst other things, restructuring small and medium

SOEs so that the enterprise rather than the state had control over certain aspects decision-making, such as marketing and procurement. Restrictions were removed on the number of workers (previously eight) that could be employed by China's growing number of entrepreneurs, and there was an increase in the categories of products and commodities that could be produced for sale on the open market rather than for distribution under the central state plan.

In an effort to align these economic initiatives with the teachings of Marxism, the party announced that China was entering a new phase of development known as the Socialist Commodity Economy. Notwithstanding the conventional Marxist antipathy towards markets, the new official line held that a limited role for market forces was not only beneficial to China's socialist development, but essential. Although the state plan remained an important part of the socialist economy (especially in relation to large SOEs where the state continued to set production targets and allocate funds and resources), a commodity economy based on supply and demand was an ideal means of stimulating production at the medium and lower levels of the economy. As party theorists Liu Guoguang et al. (1979, p. 15) explained 5 years earlier 'the state plan can only reflect the needs of society in totality, but cannot reflect correctly and flexibly the kaleidoscopic needs of our economic life'.

This rationale demonstrated a commendable degree of conceptual innovation, but the end product did little to reunite China's rapidly shifting economic situation with the party's Marxist ideology. In effect, what the CCP appeared to be suggesting was this: if an economic model is good for the development of production and the productive forces, then it can be usefully defined as socialist. This kind of open-ended, "anything goes" approach came to characterise subsequent attempts to revise Chinese Marxism during the 1980s and 1990s.

The failure to present an adequately Marxist explication of the Socialist Commodity Economy ignited a mini-debate in the Chinese media over the continuing relevance of Marxism to post-Mao China. The forum for the debate was none other than the party's official mouthpiece, the People's Daily. On 7 December 1984, a front-page commentary in entitled 'Theory and Practice' announced that:

[Marx's] works were written more than 100 years ago. Some were his tentative ideas at that time, and things have changed greatly since then. Some of his ideas were not necessarily very appropriate. We cannot expect the writings of Marx and Lenin of that time to provide solutions to our current problems. (Goldman 1994, pp. 136–137)

On the following day, the People's Daily partially retracted this statement by announcing (conveniently) that a typing omission had been made so that the last sentence should have read 'we cannot expect the writings of Marx and Lenin of that time to provide solutions to *all* our current problems' [emphasis added] (Goldman 1994, p. 137). However, two weeks later, the same newspaper published another front-page article (entitled 'More on Theory and Practice') this time claiming that Marxism may not only be irrelevant to the reforms, but could even be detrimental to them. In particular, the author challenged Marx's assertion that socialist society did not need money or commodities, arguing on the contrary that 'the practice of China's socialist construction has proved that commodities and money are necessary for socialist society and that we must develop commodity production'. In a thinly veiled attack on Marxism, the author called for the elimination of 'outdated ideas, customs and conventions' that 'hinder' China's development (Goldman 1994, p. 137).

Any further contributions to this debate were hurriedly circumvented, and this was quickly followed by a campaign against intellectual and press freedom organised by propaganda head Deng Liqun with the backing of Deng Xiaoping (Goldman 1994, pp. 150–165). However, this could not disguise the realisation that Chinese Marxism was rapidly losing touch with the economic realities of mid-1980s China and was increasingly seen as irrelevant to the needs and aspirations of the Chinese people. Following a brief period of economic slowdown in 1985 (primarily as a result of the Deng Liqun's campaign), the reforms intensified, and it was only a matter of time before official theorists were called upon again to try and reconcile the seemingly irreconcilable.

Primary Stage of Socialism

This next attempt came in 1987 in the form of the Primary Stage of Socialism, expounded by Zhao Ziyang. In a considerable departure from the conventional Marxist understanding of the socio-economic transition towards communism, Zhao insisted that, notwithstanding China's claims to be a communist state, China was still an underdeveloped nation and remained in the initial or primary stage of socialism. During this intermediary phase before the inexorable shift into communism, the priority of the day was the rapid development of the means of production. In order to realise this objective, Zhao argued, it was permissible to introduce an eclectic range of economic policies, including overtly capitalist measures. Zhao acknowledged that the more orthodox members of the party leadership were uncomfortable with the pace of economic reform. However, if China was ever to lift itself out of its protracted state of economic backwardness and finally advance towards the higher phase of socialism as envisaged by Marx (i.e. communism), it was necessary to adopt a more flexible and pragmatic approach to economic policy.

Essentially, Zhao was arguing that after 1949 China tried to "jump" the capitalist stage of development straight into communism only to find that its economic conditions were not sufficiently developed to accommodate this final phase. Marx himself believed that capitalism was the necessary penultimate stage of development because it created the material abundance necessary for the realisation of communist principles of distribution referred to as "from each according to his work to each according to his need." But Chinese conditions were not ready for communism, Zhao insisted, so it was necessary for the CCP to create the right conditions by implementing, amongst other things, economic policies of a capitalist nature, although Zhao was very careful to avoid using the term "capitalism."

Reformers in the party leadership were delighted with Zhao's novel approach for several reasons. Firstly, it helped explain why China remained poor despite almost 40 years of CCP rule. This was not down to the party but was due instead to objective historical circumstances. As Kluver (1996, p. 88) explains, theorists argued that the party 'could not be expected to change historical progression itself, it could only guide the nation through historical stages that in themselves are immutable'. Secondly, Zhao's theory accounted for the party's embrace of economic reform using the required Marxist terminology. Despite appearances, China had not become a capitalist country but was simply utilising capitalist mechanisms in order to arrive at communism. In other words, capitalism was a means to communist ends. Thirdly, it gave the reformist wing of the leadership carte blanche to continue implementing economic reform for the foreseeable future. According to Zhao, it would take at least 100 years from the date of the revolution for China to reach an advanced state of socialism, a process that would therefore be achieved sometime around 2050.

Although Zhao's theory was an ambitious attempt to bring Marxist ideology into line with economic policy, it fell short on a number of counts. For example, it failed to provide a realistic prognosis of any kind of communist future in China since the crucial question of when communism would be realised was conveniently deferred. Nor did it provide committed party members with the degree of inspiration required from Marxist theory. In contrast to the predictive and utopian nature of orthodox Marxism, the primary stage theory (like the Socialist Commodity Economy) seemed to imply that anything could be called socialist as long as it boosted Chinese economic growth. This led some party theorists to dub it 'the theory a hundred treasure bag', 'a ragbag into which anything can be stuffed' (White 1993, p. 162). Ultimately, the primary stage theory exposed the increasing irrelevance of Marxist ideology in the modern era of Chinese economic reform and underlined the increasing failure of ideology to act as a legitimising force for CCP rule. As Dirlik and Meisner (1989, p. 365) conclude:

> The distinctive features of Ideology—its ability to motivate and guide the political elite; its claim to provide a framework for a long-term strategy leading towards a credible future; its aim to establish a coherent and credible set of moral principles to provide a new social identity for the members of a 'socialist' society—seem to have atrophied. In the political world of Chinese reformism, Ideology has increasingly become residual.

THE PATRIOTIC EDUCATION CAMPAIGN

The continuing decline of the party's Marxist legitimacy, together with the fragility of its economic legitimacy as illustrated by the Tiananmen demonstrations, forced the CCP to broaden its popular appeal to incorporate a much stronger nationalist element.

This took the form of an aggressive, often anti-foreign type of nationalism precipitated in the main by the international fallout from the military crackdown that ended the demonstrations with such shocking finality. The mass shooting of Chinese citizens on 4 June 1989 unleashed an outpouring of condemnation by much although not all of the international community (e.g. Japan) and turned China into a pariah state almost overnight. This was followed shortly afterwards by the imposition of sanctions against China by Western nations, particularly the USA. In the military sphere, US sanctions included the suspension of all government-to-government military sales (worth US$601.5 million) and a ban on all commercial exports of weapons to China (valued at US$85 million in 1988). The 1985 Nuclear Co-operation Agreement between the USA and China was also suspended. In the economic sphere, US sanctions (noticeably less punitive) included the suspension of investment guarantees by the Overseas Private Investment Corporation and the recommendation that all international lending institutions suspend loans to China, estimated at US$1.3 billion (McGurn 1990). The US administration also suspended high-level government and military exchanges with China, although it covertly continued to liaise with the Deng regime less than three weeks after the crackdown (despite claims to the contrary) when National Security Adviser Brent Scowcroft and his assistant Lawrence Eagleburger were sent to Beijing (Safire 1989). In addition, according to the Washington Post, George Bush made a personal telephone call to Deng Xiaoping on 8 June, only to be told that Deng was unavailable because it was early morning in Beijing and in any event it is not customary to hold direct calls between Chinese and foreign leaders. No return call was made by Deng to Bush (Harding 1992, p. 227).

The Chinese response to international criticism of the Tiananmen crackdown and the imposition of sanctions was to accuse Western governments of meddling in China's internal affairs. This was frequently expressed, in angry tones, as a flagrant violation of Chinese national sovereignty. The Western stance was also portrayed in more sinister tones as part of a wider conspiracy to hold down and suppress a resurgent China in an effort to prevent it from resuming its "rightful" place in the international community (Guo 1991, pp. 18–19).

Emerging from this indignant and accusatory riposte was the Patriotic Education Campaign, a concerted attempt by the CCP to whip up a sense of public outrage against the West by reminding the Chinese people of past suffering inflicted during the Century of Humiliation and at the same time to encourage public support for the CCP in its quest to safeguard China's interests from an interfering West. There was certainly a potential market for this kind of approach. Callaghan (2006, p. 185) notes that 'according to the records of the National Library of China, no new books about "national humiliation" were published in China between 1947 and 1990'. So, the CCP exploited this opportunity starting in May 1990, when as part of a joint commemoration to mark the 1919 May Fourth Movement and the 150th anniversary of the beginning of the First Opium War Jiang Zemin told over 3000 attending students that the First Opium War symbolised the beginning of China's humiliation by foreign imperialists. Not only this, but that certain Western nations were still intent on humbling and embarrassing China, as demonstruted by the sanctions and pious chastisement. A few weeks later, under the heading 'Hold Much Higher the Great Flag of Patriotism', the People's Daily wrote an article on the First Opium War which concluded that 'we have to open our country to the world, but we cannot advocate total Westernisation and must resist the pressure from the West' (Xu 2001, p. 156). A few days later, the Liberation Army Daily insisted that:

> Since the [First] Opium War, the West has never stopped its aggression against China. After the PRC was established, the West first imposed an economic embargo on China and then isolated and contained the new socialist country in order to overthrow this government in its cradle. (Xu 2001, p. 156)

Along side these and other indignant proclamations by the Chinese media, the party began to release official documents which pushed the aggressive nationalist line even harder under the auspices of Jiang Zemin and Li Ruihuan (a specialist in ideological matters). This included the 1991 'Notice about Conducting the Education of Patriotism and the Revolutionary Tradition', the 'Circular on Fully Using Cultural Relics to Conduct Education in Patriotism and Revolutionary Traditions' and the 'General Outline on Strengthening Education in Modern and Contemporary History and National Conditions' (Wang, Z 2008, p. 789). The latter document, in particular, included a scathing attack on foreign imperialism during the Century of Humiliation, identifying Britain, the USA and Japan as the key culprits and the CCP as the saviours of the Chinese nation through their 'determined resistance against foreign invaders' (Wu 2012, p. 40).

Local party leaders were instructed on how to propagate the new campaign at the local level through public meetings and study sessions. As noted in the previous chapter, the campaign was particularly focused on the youth where primary school children learned patriotic songs and were taught at length about the Century of Humiliation, after which they were encouraged to articulate their feelings of disgust towards Western nations. First-year university students were required to take a course in modern Chinese history highlighting the suffering imposed by the imperialists and students of all ages were encouraged to visit newly established patriotic education bases. These included the Memorial Hall of the War to Resist US Aggression and Aid Korea in Dandong, the Memorial Hall of the War of Resistance Against Japan in Beijing and the ruined site of Yuanmingyuan (Wang, Z 2008, pp. 795–796).

This emphasis on indoctrinating the youth, particularly at the student level, was a clear attempt by the CCP to divert attention away from the pressing socio-economic issues that had precipitated the Tiananmen demonstrations, many of which remained highly relevant in the early 1990s. The focus of student critical attention should instead be on foreign powers for all the terrible things they did to China during the Century of Humiliation and were still trying to do in the early post-Tiananmen era. As Callaghan (2006, p. 186) puts it, 'a patriotic education policy was formulated not so much to re-educate the youth (as it was in the past), as to redirect protest toward the foreigner as an enemy, as an external Other'.

As part of the Patriotic Education Campaign, the CCP sharpened the tone of its foreign policy by developing the concept of international containment. This theory held that the USA and other Western powers were covertly working together to prevent China from evolving naturally as a major international force with the ultimate aim of destroying Chinese socialism altogether. Although the Cold War had ended, it was argued, the West remained intent on expanding its power and influence overseas, particularly with regard to China. Indeed, the relaxation of international tensions following the demise of socialism in Eastern Europe and the old Soviet Union had made Western forces even more arrogant and even more determined to constrain China, as evidenced by the more robust Western position on highly sensitive issues of Chinese sovereignty. Growing Western criticism of China's human rights policy in Tibet and its confrontational stance towards Taiwan particularly angered Chinese leaders. The West, especially the USA, was also blamed for the protracted delays to China's accession to the WTO and for its failure to win the bid to host the 2000 Olympic Games, a source of particular anguish for many Chinese. The passing of a US Congressional resolution in July 1993 against China's Olympic bid was seized upon as evidence of a US conspiracy against China.

The Human Rights Campaign

Shortly after Tiananmen, in response to Western criticism of the crack-down and of China's record on human rights in general, the CCP for the first time in its history began to articulate an official Chinese position on human rights through a series of press releases, official statements and government white papers on the subject. The main objective was to construct a uniquely "sinified" notion of rights to show how this differed from what was perceived as the Western model. According to the 1991 State Council white paper on human rights (the first of many) entitled 'China's Human Rights Situation' (IOSC 1991):

> A country's human rights situation cannot be judged in total disregard of its historical and national conditions, nor can it be evaluated according to the preconceived model or standard of another country or region. Such is the practical attitude of seeking truth from facts. From their own historical circumstances, the realities of their own country and their long practical experience, the Chinese people have derived their own viewpoints on the human rights issue and have formulated the relevant laws and policies.

More importantly for our purposes, another aim, in keeping with the strictures of the Patriotic Education Campaign, was to remind the public of the legacy of foreign imperialism in China and the violations of Chinese human rights that this entailed. As the 1991 white paper put it:

> The imperialists massacred people in untold numbers during their aggressive wars. In 1900, the troops of the Eight Allied Powers—Germany, Japan, Britain, Russia, France, the United States, Italy and Austria—killed, burned and looted, raising Tanggu, a town of 50,000 residents to utter ruins, reducing Tianjin's population from one million to 100,000 and killing countless people when they entered Beijing, where more than 1700 were slaughtered in Zhuangwanfu alone. During Japan's full scale invasion which began in 1937, more than 21 million people were killed or wounded and ten million people mutilated to death. In six weeks beginning on 13 December 1937, the Japanese invaders killed 300,000 people in Nanjing. (IOSC 1991)

Using a similarly inflammatory tone, the white paper further stated that:

> Under the imperialists' colonial rule, the Chinese people had their fill of humiliation and there was no personal dignity to speak of. The foreign

aggressors enjoyed "extraterritoriality" in those days. On December 24, 1946 Peking University student Shen Cong was raped by William Pierson, an American GI, but, to the great indignation of the Chinese people, the criminal, handled unilaterally by the American side, was acquitted and released.

These stark reminders of the bad old days were not just stand-alone statements. They were also used to describe how the Chinese concept of rights has been shaped over the years. So, for example, in explaining the priority attached to subsistence rights (e.g. food, accommodation and clothing) in Chinese thinking, party theorists argued that the attainment of such rights was linked inextricably to China's long and arduous struggle for national independence from imperialism. According to the party line, following the First Opium War 'imperialist powers waged hundreds of wars on various scales against China, causing immeasurable losses to the lives and property of the Chinese people'. The imperialists 'sold, maltreated and caused the death of numerous Chinese labourers, plunging countless people in old China into an abyss of misery'. Little changed after the establishment of the Republic in 1912 which categorically 'failed to deliver the nation from semi-colonialism'. It was only after the founding of the PRC that the Chinese people 'stood up as the masters of their own country' and 'won the basic guarantee of their life and security' (IOSC 1991).

The party has since adopted a similar position on democracy. In addition to the constant reminders about Western imperialism, the party has explained how this imperialism has shaped Chinese thinking on democracy. In a white paper entitled 'The Building of Political Democracy in China' (IOSC 2005). As with China's discourse on rights, the realisation of democracy is portrayed as the victorious outcome of a struggle against Western imperialism. With the First Opium War used again as the starting point, the authors claim that 'Western imperialist powers launched, time and again, aggressive wars against China' and 'for nearly 110 years after that, China became a target of plunder for almost all imperialist countries, big and small'. This created a situation in which 'the Chinese people had no democratic rights whatsoever'. According to the white paper, the Chinese people have given consideration to Western-style democracy 'through painstaking exploration and hard struggle.' But they came to the conclusion that 'mechanically copying the Western bourgeois political system and applying it to China would lead them nowhere'. Instead, in order 'to accomplish the historic task of saving China, the Chinese people developed their own new thought and new theories to open up a new road for the Chinese revolution'.

Reinforcing Patriotism

Scholars such as Wang Zheng (2008, 2012) and Xu Guangqiu (2012) have identified newer approaches to the promotion of the Patriotic Education Campaign during the twenty-first century which have abandoned the anachronistic techniques of repetitious political sloganeering, no longer deemed to be appealing (if they ever were) to the general public and young people in particular. There has also been much greater involvement in the campaign from state-run newspapers and magazines, featuring full-length articles and carefully controlled debates on the importance of patriotic education. Similarly, radio and television channels have aired a number of special programmes on the subject (Wang, Z 2012, p. 108).

Apparent, once again, has been the utilisation of history and historical memory to disseminate the nationalist message. So, for example, as part of an initiative to use entertainment to propagate the campaign (in accordance with the guidance contained in the 2004 'Opinions on Strengthening and Improving the Work of Patriotic Education Bases'), the public has been encouraged to watch 100 "red" films, read 100 "red" books and sing 100 "red" songs' in what was known as the Three One Hundred for Patriotic Education. Each of the films, books and songs was jointly recommended by the Ministry of Education and the Propaganda Department and each of them 'focus on Chinese national humiliation', according to Xu (2012, p. 115). Indeed, one of the selected books is even entitled 'Never Forget Our National Humiliation'. What is noteworthy about the Three One Hundred for Patriotic Education movement is the intended inseparability of the role of the CCP from the cause of nation-building, the inextricable linking of "red" to "nation." In addition, Chinese artists 'were summoned to propagate historical myths and trauma through literature, theatre and films' such that the campaign 'permeates all Chinese pop culture and media' (Wang, Z 2012, p. 108).

The party has also accelerated its construction of museums and public monuments devoted to patriotic causes and increased the number patriotic education bases. By 2006, Beijing, Hebei, Jiangsu, Jiangxi and Anhui had together established more than 400 provincial level bases and nearly 2000 county level bases. In an effort to encourage people to visit these bases, the party launched a "red tourism" campaign which helped to subsidise the cost of these visits. Consequently, from 2004 to 2007, more than 400 million people participated in the tourism campaign, visiting destinations such as Mao's birthplace in Shaoshan and various sites at the party's revolutionary base in Yanan (Xu 2012, pp. 115–116).

Another way of reinforcing the national message from a historical perspective (although not necessarily exclusive to this century) has been to recall the humiliations of the past inflicted by foreign powers when the party believes that such powers are still behaving aggressively towards China. In response to the May 1999 US-led NATO bombing of the Chinese Embassy in Belgrade, the Chinese media published a number of articles comparing the incident to the Anglo-French incineration of Yuanmingyuan (of which more in the next chapter) even though neither Britain nor France were involved in the Belgrade bombing. Angry comparisons were also made to the First Opium War, the Sino-French War of 1884–1885 and the unfair terms of the loan agreement made between the US administration and the Yuan Shikai government in 1913. One article entitled 'This is not the China of 1899' asserted that China had become much stronger since the terrible days of the past and would no longer tolerate any Western "bullying":

> This is a China that defeated the Japanese fascists, this is a China that had a trial of strength and won victory over the United States on the Korean battleground. The Chinese people are not to be bullied and China's sovereignty and dignity are not to be violated. The hot blood of people of ideas and integrity who opposed imperialism for over 150 years flows in the veins of the Chinese people. US-led NATO had better remember this (RMRB 1999).

A similar approach is taken when Japan acts in a way that angers or offends China. As we will see in more detail in chapter 4, the numerous spats with Japan over long-running sovereignty claims to the Diaoyu islands often precipitates accusations that Japan, in asserting its rights to the islands, is still behaving like an imperialist power, with references made to the Japanese occupation of Manchuria and the Nanjing Massacre. A similar response arises following regular Japanese prime ministerial visits to the controversial Yasukuni Shrine and the alleged whitewashing of wartime atrocities in China from Japanese history books.

Foreign support for Tibetan independence also triggers official reminders of past humiliations at the hands of foreign powers. Attempts to disrupt the Beijing Olympics torch relay (particularly in France) in protest at China's human rights record in Tibet drew ugly comparisons with the spectre of Yuanmingyuan. This and other expressions of support for Tibet around the time of the Olympics led to the publication of a State Council white paper (IOSC 2009) entitled 'Fifty Years of Democratic Reform in Tibet' in which foreign critics were dismissed as 'Western anti-China forces', accused of hypocrisy in light of their own dismal record of human rights violations in China and of trying to hold China back from its re-emergence on the international scene.

THE INITIAL PUBLIC RESPONSE

It is, of course, difficult to gauge public opinion accurately in any country, not least in a country which is as populous as China and where the state still plays such an active role in screening and regulating the freedom of speech and expression. Moreover, there will always be doubts about the "national" applicability or representativeness of, for example, an opinion poll or a public protest. But if we examine the information that is available to us, it is possible not only to identify a wide-ranging public response to the party's post-Tiananmen emphasis on nationalism, but also a shift in that response in a direction which the party would not have intended.

Initially, it appears that the Chinese public responded in a manner that was supportive of the CCP's aims and objectives. In the intellectual arena, for example, there was a rapid proliferation of anti-Western scholarly literature during the early to mid-1990s which built further on the containment theory expounded by the CCP in the immediate aftermath of Tiananmen. This was in stark contrast to the more cosmopolitan, pro-Western works of the 1980s, noted earlier. A number of new academic journals came into circulation (e.g. Strategy and Management), focusing exclusively on topics of national concern and giving a strong voice to the new wave of chauvinistic cultural conservatism that was sweeping through China's academic ivory towers. In addition, new cultural academies were established (e.g. Beijing University's Institute of Chinese Culture) reflecting an often xenophobic interest in customs and the culture of traditional China (Zhao 1997).

Mainstream commercial literature experienced an increase in anti-foreign publications, even before the Patriotic Education Campaign was launched. The book 'Winds Over the Plains' published in 1990 by Yuan Hongbing (now a political dissident exiled in Australia) claimed that the Chinese race was destined to survive and prosper at the expense of Western nations and criticised those in China who put forward Western theories and values to solve Chinese problems. Yuan's volume proved to be extremely popular, particularly with students. In 1991, General He Ming's 'The Blood of Human Rights Debt' became an instant best-seller. General He fought in the Korean War and insisted that the USA was guilty of war crimes during that campaign. Another book entitled 'Chinese Woman in Manhattan' sold over 200,000 copies in 1993. In it, the author portrayed American society as dishonest and money obsessed. A similar image of the USA was portrayed in a popular TV series entitled 'Beijing Man in New York' televised in 1993 (Xu 2001, p. 153).

Opinion polls reflected a growing wave of anti-foreign sentiment in China. In a 1995 poll carried out by the China Youth Daily, over 87% of respondents said they perceived America as the country which was "least friendly" to China, whilst more than 57% said they felt more negative towards America than towards any other country in the world, including Japan. Over 85% believed that the USA had intervened in the 1990–1991 Gulf War "out of its own interests" (Fewsmith 2001, p. 155). In a separate poll conducted in 1996 by the Youth Research Centre, more than half of the respondents said that they thought American culture was "empty," that American society had a "low morality" and that corruption in the USA was a serious cause for concern. Over 90% said that they thought drugs were a big problem in America (Xu 2001, p. 158).

Japan was also singled out for public criticism at this time. In a 1996 survey, 84% of respondents said that they associated the word Japan with the Nanjing Massacre, whilst 81% said they immediately thought of the Second Sino-Japanese War and Japan's alleged denial of its wartime aggression in China. Another question in the survey asked which twentieth-century Japanese person was most representative of Japan. First place (29%) went to Hideki Tojo, the Japanese political and military leader who ordered the attack on Pearl Harbour in 1941. When asked to identify a personality trait most closely associated with Japanese people, over 56% chose "cruel" (Fewsmith 2001, p. 261). Japan did not fare much better in a 2005 survey conducted by the Japanese think tank Genron NPO, in partnership with Beijing University and the China Daily. More than 63% had a "very bad" or "not very good" impression of Japan. A further 93% said Japan should take sole responsibility for the ongoing friction in Sino-Japanese relations (Fewsmith 2001, p. 261).

THE FIRST SIGNS OF DISSENT

Hays Gries (2004) asserts that despite Western perceptions of a post-Tiananmen mode of nationalism exclusively controlled by the state, much of China's nationalist activity has come from independently organised, grass-roots movements or sometimes just individuals with no affiliation. This is apparent in the growth of populist publications on the subject, in the increasingly vibrant commercial media (Liu and McCormick 2011) and in the new public space created by the Internet (Thornton 2010) which has seen millions of netizens articulating their views on issues of national concern. What is significant about the emergence of this populist, unofficial form of nationalism is the challenge that it poses to the CCP. Far from obediently supporting the party's claim to be the sole representative of China's national interest, some nationalists have argued that the party is not doing enough to stick up for China, that the CCP is not nationalistic enough.

We will see in Chap. 4, how one of the first signs of a dissenting nationalist voice came in 1996 after the right-wing Japan Youth Federation landed on the Diaoyu islands and set up a makeshift lighthouse as a symbol of Japanese sovereignty. This precipitated a series of spontaneous anti-Japanese public protests which, although quickly suppressed, did not prevent dissent from being articulated through other channels such as letter writing, petition signing and interviews with the media in which concerns were expressed about CCP "weakness" on Japan.

The challenge posed by popular nationalism was even more evident with the publication in 1996 of the best-selling book 'China Can Say No' (Song Qiang et al. 1996). Released just before the lighthouse incident the book was an impassioned manifestation of the widely held view that the West and America, in particular, was trying to hold China down by lecturing China on issues of morality, disrupting the Chinese economy and creating domestic uncertainty about the current political regime. The five authors (each from non-scholarly backgrounds) cited, amongst other things, Western sympathy for Tibet and Taiwan as evidence of an anti-China conspiracy. They also attacked Western denunciations of China's human rights record, questioning whether the West had the moral high ground on this subject given its legacy of imperialism in China and elsewhere. Although these viewpoints dovetailed perfectly with the party's own position, the authors deviated from the party line in their virulent assertion that China should be bolder in standing up (or "saying no") to America and the West on these and other issues of national importance and should even be prepared to bear arms against its foreign detractors. Although not overtly critical of Chinese foreign policy, there was an inherent implication that the CCP had been too soft in its dealings with the West.

At first, the party enthusiastically endorsed the publication of 'China Can Say No'. Yu Quanyu (Deputy Chair of China's Human Rights Commission) described the book as closely reflecting popular opinion, whilst several editorials in the state-controlled media heaped praise on the book (Fewsmith 2001, p. 155). But when the underlying critical tone of the book became more apparent, the party abruptly changed its stance, condemning the book as an unwarranted attempt to interfere in foreign policy matters by people who were unqualified to understand such matters. By this time, however, the book had already sold hundreds of thousands of copies (all 50,000 copies of the first edition were sold immediately), becoming the single most popular book in China in the 1990s and drawing numerous letters of support from all over the country. The book also spawned a burgeoning cottage industry of similarly themed (and unimaginatively named) publications such as 'China Can Still Say No' and 'Why Does China Say No?' which were more directly critical of Chinese foreign policy and, by implication, the CCP.

The resultant banning of the "say no" series of works and other popular anti-foreign tracts was hardly an unprecedented move by the CCP. It was, however, highly significant in that it exposed a realisation that this new wave of popular nationalists had, on the face of it, become more representative of public opinion on the question of nationalism than the party itself. This was deemed (rightly so) to constitute a direct threat to the party's nationalist legitimacy.

Subsequent expressions of popular nationalism were even more pronounced, forcing the party to alter its approach to the dissenters moving from suppressing them to accommodating them, as noted in the previous chapter. This was particularly apparent during the public protests which took place following the American bombing of the Chinese embassy in Belgrade in May 1999. As the US and Chinese governments deliberated over the full extent of any apology to be given by the Clinton administration, street demonstrations erupted in over 100 Chinese cities comprising participants from all generations and a variety of social backgrounds. Whilst many protestors were angry with the USA, public attention also focused on the party's alleged unwillingness to confront the USA, preferring, as one protestor claimed, to adopt a policy of "merely lodging fierce protests". The diversity of the participants was further manifested by the 281 condolence letters delivered to the Guangming Daily which came from 26 Chinese provinces as well as from outside China. Those sending the letters included students, teachers, members of the party-state and media workers, and here again criticism was directed both at America and the CCP (Hays Gries 2004, pp. 129–131).

Unable to control the demonstrations (despite a nationally televised plea for calm from Hu Jintao) and anxious that they might rapidly evolve from being anti-US to anti-CCP in the light of the approaching tenth anniversary of the Tiananmen crackdown, the authorities in Beijing moved quickly to accommodate the protestors by providing a bus service, mainly for students from the outer regions of the city to the central embassy district. The students were then allowed (albeit closely watched by the police) to walk past the US ambassador's residence, the embassy building and then the chancellery, throwing bricks, ink and faeces as they went. As Fewsmith (2001, p. 213) points out:

> It was certainly better, from the Party's point of view, to have such public anger directed at the United States than to have students throw stones at Zhongnanhai (the compound in which the leadership lives), which they certainly would have done had the Party's reaction been perceived as weak.

These examples of nationalist dissent against the party are a snapshot of the early stages of an adverse public response. We will see in later chapters how this dissent has since developed in a manner which is more bold and overtly critical. We will also see how, just as the party has used history and historical memory as a means of bolstering its nationalist legitimacy, so the popular nationalists have used it to challenge this legitimacy. We will begin with our first example of this: the destruction of Yuanmingyuan.

References

Baum, R. (1997). The road to Tiananmen: Chinese politics in the 1980s. In R. MacFarquhar (Ed.), *The politics of China: The eras of Mao and Deng* (pp. 340–471). Cambridge: Cambridge University Press.

Breslin, S. (1996). *China in the 1980s: Centre-province relations in a reforming socialist state*. London: Macmillan.

Callaghan, W. (2006). History, identity, and security: Producing and consuming nationalism in China. *Critical Asian Studies, 2*(38), 179–208.

Chang, C. (1985). The Hainan vehicle trafficking scandal. *Issues and Studies, 21*(9), 5–7.

Dirlik, A., & Meisner, M. (Eds.). (1989). *Marxism and the Chinese experience.* London: M.E. Sharpe.

Domes, J. (1985). *The government and politics of the PRC: A time of transition.* Boulder: Westview Press.

Fewsmith, J. (2001). *China since Tiananmen: The politics of transition.* Cambridge: Cambridge University Press.

Goldman, M. (1994). *Sowing the seeds of democracy in China.* Cambridge, MA: Harvard University Press.

Gong, W. (1989). The legacy of confucian culture in Maoist China. *Social, 26*(4), 363–374.

Goodman, D. (Ed.). (1989). *China's regional development.* London: Routledge.

Guo, Q. (1991). *Zhongguo zai Renquan de Jiben Lichang he Jiben Shijian* [The basic position and practice of human rights in China]. *Qiushi* [Seek Truth], *23,* 14–19.

Guo, Y. (1998). Patriotic villains and patriotic heroes: Chinese literary nationalism in the 1990s. *Nationalism and Ethnic Politics, 4*(1/2), 163–188.

Harding, H. (1992). *A fragile relationship: The United States and China.* Washington, DC: Brookings Institution.

Hays Gries, P. (2004). *China's new nationalism: Pride, politics and diplomacy.* Berkeley: University of California Press.

IOSC. (1991). *Human rights in China.* Beijing: Information Office of the State Council. Retrieved from http://big5.news.cn/gate/big5/news.xinhuanet.com/employment/2002-11/18/content_633179.htm.

IOSC. (2005). *The building of political democracy in China.* Beijing: Information Office of the State Council. Retrieved from http://big5.news.cn/gate/big5/news.xinhuanet.com/english/2005-10/19/content_3645750.htm.

IOSC. (2009). *Fifty years of democratic reform in Tibet.* Beijing: Information Office of the State Council. Retrieved from http://big5.news.cn/gate/big5/news.xinhuanet.com/english/2009-03/03/content_10931976.htm.

Kluver, A. (1996). *Legitimating the Chinese economic reforms: The rhetoric of myth and orthodoxy.* New York: State University of New York Press.

Liu, G., Wu, J., & Zhao, R. (1979). The relationship between planning and the market as seen by China in her socialist economy. *Atlantic Economic Journal, 7*(4), 11–21.

McGurn, W. (1990). The US and China: Sanctioning Tiananmen. In G. Hicks (Ed.), *The broken mirror.* Essex: Longman Group.

Meany, C. (1991). Market reform and disintegrative corruption in urban China. In R. Baum (Ed.), *Reform and reaction in post-Mao China: The road to Tiananmen* (pp. 124–142). London: Routledge.

Naughton, B. (1989). Inflation and economic reform in China. *Current History*, (September), 270.

Naughton, B. (1990). Economic reform and the Chinese political crisis of 1989. *Journal of Asian Economics*, *1*(2), 349–361.

Qiang, S., et al. (Eds.). (1996). *Zhongguo Keyi Shuo Bu: Lengzhanhou Shidai de Zhengzhi yu Qingan Jueze* [China can say no: Political and emotional choices in the post-cold war era]. Beijing: Zhonghua Gongshang Lianhe Chubanshe.

Qing, L., & McCormick, B. (2011). The media and the public sphere in contemporary China. *Boundary 2*, *38*(1), 101–134.

RMRB. (1999a, May 12). *Zhongguo bu shi Yibai Jiujiu* [This is not the China of 1899]. *Renmin Ribao* [People's Daily]. Retrieved from http://huylpd.twin-bridge.com.

Rosen, S. (1990). The Chinese communist party and Chinese society: Popular attitudes towards party membership and the party's image. *Australian Journal of Chinese Affairs*, *24*, 51–92.

Safire, W. (1989, December 27). The Scowcroft visit to Beijing in July was leaked by a Chinese official to Cable News Network. *New York Times*, 1.

Saich, T. (1991). Urban Society in China. *Nordic Proceedings in Asian Studies*, *2*, 558–599.

Teiwes, F., & Sun, W. (2011). China's new economic policy under Hua Guofeng: Party consensus and party myths. *China Journal*, *66*, 1–23.

Thornton, P. (2010). Censorship and surveillance in Chinese cyberspace: Beyond the great firewall. In P. Hays Gries & S. Rosen (Eds.), *Chinese politics: State, society and the market* (pp. 179–198). Abingdon: Routledge.

Wang, Z. (2008). National humiliation, history education, and the politics of historical memory: Patriotic education campaign in China. *International Studies Quarterly*, *52*(4), 783–806.

Wang, Z. (2012). *Never forget national humiliation: Historical memory in Chinese politics and foreign relations*. New York: Columbia University Press.

Weatherley, R. (2006). *Politics in China since 1949: Legitimizing authoritarian regimes*. London: Routledge.

Weatherley, R. (2010). *Mao's forgotten successor: The political career of Hua Guofeng*. London: Palgrave.

White, S. (1986). Economic performance and communist legitimacy. *World Politics*, *38*(3), 462–482.

White, G. (1993). *Riding the Tiger: The politics of economic reform in post-Mao China*. Stanford: Stanford University Press.

Wong, C. (1985). The second phase of economic reform in China. *Current History* (September edition), 260–263.

Wu, Z. (2012). *The effects of patriotic education on Chinese youths' perceptions of Japan*. MPhil Thesis, Lingnan University.

Xu, G. (2001). Anti-western nationalism: 1989–1999. *World Affairs, 163*(4), 151–162.
Xu, G. (2012). Chinese anti-westernism, 2000–2010. *Asian and African Studies, XVI*(2), 109–134.
Zhao, S. (1997). Chinese intellectuals quest for national greatness and nationalistic writings in the 1990s. *China Quarterly, 157,* 725–745.

CHAPTER 3

Aggressive Nationalism: Utilising the Yuanmingyuan Incident

On 18 October 1860, Britain's High Commissioner to China Lord James Elgin (son of Thomas Elgin of Elgin Marbles fame) ordered more than 3,500 British troops to set fire to Yuanmingyuan, comprising a vast complex of residential palaces, temples, ancestral shrines, libraries and art galleries situated in north-west Beijing. As the final act of the Second Opium War, the destruction of Yuanmingyuan was carried out in direct retaliation for the kidnap and torture of a small delegation of Anglo-French emissaries who had arrived in Beijing to insist on the enactment of the terms of the 1858 Treaty of Tianjin. Twenty members of the group died in captivity, including a correspondent for the London Times. The other sixteen, including the British envoys Henry Loch and Harry Parkes, were released after surviving for almost two weeks in the infamous Chinese Board of Punishments (Wolsey 1862; BBC 2015a). Prior to igniting the palaces, British and French troops stole thousands of priceless antiques, many of which are now displayed in museums around the world. Shortly after the site had been reduced to ruins, a sign was erected with the inscription 'this is the reward for perfidy and cruelty'.

Yuanmingyuan was ransacked again in 1900 during the Boxer Rebellion when anti-Qing Chinese looters broke into the gardens to thieve precious timber and raze the buildings that had been repaired after 1860 at the instruction of the Qing court. The troops of the Eight-Nation Alliance which had been dispatched to suppress the Boxers and relieve the siege of the foreign legations stole whatever remained of artistic or monetary value, including bronze statues, stone carvings and ceramic ornaments. Ironically, given the nationality of those who ordered its annihilation, all that remains of the original site are the ruins of the European-style palaces which were never fully destroyed because they were made of stone and marble.

Although the destruction of Yuanmingyuan was largely ignored during the Mao era, the launch of the Patriotic Education Campaign saw a sharp increase in official references to the incident and this has continued in more recent years, especially in the build-up to the 150th anniversary of the incident. Sometimes the focus is on the wisdom of whether or not to restore the ruined site to its former glory. Sometimes there are impassioned calls for the return of the stolen antiques to their rightful home. In each case the CCP's objective is the same: to remind the Chinese people of the misery of foreign imperialism in an attempt to incite a sense of anger and indignation against foreign, particularly Western nations. This is what we refer to in this chapter as aggressive nationalism. In so doing, the CCP is also seeking to bolster its own nationalist credentials as the party which liberated China from the Century of Humiliation and has since transformed the motherland into a major international power.

However, as we will see below, the public response to the CCP's aggressive nationalist stance on Yuanmingyuan has not always been palatable for the ruling party. Whilst there is plenty of public outrage over the issue, not all of it is directed towards foreign powers. Some of it is directed at the party. Some critics suggest (no doubt correctly) that the official narrative on the burning and looting of the site has been extravagantly finessed by the party for its own propaganda purposes. Others question the appropriateness of the CCP's choice of Yuanmingyuan as a symbol of national suffering given the era of elitism and inequality during which it was built. Some are scathing about the time and money spent by the CCP in keeping the legacy of the incident alive, particularly given some of the more pressing socio-economic issues facing the PRC. Most significant of all are the accusations that China is still too submissive in its dealings with foreign powers, despite the party's claims to have freed the nation from imperialist subjugation. The irony here is that rather than strengthening its nationalist legitimacy, the debate that has arisen over Yuanmingyuan may well be serving to erode that legitimacy.

THE TRAGEDY OF YUANMINGYUAN

The origins of Yuanmingyuan date back to the Ming Dynasty (1368–1644) when a collection of private gardens were created in an area of Beijing that was already resplendent with natural springs and scattered hills. Successive emperors from the early Qing Dynasty (1644–1911) authorised an increase in the number of gardens, together with the construction of a summer residence around the gardens where emperors could retreat from the stifling ceremonial formality of the Forbidden City. But it was the Qianlong Emperor (1711–1799) who gave Yuanmingyuan its definitive identity, overseeing the creation of a vast complex of villas, pavilions, gardens, lakes and hills. Translating as Garden of Perfection and Brightness, Yuanmingyuan is better known to foreigners as the Old Summer Palace because of its status as the emperor's residence prior to the construction of the nearby Yiheyuan (or the Summer Palace). But it was more than just a summer residence. It served as a suburban administrative base for five successive generations of Manchu rulers from where they carried out their official business, including receiving foreign tributaries and convening important political conferences.

The tragedy of Yuanmingyuan's destruction is difficult to overstate. This is verified by descriptive eye witness accounts. When the French General de Montauban and his troops arrived in the gardens to begin the attack, he was apparently spellbound by what he saw, describing it as 'a vision of the Thousand and One Nights, one such that no wild imagination could dream the tangible reality that stood before one's eyes' (Broudehoux 2004, p. 58). According to Charles Gordon, captain of the British Royal Engineers who also participated in the attacks, 'we went out, and, after pillaging it, burned the whole place, destroying in a vandal-like manner'. Noting that it took more than three days to burn Yuanmingyuan to the ground, Gordon lamented that:

> You can scarcely imagine the beauty and magnificence of the palaces we burnt. It made one's heart sore to burn them; in fact these places were so large, and we were so pressed for time, that we could not plunder them carefully. Quantities of gold ornaments were burnt, considered as brass. It was wretchedly demoralising work for an army. (Opoku 2009)

Before the destruction commenced in full, many of Yuanmingyuan's finest art works were extracted and sent to England and France, sometimes straight to the residences of Queen Victoria and Napoleon III. Queen Victoria received a Pekinese dog from Yuanmingyuan, the first of its kind to be seen in Europe, which she appropriately (or perhaps inappropriately) called Looty. Another irony was that the artefacts stolen from Yuanmingyuan had originally been gifts to the Emperor from European monarchs. Charles Gordon managed to steal an entire imperial throne which he donated to his regimental headquarters in Chatham, England, where it still stands today. Some items that were too cumbersome to carry away were sold to Beijing merchants. Other antiques were mindlessly destroyed, including ornate statues in the temples which were bayoneted in the search for the jewels they might contain (Broudehoux 2004, p. 58).

One consolation for the Chinese (if you can call it that) was that the Anglo-French troops preferred to steal the vast quantities of porcelain on display in the palaces rather than the bronze antiques, many of which dated back to the Shang (1556–1046 BC), Zhou (1046–256 BC) and Han dynasties (206 BC–220 AD). But not all the bronze was overlooked. Sculptures of the famous twelve zodiac animals were stolen, and their return to China has become a focal point of intense public attention, as we will see shortly.

One of the most high-profile foreign critics of the Yuanmingyuan incident was the French poet, novelist and dramatist Victor Hugo who famously wrote a letter in November 1861 to the English Captain Butler in which he condemned the Anglo-French actions:

> One day two bandits entered the Summer Palace. One plundered, the other burned. Victory can be a thieving woman, or so it seems. The devastation of the Summer Palace was accomplished by the two victors acting jointly. (Opoku 2009)

Hugo continued:

> All the treasures of all our cathedrals put together could not equal this formidable and splendid museum of the Orient. It contained not only masterpieces of art, but masses of jewellery. What a great exploit, what a windfall! One of the two victors filled his pockets; when the other saw this he filled his coffers. And back they came to Europe, arm in arm, laughing away. Such is the story of the two bandits. We Europeans are the civilised ones, and for us the Chinese are the barbarians. This is what civilization has done to barbarism. (Opoku 2009)

It appears that Hugo never actually travelled to China to view the site of the ruined palaces. Moreover, despite his apparent outrage at the incident, Hugo later admitted to having purchased some of the Chinese silk stolen from Yuanmingyuan by British officers (Broudehoux 2004, p. 59). Nevertheless, his critical words have been gleefully cited time and time again by the CCP in its efforts to keep the Yuanmingyuan incident firmly in the public consciousness.

NEGLECT OF THE SITE UNDER MAO

Despite the often anti-Western rhetoric of the Mao regime, official denunciations of the Yuanmingyuan incident were surprisingly rare under Mao. The apparent lack of significance attached to this incident was reflected in the physical neglect of the site, with little effort expended on protecting it despite the area being declared a municipal park at the request of Zhou Enlai. During the 1960s, much of Yuanmingyuan was allocated to local peasants and this led to further neglect and decay. As Haiyan Lee (2009, p. 161) explains 'in the years following the Great Leap Forward nearby production teams began to cut down trees, flatten the hills and fill the lakes and waterways, make rice paddies, build hog and poultry farms and set up factories and workshops'. By the mid-1970s, there were 15 work units, 20 villages and 270 families occupying the walled-off south-western part of the site (Broudehoux 2004, p. 24). This area has remained walled-off and was scathingly described by one disgruntled observer as follows:

> This sacred site – 'the garden of all gardens' – has now become a festering ground crowded with garbage heaps, vegetable plots, pigsties, and beancurd presses! Motley groups of peasant and migrant families have converged here in the thousands to make a living and to multiply in a disorderly and slipshod manner, generating pollution at a shocking speed and hastening the final deterioration of Yuanmingyuan. (Wang 1999, p. 800)

Another observer bemoaned the woeful disregard of the site, concluding poignantly that 'no one with the slightest knowledge of Yuanmingyuan's history could stand amid such things and hold back their tears. Where were the world-renowned royal gardens? Where were the famed creations of the ingenious Chinese people?' (Wang 1999, p. 815).

It was not until the 1980s that the CCP began to turn its attention to Yuanmingyuan. A government bureau and a scholarly committee were formed, symposia and writing forums were held, and the party reclaimed Yuanmingyuan as a historical site, authorising the creation of the Yuanmingyuan Ruins Park which has been open to tourists for some years (Lee 2009, p. 156). The west side of Yuanmingyuan was modestly renovated in 2005, several small temples have been rebuilt, and there are a number of tourist attractions including a museum, a small funfair, countless souvenir shops and even jet-ski rides on one of the main lakes. Tourists are allowed to trample around and touch the ruins with no restrictions placed on photography. Julia Lovell (2011, p. 345) believes that the CCP is finally capitalising on the propaganda value of the Yuanmingyuan ruins, 'replacing the pigsties and piles of rubbish with new signs littered across the gardens reminding visitors of what would have been there, if the British and French had not burnt or stolen it first'. But taken as a whole, the site remains largely untouched as the CCP contemplates what to do with it.

Constructing a Historical Legacy

In contrast to the physical fate of the site, the party has acted much more decisively over its historical legacy, placing this firmly on the Chinese political agenda and using its best endeavours to keep the incident firmly in the public memory. This was first apparent with the launching of the Patriotic Education Campaign. The 1991 'Circular on Fully Using Cultural Relics to Conduct Education in Patriotism and Revolutionary Traditions' noted in the previous chapter made direct reference to the destruction of Yuanmingyuan and stressed the importance of retrieving the antiques that were stolen by the Anglo-French forces, describing this as the patriotic duty of all Chinese citizens. As the campaign spread into the education sector, school children, including those at primary school level, were taught in great detail about the indignity suffered at Yuanmingyuan within the wider context of the Century of Humiliation. Compulsory first-year university courses on modern Chinese history which highlighted the suffering inflicted by the imperialists made explicit references to the Yuanmingyuan incident. Yuanmingyuan was designated as one of a number of patriotic education bases established throughout China during the early 1990s that students of all ages are required to visit (Wang 2008, p. 796). Anecdotal evidence suggests that, during such visits, students are encouraged to articulate their feelings of disgust towards former imperialist nations and then to repeat this process once they are back in the classroom. In addition, numerous signs have been erected in and around Yuanmingyuan reminding visitors of the incident. There is even a 'Never Forget National Humiliation' memorial wall on which is inscribed details of 'the sordid history of European and American incursions into China, of opium dealing, and the imposition of unequal treaties that made up the century of humiliation' (China Beat 2009).

Another way in which the party has sought to preserve the memory of Yuanmingyuan is to recall the incident when it believes that the West is still acting aggressively towards China, using the state-controlled media to articulate its views. So, for example, following the US bombing of the Chinese Embassy in Belgrade in May 1999, an article published in the People's Daily made a direct comparison between the bombing and the destruction of Yuanmingyuan, stating dramatically that 'through the Embassy riddled with bullet holes covering the charred building, I can see reflected the destroyed ruins of Yuanmingyuan' (RMRB 1999b). Another People's Daily article angrily insisted that China would never again be downtrodden by Western powers, citing the burning of Yuanmingyuan as one in a series of past humiliations that must never be repeated:

> This is not a period when Western forces can plunder the imperial palace at will, burn down Yuanmingyuan and snatch Hong Kong and Macao, nor is it the same period as when the corrupt Qing government or Chiang Kai-shek ruled. China has already stood up. (RMRB 1999a)

Similar impassioned analogies to the Yuanmingyuan incident were made to mark the tenth and fifteenth anniversaries of the US attack.

The hosting of international events in China has also been used by the CCP to resurrect the memory of Yuanmingyuan. This was first apparent during the 1990 Asian Games in Beijing when a number of newspaper articles made reference to the incident. One article suggested that China was much stronger domestically in 1990 than it was in 1860 and was in a much better position on the world stage as it moved towards the twenty-first century (JFJB 1990).

There were further references to Yuanmingyuan in the build-up to the 2008 Beijing Olympics. For example, the Xinhua News Agency used the Olympics to draw a symbolic comparison between the ruins of Olympia and the ruins of Yuanmingyuan. A further comparison was made between the flames of the Olympic torch and the flames that engulfed the palaces (XZX 2008). The tone became confrontational in Chinese state media reports about overseas demonstrators disrupting the Olympic torch relay in protest at China's human rights record in Tibet. Particular venom was directed towards French protestors and the perceived support given to them by the French government and media who were accused of gross hypocrisy in light of their participation in destroying Yuanmingyuan. As the People's Daily put it 'if France wants to talk to China about human rights, they first need to apologise for what they did to Yuanmingyuan and then return the great quantity of Chinese relics that they stole' (RMRB 2008a). Following this, public opinion polls in China (cited enthusiastically in the People's Daily) showed a sharp decline in positive feelings towards France (RMRB 2008b) and a sudden increase in the public boycotting of French goods (XHW 2008).

Another high-profile event that provided an opportunity to evoke the memory of Yuanmingyuan was the return of Hong Kong to China in 1997. In an article published by the People's Liberation Army Daily entitled 'Together the Military and Civilians Celebrate the Return of Hong Kong', the authors declared that the handover 'had finally removed the stains from the imperialists' burning of Yuanmingyuan' (JFJB 1997).

The media often publishes dramatic personal accounts made by visitors to the site. One article claims that 'in Yuanmingyuan's scorched ruins, I see a pool of blood' (RMRB 2009). Another article laments Yuanmingyuan's 'former imperial glory that has been reduced to a royal scar' (RMRB 2010a). A report in China Aviation News describes the ruins as 'like a bleeding wound, still tingling in each Chinese descendant' (ZHTB 2010). Even articles which refer fleetingly to Yuanmingyuan rarely fail to make mention of its destruction. A seemingly innocuous article about the completion of the Beijing Number 4 subway line observes how the new line passes through Yuanmingyuan and then automatically defaults to anguished and protracted descriptions of its annihilation, completely changing the original focus of the article (GZRB 2009).

We noted earlier the critical comments made by Victor Hugo and how these have often been recalled by the CCP by way of reminder of the incident. In a strongly worded article published by the People's Liberation Army Daily entitled 'Hugo's Letter Exposes the Face of the Two Robbers,' the authors insisted that 'we must not forget the bullying and oppression during that period of history and we must not forget this righteous Western author's loud calls from over 100 years ago' (JFJB 1995). A later article in People's Liberation Army Daily included a reading of the letter by Hugo's great granddaughter to mark the anniversary of his 200th birthday which was celebrated throughout China (JFJB 2002). Delegations of Chinese officials have visited Hugo's former residence in Paris, almost like a sacred pilgrimage and in 2010 a statue of Hugo was erected in Beijing (CQWB 2010). Media debates about whether or not to restore the ruined site invariably refer to Hugo (ZZX 2002) as do discussions about returning the stolen antiques to China (GZRB 2009).

The media interest in Yuanmingyuan reached its peak in the build-up to the 150th anniversary of its destruction on 18 October 2010. The first commemorative articles started appearing as early as January 2010, with the Wenhui Bao suggesting (somewhat controversially as it turned out) that China was considering inviting an Anglo-French delegation to attend the anniversary ceremony (WHB 2010). This was followed by a plethora of other articles and news reports about, for example, the month-long schedule of events prior to the anniversary date culminating in a live performance by Jackie Chan (XZX 2010a) and a salt sculpture exhibit in Taibei replicating the looted and much-heralded twelve zodiac animals, thereby emphasising the cross-strait significance of the occasion (ZXS 2010). There was also a story covering an official essay-writing contest about the ruins, specifically designed 'to arouse the population's patriotic passion and encourage the public to give more attention to the Yuanmingyuan incident' (ZJCB 2010).

THE NATIONALIST RATIONALE

The rationale for resurrecting the memory of Yuanmingyuan in such a deliberate, concerted and often provocative manner draws directly on the CCP's quest for nationalist legitimacy. We noted in the previous chapter how, after Tiananmen, the party was forced to redirect its popular appeal towards nationalism, presenting itself as the sole defender of Chinese national interests in the face of a seemingly hostile West. A key aspect of this approach has been to utilise the legacy of Yuanmingyuan which it has done in two inter-related ways. Firstly, Yuanmingyuan reminds the Chinese people just how bad life was during the Century of Humiliation. The destruction of the palaces, with their ruins still visible today, is ideal for these purposes, carefully depicted as the living epitome of a terrible period in China's history. By the same token, Yuanmingyuan is a reminder of just how good life is under the CCP, or so the propagandists would have us beleive. After liberating China from foreign imperialism in 1949, the CCP is guiding China single-handedly towards superpower status and restoring China to its rightful place in the world. So the dual objective is to create public antagonism towards the West and simultaneously to create public gratitude towards the CCP.

Much of the party's rhetoric bears this out. We noted earlier a reference in the People's Daily to the West no longer being able to 'plunder the imperial palace at will, burn down the Yuanmingyuan and snatch

Hong Kong and Macao'. The message from this is clear: the Century of Humiliation is now over and the CCP ended it. Similarly, the claim that 'China has already stood up', drawing conveniently on Mao's words at the Gates of Heavenly Peace on 1 October 1949, strongly implies that the CCP is responsible for this standing up. Likewise, the references to Yuanmingyuan when China hosts major international events such as the Asian Games and the Olympics is intended to contrast the humiliations of the past with the triumphs of the present, again brought about by the CCP. Both of these events were depicted as epitomising national rejuvenation, proof that China, under the CCP, is no longer the "sick man of Asia".

THE DEBATE OVER RESTORATION

The increased focus on the Yuanmingyuan incident has given rise to a number of domestic debates. One of the most prominent concerns whether to restore the site to its former glory or leave it in its current ruinous state. Putting aside issues to do with reconstruction costs, the protection of the local environment and the aesthetics of a rebuild, the most important aspect of the debate for our purposes concerns the historical and political implications of restoring the site or leaving it be. The objective for participants on both sides of the argument is to ensure that Yuanmingyuan retains its symbolic role either as a powerful reminder of imperialist subjugation or as a symbol of China's new-found wealth and prosperity. For the CCP, seemingly undecided on precisely where it stands, the issue at hand is which route offers the best means of further enhancing its nationalist legitimacy.

Leave Alone

Those who want the site left alone insist that this is the only way to ensure the suffering inflicted on the Chinese people during the Century of Humiliation will never be forgotten and will retain its potency as evidence of a bygone era to which China must never return. According to one scholar cited in China Business News, the existing ruins are 'an eternal commemoration of the country's humiliation, such that to restore it would squander its historical, cultural and educational value'. He continues, 'Yuanmingyuan's primary worth today is not the splendour of the palace courtyard or imperial gardens from long ago, but the disgrace that remains from the destruction reaped by the invading armies' (ZGSB 2004).

Ye Yanfang from the Chinese Academy of Social Sciences (CASS) agrees with this perspective. Ye insists that the destruction of Yuanmingyuan is 'like a scar left by the powerful Western nations on the back of the Chinese nation'. For Ye it is crucial to leave the site in its dilapidated state because 'preserving the ruins in Beijing would protect the true facts of history' (China.org 2006). Similarly, Ruan Yisan, Director of the State Institute of Famous Historical and Cultural Cities at Tongji University in Shanghai asserts that 'the present day ruins serves as a testimony to that period of humiliating history' (China.org 2006).

Another opponent of restoration is the internationally acclaimed writer Cong Weixi who suggests that most other countries in the world would not dream of rebuilding their historical monuments. Noting that a Berlin church steeple damaged during the Second World War remains in its original state of disrepair right in the middle of a modern shopping centre, Cong concludes that the intention is 'to remind Germans of a past they dared not forget' (Kutcher 2003, p. 32). For the same reason, Cong suggests, a pillar in Koblenz on which once stood a bronze statue of Germany's combative last emperor, Wilhelm II, has never been replaced after it was completely destroyed during the Second World War. By contrast, Cong believes 'if there had existed such a statue in my country, it would long ago have been replaced. We Chinese have always preferred to repair our history' (Kutcher 2003, p. 32).

A slightly different argument from the anti-restorationist camp is that to rebuild the site would bring yet further shame and embarrassment to China. One frequently made point is that the Western tradition of non-restoration is the better way and to create what some people deride as a fake antique on such a historic and sacred site would simply demonstrate that China remains a backward and inferior nation. According to an article carried by the Xinhua News Agency entitled 'Netizens Against Rebuilding the Yuanmingyuan', this point is commonly made by Chinese internet users. The article also claims that the general online consensus is hostile towards restoration (China.org 2007).

Liao Baoping of the Yancheng Evening News shares this perspective. He believes that Yuanmingyuan, as it once was, comprised a symbol of all that was wrong with China, a self-indulgent nation blinded by its own superiority complex and woefully ignorant of the giant strides in economic and military development being taken by Western nations. As Liao puts it, 'while the West was making great headway in science, technology, and navigation and began imperialist expansion around the world, the Qing Dynasty rulers were immersed in the illusion of a prosperous era'. To rebuild the palaces would simply remind the Chinese people of 'the extravagance of the Qing Dynasty' (Beijing Review 2011).

Some opponents of restoration believe that proposals to rebuild the old site are purely motivated by financial gain. The architectural historian Chen Zhihua has branded restoration proposals as an exercise in money worship. He points to a reconstructed section of the Great Wall at Badaling where a KFC restaurant and a crowd of noisy vendors have destroyed the rich history of that frontier fortress. Rebuilding Yuanmingyuan, Chen suggests, would ensure the same ghastly outcome (Kutcher 2003, p. 32).

Restore

The most famous exponent of restoring Yuanmingyuan was Zhou Enlai who believed that renovation work could be carried out when national conditions were right. This is seized upon by modern-day restorationists who argue that national conditions are now right. As the second largest economy in the world destined to overtake the USA in the not too distant future, China has a vast reservoir of financial reserves with which to bankroll a major reconstruction project. More importantly, to do so would send the following powerful statement to the rest of world: just as the torching of Yuanmingyuan symbolised a China that was weak, submissive and easy to invade, the reconstruction of the site would symbolise China's spectacular re-emergence on the international scene and laying to rest its legacy of misery and humiliation (ZQZX 2010). This point is also made by Xu Wenrong, chairman of the Hengdian Social and Economic Federation, which completed the largest part of a full-size replica of Yuanmingyuan in Hengdian (Zhejiang Province) in May 2015. According to Xu 'the Old Summer Palace is the pain and pride of China. I want to prove that the Chinese people have the ability to rebuild it on our own' (Global Times 2015). Ironically, the replica Yuanmingyuan has caused almost as much controversy as the original in Beijing, with the administrative department of the latter threatening to sue Xu for breach of intellectual property (Global Times 2015).

So as to accentuate the point that a "new" Yuanmingyuan implies national strength, some restorationists insist that only the Chinese-style quarters should be restored to their earlier dazzling splendour, whilst the stone and marble Western architectural ruins should remain completely untouched.

According to an article in the Chongqing Evening News, to do this would draw a perfect contrast between the vitality of contemporary China and the erosion of modern-day Western power and influence (CQWB 2011). Restoration of the Chinese-style areas only would also allow Yuanmingyuan to retain its currency as a symbol of Western imperialism. As Liu Yang of the Beijing Times suggests 'on the one hand, the grandiosity of the garden can be partly restored. On the other hand, reconstruction and renovation will not demolish the evidence of a Western invasion' (Beijing Review 2011). Likewise, not to restore at least some features of Yuanmingyuan would be to completely squander its value as a reminder of Western imperialism, it is argued. According to Liu, without immediate renovation much of the site will erode completely: 'when the relic site is no longer there, how can you still expect to see the symbol of national humiliation? To reconstruct it aims to better protect it' (Beijing Review 2011). This is a view shared by others such as Tong Shujie of the Dazhong Daily (Beijing Review 2011) and Xu Wenrong (XHNA, 2006).

It is worth noting that Yiheyuan, also situated in north-west Beijing and known simply as the Summer Palace, was likewise decimated in 1860 by the British and French. After being rebuilt during the 1880s, it was attacked again during the assault by the Eight-Nation Alliance in 1900 and then restored again shortly afterwards. According to Robert Weil (2013, p. 96) the funds for the reconstruction were diverted away from reserves originally intended to help fortify the Chinese military against further foreign encroachments, the most striking symbol of which 'is the magnificent marble boat that sits dead in its waters, a useless mimic of the real navy that the country desperately needed to repel the modern gunboats of the imperialist invaders'. Weil describes the restoration of Yiheyuan as something which 'speaks to Chinese efforts over the centuries to hold onto and restore their glorious past'. But perhaps the more important point is that the restoration has removed the historical significance of the site as somewhere that epitomised their humiliating past. As Weil puts it, the numerous tourists 'who flock to its grounds are largely spared any sense of its past destruction'.

As noted earlier, the CCP's stance on the restoration debate is not altogether clear, most likely because it can see benefits on both sides of the argument. To leave Yuanmingyuan in its current state as a vast wasteland punctuated by Western-style ruins helps to send a chilling reminder to the Chinese people of Western imperialist subjugation. This gives the party scope to continue using the site as a means of inciting a public frenzy of anti-foreign jingoism as and when it is deemed necessary, an approach referred to in this book as aggressive nationalism. On the other hand, the full restoration of the site would make a powerful statement about China's ascendancy. The CCP could use this to demonstrate that China has returned as a great power and that the CCP is entirely responsible for this greatness. What better way for the party to prove its worth to the nation than to lavish millions on restoring an ancient monument so close the public's heart? The restoration of about ten per cent of the site in the last few years suggests that the CCP is veering towards full restoration. But the fact that the site remains only partially restored suggests that the party wants to carry on enjoying the best of both worlds.

Returning the Booty

Whilst the restoration debate can be divided broadly into two camps, there is a much greater consensus about what should be done with the thousands of relics that were looted by the British and French in 1860 and are now scattered throughout the world—they should all be brought back to China, to their rightful home. The number of Yuanmingyuan artefacts situated overseas is difficult to quantify. According to a CNTV (2010a) news report, UNESCO has estimated that of the 1.6 million Chinese antiques stored in more than 200 museums across 47 countries, about one million were stolen from Yuanmingyuan. These include a two-metre-high Buddhist stupa currently housed at the Chinese pavilion in the Fontainebleau Palace near Paris and a painting of one of the "forty scenic sites" of Yuanmingyuan displayed in the Paris National Library.

Although there was sporadic media coverage of the lost antiques during the 1990s (JFJB, 1998), the China Youth Daily identifies 2009 as the year in which there was a significant increase in public demand for the return of the stolen relics, noting a massive rise in internet blogging and newspaper articles on the subject (ZQB 2009). During the same year, a group of Chinese lawyers working overseas formed a "patriotic alliance" for the return of the lost relics, seeking to apply international law to resolve the situation (China View 2009). In 2010, the CCP paid for a team of experts to travel across the world and make contact with foreign museums in an effort to bring back the stolen items (XZX 2010b).

The nationalist symbolism associated with the stolen treasures is palpable and has been enthusiastically developed and exploited by the CCP in its quest to whip up a nationalist zeal against former imperialist powers. For example, the theft of the treasures is depicted as a devastating wound struck at the very heart of the Chinese nation, a wound which can only be fully healed once all the treasures are returned to China. One newspaper has likened the return of the antiques to 'a long and arduous road towards national salvation' (JFJB 2009a). When certain items have been returned (see immediately below), this is seized upon as a great victory for the Chinese nation (BJRB 2011). But it is only a partial victory. The state-controlled media frequently reminds the Chinese public that many antiques remain scattered throughout the world and this constitutes a continued humiliation for China (JFJB 2009b).

The strength of feeling over the return of the Yuanmingyuan treasures is reflected by the astronomical prices paid for them by Chinese bidders at auctions across the world. At a 2007 Christie's auction in Hong Kong, a bidder from Macao called Ho Hung-sun paid 70 million Hong Kong Dollars for a horse head sculpture, one of the stolen twelve zodiac animals (CNTV 2010a). Three years later, Ho purchased two more bronze pieces for 76 million Hong Kong Dollars, donating both of them to the Yuanmingyuan Museum in Beijing (CNTV 2010b).

The return of Yuanmingyuan antiques to China by Chinese bidders is welcomed by the Chinese media. There has been much praise for the actions of Ho Hong-sun. In addition, praise was heaped on a New Zealander called Mary Kempson who returned two porcelain vases looted by her ancestor Major William Kempson who served in the British 99th Regiment. Kempson travelled with the vases to Beijing where she attended a special ceremony put on in her name and 'apologized to the Chinese people' (CNTV 2010c).

However, sometimes reports on foreign auctions of the Yuanmingyuan antiques are designed to generate public resentment and anger, especially when Chinese bidders pay a fortune to buy back what was stolen from China in the first place. The Liberation Army Daily derided these auctions as an affront to China's national dignity 'going against the spirit of international conventions and inflicting serious harm on China's cultural rights and national emotions' (JFJB 2009b). A People's Daily article condemned foreign claims that there was nothing wrong in auctioning the antiques as an example of the continuing 'undisguised gangster logic' and the 'cultural hegemony' of Western nations (RMRB 2010b).

The most high-profile foreign auction of Yuanmingyuan relics took place in Paris in 2009. When Christie's offered for purchase the rat and rabbit zodiac heads collection owned by the late fashion designer Yves Saint Laurent and his business partner Pierre Berge, there was widespread condemnation in China and demands that the statues should be given back to China free of charge. There was particular outrage at comments made by Berge after he said that he would happily return the antiques if China improved its human rights record, returned Tibet to the Tibetans and authorised the safe return of the Dalai Lama (JFJB 2009b). This sparked a number of angry protests in China, and numerous petitions were signed demanding that the antiques be handed back immediately not sold at auction (Weil 2013, p. 132). A group of 81 Chinese lawyers filed a suit in France in an attempt to halt the proposed auction (Weil 2013, p. 132). Meanwhile, Chinese Foreign Ministry spokesman Ma Zhouxu condemned the hypocrisy of Western nations on the question of human rights and noted that 'Western imperial powers have looted a lot of Chinese cultural relics. These cultural relics should be returned' (New York Times 2009).

In the end, the auction went ahead but ended in farce. Although the antiques were "sold" to Cai Mingchao, an established Chinese collector and adviser to China's National Treasures Fund for 15 million Euros each, Cai refused to pay, claiming, in what can only have been a publicity stunt approved by the party, that his bid was made purely 'on patriotic grounds' (BBC 2009). Cai was hailed as a hero back in China, but Christie's declared his actions unlawful and threatened to bring a suit against him. Ownership of the two heads reverted back to Pierre Berge. However, in April 2013 they were returned to China by the family of the French billionaire Francois-Henri Pinault who now owns Christie's. Neither Christie's nor the family office would confirm whether or not the Pinaults has purchased the heads from Berge prior to their return. However the gesture was a clear attempt at strengthening economic ties between France and China since it coincided with an official visit to China by Francois Hollande, accompanied by Francois-Henri Pinault (Bloomberg 2013).

Norway has also sought to enhance relations with China by returning Yuanmingyuan relics at a strategic moment. Seven Yuanmingyuan marble columns, acquired more than a century ago by a former Norwegian cavalry officer who had settled in China, were "presented" to the private real estate developer Huang Nubo by the Kode Art Museum in

Bergen where the columns had been displayed for almost eighty years. In return, Huang donated ten million Norwegian Krone to the museum and arranged for the columns to be displayed at Huang's alma mater Beijing University, located adjacent to Yuanmingyuan and which has an academic cooperation programme with the art museum. Although both Huang and the Norwegian Foreign Ministry played down any political element to this transaction, it is widely thought to have been an attempt by Norway to thaw relations with Beijing after the Norwegian Nobel Committee awarded the 2010 Peace Prize to the Chinese democracy activist and bête noir of the CCP, Liu Xiaobo (New York Times 2014).

Public Discord

In his book entitled 'What Does China Think?', Mark Leonard (2008 p. 10) has described the destruction of Yuanmingyuan 'as an open wound that can be salted whenever citizens need to be mobilized or reminded of how the Communist Party saved China from foreign defeat'. To some extent, Leonard's analysis is accurate. In response to the frequent official reminders of the incident, some people have obediently towed the party line by expressing their outrage at the incident. The blogger Wei Yahua (2012) who was active on the neo-Maoist website Utopia (since shut down by the CCP) proclaimed angrily in a blog entitled Is the Humiliation of the Burning of Yuanmingyuan Repeating Itself? that the imperialists entered the territory unhindered, like a wolf entering a flock of sheep. Wei continued this was not a war, it was a slaughter. Another blogger known only as Miriam (2012) insisted that China will never fully recover from the devastation inflicted in 1860, despite the passing of more than 150 years and the re-emergence of China on the international scene: 'history's smoke may have cleared, but it has solidified in our hearts as eternal pain'. One commonly made observation is that although China is on the rise, the Chinese people should remain vigilant against the West and must never forget Yuanmingyuan otherwise something analogous may happen in the future. In a blog entitled The Regret of the Yuanmingyuan, the writer Jia Chenxi (2011) warns that 'we cannot forget our past history, otherwise the nightmare will repeat itself!'. This resonates closely with the CCP's approach, especially, as noted earlier, when it feels under threat by a perceived act of foreign aggression.

Expressions of outrage over the destruction of Yuanmingyuan also occur at the site itself. Robert Bickers (2011) in his article China's Age of Fragility recalls how, as an Englishman, he encountered direct hostility from a group of Chinese school children on a visit to Yuanmingyuan. Anecdotal evidence confirms that it is wise not to reveal your true nationality to inquisitive passers-by if you are a British or French visitor to the site. Speaking from personal experience as one of the authors of this book, it is not unusual to face racial abuse as an Englishman visiting the site.

Others are more positive about the legacy of Yuanmingyuan. Instead of dwelling mournfully on the past, they believe that the Chinese people should exploit the incident as a means of embracing and celebrating the present. Writing in 2008 about the national significance of the Olympics being staged in Beijing, Wei Guihua (2008) noted with reference to Yuanmingyuan that 'China was once called the sick man of Asia, but is now able to host the Olympics, in itself a type of pride, a type of validation'. In line with Leonard's observation, some people insist that China's rise from the ashes of Yuanmingyuan is solely attributable to the CCP. According to a blogger known only as Cedar (2012) 'this glorious victory of modern history is down to the CCP, which, as before, has risen up as the backbone of Chinese people, uniting everyone to bring about a unity of strength'.

Fabricating History

But not everyone automatically rallies behind the CCP at the mere mention of the Yuanmingyuan incident. We will see in Chap. 5 that there is growing disaffection over the CCP's true role in the Second Sino-Japanese War, with some very serious accusations being made that the party deliberately fabricated the official war history to suit its own political purposes. Accusations of a similar nature have been made about the official narrative on Yuanmingyuan. A particularly vocal critic with the blog name Dai35408 (2010) vehemently rejects the party's interpretation of the incident, dismissing it as riddled with 'politically motivated biases and inaccuracies' which have culminated in 'more than half a century of patriotic education brainwashing'. The basis of Dai's accusations derives from the convenient paucity of information in Chinese text books and media coverage about the brutal maltreatment of the Anglo-French delegation prior to the burning and looting of the palaces. Another blogger Li Wei (2012) criticises the scant official references to the plundering of the site that took place during the Boxer Rebellion, the vandalism and theft inflicted by Chinese warlords during the Republican era and the sporadic Red Guard attacks during the Cultural Revolution. Instead, the destruction is conveniently linked to the attack in 1900 by the Eight-Nation Alliance sent to quell the Boxer Rebellion.

The Shenzhen-based writer Yan Changhai (2014) has also criticised the CCP's unbalanced portrayal of the Yuanmingyuan incident. In a blog entitled 'Why Don't You Ask Why Yuanmingyuan Was Burnt', Yan blames the destruction of the palaces (and the start of the Second Opium War) on what he describes as the provocative actions of the Qing government under Emperor Xianfeng, most notably the torture and execution of the Anglo-French delegation. Like other bloggers, Yan notes how this fact is deliberately omitted from the CCP narrative on the incident. Leading on from this, Yan accuses 'corrupt CCP officials' of using nationalism for their own political purposes as 'a tool to fan up populism'. Yan then draws parallels with other examples of state-controlled popular nationalism that have allegedly been used as a smokescreen for illegal financial gain:

> Let us take the oilfields in the South China Sea which caused confrontation, as an example. What quantity of the resources eventually went into the pockets of corrupt Chinese party officials? How much of it actually ended up in the treasury? How much of it has been used to the benefit of the Chinese people? These are the questions that mainland China never dares to confront.

Blaming China

A less vociferous, but no less critical perspective on the imbalances of the party line on Yuanmingyuan has come from Yuan Weishi (2010a), an historian at the Sun Yat-sen University in Guangzhou. In an article published in the journal History Reference to coincide with the anniversary of the founding of the PRC, Yuan argued that the Qing government must share some of the blame for the incineration of the palaces due to a series of grave diplomatic blunders. This included not only the maltreatment of the Anglo-French delegation when they arrived in Beijing, but incidents that took place before their arrival such as the Chinese attack on Anglo-French forces at the fort of Dagukou in Tianjin and the execution of a French missionary in Guangxi Province. According to Yuan, these and other similar acts were the 'terrible consequence of the insularity and ignorance of both the Qing court on high and the masses below. In other words, the disaster resulted from the gap between ignorance and civilisation'.

Whilst this statement in itself is not overtly critical of the CCP, Yuan concluded the article with a subtle dig at the party's tendency to focus exclusively on the evils of foreign imperialism when discussing the Yuanmingyuan incident, whilst deliberately glossing over any contribution that China may have made to its own downfall:

> As a nation that suffered a lot from aggression and oppression, the Chinese should remember history. We should truthfully remember that our suffering was not only caused by outside invaders, but to an even larger extent, it was a result of our own backwardness and insularity.

Yuan (2006) made a similar claim a few years earlier in article entitled Modernisation and History Textbooks published by the Bingdian Weekly, a supplement to the China Youth Daily. In this article Yuan's focus was on a propensity for Chinese history textbooks to ignore or underplay the late Qing role in the collapse of the empire across a range of incidents (e.g. the Boxer Rebellion) not just Yuanmingyuan. However, on Yuanmingyuan, Yuan wrote that:

> In the face of aggressive and strong enemies, the Qing empire was in a weak position and would have been wise to strictly enforce the existing treaties, avoid a head-on confrontation and try to win time to reform and develop itself. But the government and officials at the time were completely under the influence of extreme emotions and foolishly violated treaties on small matters, leading to a catastrophe. Had the Qing decision-makers and the relevant local officials not been so ignorant, this disaster could have been avoided.

Why Remember Yuanmingyuan?

Just as doubts have been raised about the historical accuracy (and indeed honesty) of the official narrative on Yuanmingyuan, so there are doubts about the appropriateness of sporadically resuscitating the memory of the incident. Some people note that the very existence of Yuanmingyuan reflected a shameful era of elitism and inequality. It was, after all, an inordinately expensive complex of palaces and gardens inhabited by an imperial royal family, built on the back of slave labour and yet completely inaccessible to the impoverished general public. As Tong Shujie puts it, Yuanmingyuan was 'nothing but a place for the Qing Dynasty emperors to live a luxurious life. It is a symbol of a waste of money and resources and the then imperial family's greediness' (Beijing Review 2011). Likewise, Liao Baoping notes that Yuanmingyuan was 'a place for the Qing emperors to enjoy life and kill time. It was used to show the superiority of the imperial family to the ordinary people' (Beijing Review 2011).

One blogger using the name Zhexuejia gua le (2014) which translates as The Philosopher is Dead has suggested on Weibo that the common people deeply resented the greed and luxury associated with Yuanmingyuan, indeed so much so that when it was attacked by Anglo-French forces 'they did not feel a thing and many even clapped and helped the Anglo-French forces'. It has only been in recent years, to suit the CCP's nationalist purposes, that Yuanmingyuan 'has been elevated to a national event. But actually burning it made ordinary people feel avenged'. Another blogger with the name Zijia Yuanzi Li Xiongwei (2013) which translates as Li Xiongwei's Own Garden, has insisted that 'for a dynasty that did not consider the welfare of its people, the more beautiful and spectacular their buildings were, the worse their crimes'. This blogger even asserts that 'the Western powers did not do enough by burning these buildings. They should have burnt their owners too'. Yan Changhai (2014) suggests that even if Yuanmingyuan had not been burned down, it would remain inaccessible to the Chinese public, asking, in a clear dig at the continued secretiveness of the CCP, 'would it not have turned into today's Zhongnanhai [the central headquarters of the CCP]'? He continues, 'as a forbidden area, it is better for Yuanmingyuan to have been burnt. At least ordinary people are able to see the ruins'.

Other people express misgivings about the continued relevance of the incident and the amount of column space devoted to it by the Chinese media in light of current social pressures, such as passing exams, finding work and raising a family (Milkrangers 2010). A first-hand example of this is nicely captured by Lovell (2011, pp. 352–353) in conversation with a Chinese visitor to Yuanmingyuan who, in one breath, expressed his outrage at the destruction of the site, but in the next breath asked about opportunities to study at law school in England (of all places!).

Leading on from this, there is a feeling amongst some people that the CCP should not be wasting its time and more importantly public money on setting up delegations to scour the world for lost Yuanmingyuan treasures or on rebuilding the old site, albeit only partially at this stage. Instead, there are more important issues to contend with such as unprecedented environmental degradation, spiralling unemployment and official corruption. It is these ongoing issues, unattended to by CCP, which shame the nation. Wang Feng of the Qilu Evening News insists that, 'it's more meaningful to build more quality schools than to spend so much money on the reconstruction program' (Beijing Review 2011). Similarly, as one blogger poignantly remarks:

> What is national humiliation? It is when government buildings are extravagant in the extreme and village schools are shabby and leaking, this is national humiliation. When we believe that building the Birds Nest, constructing arenas and rebuilding Yuanmingyuan are able to 'restore the nation's glory' and the dignity of the Chinese people, to take ignorance and treat it as honour, that is the biggest national humiliation. (Nmghongjing 2011)

Comments such as this constitute a significant challenge to the CCP, but so too do the comments of others who fully appreciate the continued importance and relevance of the Yuanmingyuan legacy. Strongly implied within Jia Chenxi's blog cited earlier that China must beware of future foreign encroachments is the suggestion that the CCP may not be doing enough to circumvent such an eventuality and that the party should be more forceful in its dealings with foreign powers. Jia is well-known for his candid online allegations of the CCP's failure to confront Japan over the Diaoyu islands dispute, so it does not seem unreasonable to assume that he is also being critical in his references to Yuanmingyuan. Another blog about the incident entitled The Destruction of the Yuanmingyuan finishes with a statement: 'a country which remains poor, backward and weak is likely to come under attack once again' (Benniu007 2012). This blogger, like Jia, is well-known for his online accusations of CCP weakness over Diaoyu.

Time to Stand up

But if some people only imply that the CCP is too timid in its interactions with foreigner powers, others are more forthright in this assertion. One impassioned blogger known as PLANavy (2012) insists that Western imperialists are still trying to degrade and embarrass China as they did at Yuanmingyuan, calling on the CCP to finally 'wake the sleeping Chinese dragon'. In a blog entitled Forgotten Memories, Zui Huayin (2010) has insisted that 'China must wake up! We cannot again lag behind, we cannot be weak again! We cannot allow a tragedy like Yuanmingyuan to happen again!'. In addition, there were reports of widespread internet anger over suggestions that the CCP was considering inviting British and French officials to the events marking the 150th anniversary of the Yuanmingyuan incident, with angry claims that China was putting 'salt in the nation's wounds' (ZZX 2010) by 'inviting the invading forces' (DFRB 2010). In the end the scale of opposition on this issue forced the party to back down on its original plans.

The US presence in the South China Sea has also triggered online criticism of China's lack of national assertiveness via historical references to Yuanmingyuan. In October 2015, a US aircraft carrier sailed inside the 12 nautical mile radius that China claims as its territorial waters around one of its recently reclaimed islands, followed shortly afterwards by a visit from the then US Defence Secretary Ash Carter whose helicopter landed on the aircraft carrier. If this caused irritation to the Chinese Foreign Ministry (BBC 2015b), it was nothing compared to the outrage expressed by a significantly large number Weibo users. The most vocal came from Yike de Weibo (2015) which translates as Stranger's Weibo:

Having slapped the left side of your face [by sailing into Chinese territory], they [the US] are coming to slap the right side of your face. Let us see how the CCP leadership will explain this to the people. Today, it is the South China Sea, tomorrow it will be Tianjin Port. Yuanmingyuan has been burnt, Yiheyuan will be next.

A similar level of anger was expressed by bloggers following comments published in the Global Times (2014) made by the former commander of the US Pacific Fleet Gary Roughead who stated that the USA would stand by its treaty with Japan, no matter what. According to dgc5 (2015) if in its negotiations with foreign powers 'China fails to make any progress, it would not be strange at all if the Eight-Nation Alliance burns Yuanmingyuan again'. In referring to Eight-Nation Alliance, the blogger means the Anglo-French Alliance, a common mistake made by bloggers on this subject.

PICKING OVER THE ASHES

We will see in the next three chapters that there has been a significant official backlash against the various dissenting views contained in those chapters, ranging from carefully worded rebuttals published in the state-controlled media to the harassment, arrest and sometimes incarceration of some dissenters. By contrast, heavy-handed government reaction on Yuanmingyuan-related discord is less apparent, with one or two exceptions. One such exception is an article published in Chinese Social Sciences Today, a theoretical publication run by CASS (Li and Wen 2010). In it, the authors criticise the views of Yuan Weishi who, as we noted earlier, suggested that the Qing government was partly to blame for the Anglo-French attack on the palaces and that the CCP has conveniently ignored this point in its historical interpretation of the incident. Without naming him directly, Yuan's views are derided as a form of 'historical nihilism' and as constituting 'a misconception that Western civilisation is good and Chinese civilisation is backward'. The authors continue:

> According to this argument, backward nations naturally lose their right to independent existence and development so that it would somehow have been natural for Yuanmingyuan to be looted and burnt. This is nothing but a Chinese version of the West's defence for its looting and burning of Yuanmingyuan!

The logic of this reposte is not altogether clear in that it does not appear to bear any obvious relevance to the main points that Yuan was trying to establish. However, it does suggest that there is an acute sensitivity in official circles to any suggestion that China was culpable for the attack on Yuanmingyuan. This is reinforced by the fact that the party shut down the Bingdian Weekly shortly after Yuan's 2006 article criticising Chinese history textbooks for their version of late Qing history, including Yuanmingyuan. The reason given was that the publication contained 'articles incompatible with the mainstream ideology which had had very bad effects'. In an open letter protesting against the closure, the editor Li Datong said that he had been handed a 'Cultural Revolution-style critique' of the article published by Yuan (UPI 2006).

One important point to be expanded upon in the concluding chapter is whether the dissent faced by the CCP on matters of national sensitivity actually impacts on how the party behaves or on the decisions that it takes. Looking at this question from a purely Yuanmingyuan-related perspective, we noted earlier the mounting internet opposition to a proposal to invite an Anglo-French delegation to attend the 150th anniversary of the incident and how, in the end, the scale and intensity of this opposition forced the Beijing authorities to jettison the idea. So the party is clearly sensitive to netizen views on this thorny issue and is seemingly prepared to act in accordance with these views.

Another indirectly related example is the success of an online campaign launched by Rui Chenggang in 2009 in getting a Starbucks café removed from inside the Forbidden City. An important part of the campaign was the use of evocative imagery of the Yuanmingyuan ruins to rally public support for the cause. According to the views of one blogger, which was very indicative of the general mood:

> When I see the Starbucks against the repaired broken wall inside the Forbidden City, I cannot help recalling the invasion of the Eight-Power Allied Forces, as well as the burning, killing, robbing, and plundering at Yuanmingyuan by the British and French Allied Forces. (Gang and Ai 2009, p. 398)

By way of summary, we have examined in this chapter the deliberate cultivation by the CCP of an aggressive mode of Chinese nationalism, relating specifically to the 1860 Yuanmingyuan incident. In an effort to bolster its nationalist credentials as the party which saved China from the Century of Humiliation, the CCP has frequently reminded the Chinese public of exactly what happened during those fateful few days. Intrinsically tied to this intended message is another message—that since 1949, the CCP has single-handedly made China strong by overseeing remarkable growth in the economy, the strengthening of the Chinese military and the (re-)emergence of China as a respected international power, thereby ensuring that China will never return to the bad old days.

For some people, however, those bad old days have never really gone away. Some critics have argued that, notwithstanding its anti-imperialist posturing, the party is no more assertive now than the Qing government was back in 1860, an accusation that is usually levelled when there is a foreign infringement of Chinese national sovereignty to which the party is perceived as not responding to with adequate force. Others have used the Yuanmingyuan discussions to accuse the party of reinventing the history of the incident for its own nationalists purposes. Some have challenged the appropriateness of spending public money on partially restoring the ruined site or sending expensive delegations overseas in an attempt to retrieve the stolen antiques when this money would have been better spent on much-need domestic projects such as repairing China's schools and hospitals. Ironically, therefore, rather than bolstering, the party's nationalist legitimacy, the backlash on Yuanmingyuan risks eroding it, a pattern which has been repeated on the subject of Japan as we will see in the next chapter.

REFERENCES

BBC. (2009, March 2). *China "Patriot" sabotages auction.* Retrieved from http://news.bbc.co.uk/1/hi/world/asia-pacific/7918128.stm.

BBC. (2015a, February 2). *The palace of shame that makes China angry.* Retrieved from http://www.bbc.co.uk/news/magazine-30810596.

BBC. (2015b, November 5). *South China sea: US defence chief Ash Carter wades into row.* Retrieved from http://www.bbc.co.uk/news/world-asia-34737051.

Beijing Review. (2011, December 15). *Is it necessary to reconstruct the Yuanmingyuan?* Retrieved from http://www.bjreview.com.cn/forum/txt/2011-12/12/content_411014.htm.

Benniu007. (2012, May 27). Yuanmingyuan de Huimie [The destruction of the Yuanmingyuan]. *Xinlang Boke [Sina Blog].* Retrieved from http://blog.sina.com.

Bickers, R. (2011). China's age of fragility. *History Today.* Retrieved from http://www.historytoday.com/robert-bickers/chinas-age-fragility.

BJRB. (2011, June 14). Si Jian Yuanmingyuan Shou Shou Jiang Jushou Wuhan [Four old summer palace animal head statues will 'Meet' in Wuhan]. *Beijing Ribao [Beijing Daily].* Retrieved from http://www.bjd.com.

Bloomberg. (2013, April 27). *Pinault family gives China $40 million disputed bronze.* Retrieved from https://www.bloomberg.com/news/articles/2013-04-26/christie-s-pinault-donates-40-million-bronzes-to-china.

Broudehoux, A.-M. (2004). *The making and selling of post-Mao Beijing.* London: Routledge.

Cedar. (2012, March 24). Zhongguoren de Shi Yao Zhongguoren Ziji Ban - Yao Gan yu Shihang Baogao [Chinese matters need Chinese self-management - responding to the world bank report]. *Xinlang Boke [Sina Blog].* Retrieved from http://blog.sina.com.

China Beat. (2009, February 24). *James Hevia on summer palace relics.* Retrieved from http://www.thechinabeat.org/?p=372.

China.org. (2006, September 27). Yuanmingyuan Park to be Rebuilt? *China.org. cn.* Retrieved from http://www.china.org.cn http://www.china.org.cn/english/travel/182412.htm.

China.org. (2007, December 21). Netizens against rebuilding the old summer palace. *China.org.cn.* Retrieved from http://www.china.org.cn/english/China/236455.htm.

China View. (2009). Lawyers abroad form alliance for return of lost cultural relics. *Xinhua News Agency*. Retrieved from http://news.xinhuanet.com/english/2009-03/04/content_10942816.htm.

CNTV. (2010a, October 20). *1.6 Million Chinese relics held by 47 museums worldwide*. Retrieved from http://english.cntv.cn/program/china24/20101020/100840.shtml.

CNTV. (2010b, October 20). *Arduous journey to recovering relics*. Retrieved from http://english.cntv.cn/program/china24/20101019/101180.shtml.

CNTV. (2010c, October 20). *New Zealander returns looted Yuanmingyuan treasures*. Retrieved from http://english.cntv.cn/program/cultureexpress/20101019/101188.shtml.

CQWB. (2010, December 17). Babai Zhuangshi Zuihou Laobing Yang Yangzheng Zou le [Yang Yangzheng, the last of the eight hundred heroes, passed away yesterday]. *Chongqing Wanbao [Chongqing Evening News]*. Retrieved from http://www.cqwb.com.cn/NewsFiles/201012/17/20100017120000412114.shtml.

CQWB. (2011, November 28). Yuanmingyuan Shifou Chongjian Yin Zhengyi [The continuing restoration debate regarding Yuanmingyuan]. *Chongqing Wanbao [Chongqing Evening News]*. Retrieved from http://news.cqwb.com.

Dai35408. (2010, October 23). Du Junli: Fang Bu Xia De Yuanmingyuan Qingjie [Unable to let go of the Yuanmingyuan complex]. *Xinlang Boke [Sina Blog]*. Retrieved from http://blog.sina.com.

DFRB. (2010, January 15). Huoshao Yuanmingyuan 150 Nian Yao Qinlue Guo Chuxi Jinian [Invitation to the invading countries to attend the commemoration of the 150th anniversary of the burning of the Yuanmingyuan]. *Dongfang Ribao [Oriental Daily News]*. Retrieved from http://global.factiva.com.

dgc5. (2015, January 26). Retrieved from http://www.weibo.com/1829885151/ClqaUyNkT.

Han, G., & Zhang, A. (2009). Starbucks is Forbidden in the Forbidden City: Blog Circuit of Culture and Informal Public Relations Campaign in China. *Public Relations Review, 35*, 395–401.

Global Times. (2014, December 8). *US, China can work together to cool disputes*. Retrieved from http://www.globaltimes.cn/content/895600.shtml.

Global Times. (2015, May 13). *Zhejiang businessman attempts to recreate old summer palace, turn it into theme park*. Retrieved from http://www.globaltimes.cn/content/921513.shtml.

GZRB. (2009, November 3). Yanzhe Beijing Si Hao Xian Chihe Wanle [Food and amusements along the Beijing number 4 line]. *Guangzhou Ribao [Guangzhou Daily]*. Retrieved from http://gzdaily.dayoo.com.

JFJB. (1990, September 23). Zhongguo: Zouxiang 21 Shiji [China: Moving towards the 21st century]. *Jiefangjun Bao [People's Liberation Army Daily]*. Retrieved from http://dlib.eastview.com.

JFJB. (1995, January 16). Yuguo Shuxin Jielu Liang ge Qiangdao Zuilian [Hugo letter exposes the face of the two robbers]. *Jiefangjun Bao [People's Liberation Army Daily]*. Retrieved from http://dlib.eastview.com.

JFJB. (1997, July 2). Junmin Gongqing Xianggang Huigui [Together the military and civilians celebrate the return of Hong Kong]. *Jiefangjun Bao [People's Liberation Army Daily]*. Retrieved from http://dlib.eastview.com.

JFJB. (1998, February 9). Dangdai Zibenzhuyi Guojia Gongren Jieji de Bianhua Deng [Working class changes in a contemporary capitalist country]. *Jiefangjun Bao [People's Liberation Army Daily]*. Retrieved from http://dlib.eastview.com.

JFJB. (2002, May 20). Yuguo de Zhongguo Xin [Hugo's China heart]. *Jiefangjun Bao [People's Liberation Army Daily]*. Retrieved from http://dlib.eastview.com.

JFJB. (2009a, February 28). Guobao Huigui Lu Manman [The road to returning the national treasures is very slow]. *Jiefangjun Bao [People's Liberation Army Daily]*. Retrieved from http://dlib.eastview.com.

JFJB. (2009b, February 25). Yi Renquan wei Qihao Qinfan Zhongguo Renmin de Jiben Wenhua Quanli shi Huangmiu de [To use the banner of human rights to infringe on the Chinese people's basic cultural rights is absurd]. *Jiefangjun Bao [People's Liberation Army Daily]*. Retrieved from http://dlib.eastview.com.

Jia, C. (2011, November 17). Yuanmingyuan de Wanxi [The regret of the Yuanmingyuan]. *Xinlang Boke [Sina Blog]*. Retrieved from http://blog.sina.com.

Kutcher, N. (2003). China's palace of memory. *Wilson Quarterly, 27*(1), 30–39.

Lee, H. (2009). The ruins of Yuanmingyuan or how to enjoy a national wound. *Modern China, 35*(4), 155–190.

Leonard, M. (2008). *What does China think?* London: Fourth Estate.

Li, S., & Wen, Z. (2010, November 2). Mingji Lishi, Mianxiang Weilai [Remember history and face the future]. *Zhongguo Shehui Kexue Bao [Chinese Social Sciences Today]*. Retrieved from http://news.ifeng.com/history/shix-ueyuan/detail_2010_11/19/3167937_0.shtml.

Li, W. (2012, September 17). Zai Minguo [In the Republic]. *Xinlang Boke [Sina Blog]*. Retrieved from http://blog.sina.com.

Lovell, J. (2011). *The opium war: Drugs, dreams and the making of China.* London: Picador.

Milkrangers. (2010, November 15). Bu Neng Wangque de Jinian [Never forget to commemorate]. *Xinlang Boke [Sina Blog]*. Retrieved from http://blog.sina.com.

Miriam. (2012, February 27). Beijing, Beijing: Jiyi Zhong de Yuanmingyuan [Beijing, Beijing: The memory of Yuanmingyuan]. *Xinlang Boke [Sina Blog]*. Retrieved from http://blog.sina.com.

New York Times. (2009, February 26). *China fails to halt sale of looted relics at Paris auction*. Retrieved from http://www.nytimes.com/2009/02/27/world/europe/27auction.html.

New York Times. (2014, February 9). *Despite frigid relations, Chinese relics coming home from Norway*. Retrieved from http://sinosphere.blogs.nytimes.com/2014/02/09/despite-frigid-relations-chinese-relics-coming-home-from-norway/?_r=0.

Nmghongjing. (2011, November 20). Shenme shi Guochi? [What is national humiliation?]. *Xinlang Boke [Sina Blog]*. Retrieved from http://blog.sina.com.

Opoku, K. (2009, October 23). Chinese research artefacts looted in Anglo-French attach on summer palace in 1860: Do Great museums not keep records? *Modern Ghana*. Retrieved from https://www.modernghana.com/news/245039/1/chinese-research-artefacts-looted-in-anglo-french-.html.

PLANavy. (2012, March 29). Nandao Yao Muyi Tianxia, Zhongguo Cai Hui Suxing Ma? [Is it possible to be the mother under heaven and earth, until China is able to wake up?]. *Xinlang Boke [Sina Blog]*. Retrieved from http://blog.sina.com.

RMRB. (1999a, May 12). Zhongguo bu shi Yibai Jiujiu [This is not the China of 1899]. *Renmin Ribao [People's Daily]*. Retrieved from http://huylpd.twinbridge.com.

RMRB. (1999b, May 25). Zhengyi de Nahan [Righteous cry]. *Renmin Ribao [People's Daily]*. Retrieved from http://huylpd.twinbridge.com.

RMRB. (2008a, April 11) Wangmin Reyi de Xinwen: Aoyun Shenghuo Chuandi Zao Xirao' [Netizens hot news: Olympic torch relay disrupted]. *Renmin Ribao [People's Daily]*. Retrieved from http://news.xinhuanet.com.

RMRB. (2008b, May 17). Cong Faguo Kan Xifang Minzhu yu Guojia Liyi de Beilun [From France we see a western democracy and national interest paradox]. *Renmin Ribao [People's Daily]*. Retrieved from http://world.people.com.

RMRB. (2009, January 13). Jiu zai Nin de Xingxiang li [Only in your image]. *Renmin Ribao [People's Daily]*. Retrieved from http://huylpd.twinbridge.com.

RMRB. (2010a, October 18). Daguo Mianzi: Yuanmingyuan 150 Nian Jiachou yu Guochi [Great power honour: Yuanmingyuan's 150th anniversary of animosity and humiliation]. *Renmin Ribao [People's Daily]*. Retrieved from http://www.people.com.

RMRB. (2010b, November 19). Wenwu Zhuisuo Shi bu Wo Dai [Cultural relic recourse waits for no one]. *Renmin Ribao [People's Daily]*. Retrieved from http://huylpd.twinbridge.com.

UPI. (2006, January 26). *China closes another liberal publication*. Retrieved from http://www.upi.com/China-closes-another-liberal-publication/74971138267495/.

Wang, D. (1999). *Yuanmingyuan: Lishi, Xianzhang, Lunzheng [Yuanmingyuan: Debates past and present]*. Beijing: Beijing Chubanshe.

Wang, C. (2008). Recent research on republican Chinese history. *Journal of Modern Chinese History*, 2(1), 89–97.

Wei, G. (2008, April 17). Aoyunhui, bu shi Yuanmingyuan [The olympic games are not the Yuanmingyuan]. *Xinlang Boke* [*Sina Blog*]. Retrieved from http://blog.sina.com.

Wei, Y. (2012, April 3). Huoshao Yuanmingyuan de Guochi Hai Hui Zhongyan Ma? [Is the humiliation of the burning of Yuanmingyuan repeating itself?]. *Xinlang Boke* [*Sina Blog*]. Retrieved from http://blog.sina.com.

Weil, R. (2013). Yuanmingyuan revisited: The confrontation of China and the west. *Socialism and Democracy*, 27(1), 99–135.

WHB. (2010, January 15). Yuanmingyuan Linan 150 Zhounian Huo Yao Yingfa Zhengyao Chuxi [British and French officials might be invited to attend the 150th anniversary of the Yuanmingyuan]. *Wenhui Bao* [*Wenhui Newspaper*]. Retrieved from http://global.factiva.com.

Wolseley, J. (1862). *Narrative of the war with China in 1860; to which is added the account of a short residence with the Tai-ping rebels at nanking and a voyage from Thence to Hankow*. London: Longman.

XHW. (2008, April 14) Aoyun Huoju Chuandi Bali Shouzu Wangmin Zhenglun "Dizhi Faguo Huo" [Olympic torch relay in Paris blocked, internet users argue for 'French goods boycott']. *Xinhua Wang* [*Xinhua Network*]. Retrieved from http://news.xinhuanet.com.

XZX. (2008, March 4). Aoyun Shenghuo Caiji yu Chuandi Quwen [Olympic torch lighting and relay story]. *Xinhuashe Zhongwen Xinwen* [*Xinhua News Agency*]. Retrieved from http://global.factiva.com.

XZX. (2010a, September 25) Yuanmingyuan Jiang Qidong Lijie 150 Zhounian Xilie Jinianhuodong [Yuanmingyuan is launching 150th anniversary commemoration events]. *Xinhuashe Zhongwen Xinwen*. Retrieved from http://global.factiva.com.

XZX. (2010b, January 18). Zhongguo Zhuanjia Cheng Haiwai Faxian Xin de Yuanmingyuan Liushi Wenwu [China expert goes abroad to discover new lost Yuanmingyuan relics]. *Xinhuashe Zhongwen Xinwen*. Retrieved from http://global.factiva.com.

Yan, C. (2014, July 22). *Why don't you ask why Yuanmingyuan was burnt?* Retrieved from http://yanchh.blogchina.com/2214016.html.

Yike de Weibo. (2015, November 5). Retrieved from http://www.weibo.com/1204278217/D2pkVyFkh.

Yuan, W. (2006, January 11). Xiandaihua yu Lishi Jiaokeshu [Modernisation and history textbooks]. *Bingdian Weekly* [*Freezing Point*]. Retrieved from http://edu.people.com.cn/GB/1055/4016350.html.

Yuan, W. (2010a, October 1). Yuanmingyuan Lijie 150 Zhounian Ji - Kunan Laiziyu Luohou he Fengbi [Marking the 150th anniversary of the Yuanmingyuan catastrophe - suffering comes from backwardness and insularity]. *Wenshi Cankao* [*History Reference*]. Retrieved from http://www.people.com.cn/GB/198221/198819/204160/12859078.html.

Yuan, W. (2010b, November 1). Mao Yushi Deng: Huishou Xinhai Bainian, [Mao Yushi et al: Reviewing the century since the 1911 revolution]. *Zhongguo Gaige Luntan* [*China Reform Website*]. Retrieved from http://www.chinareform.org.cn/explore/explore/201011/t20101101_49427.htm.

ZGSB. (2004, September 11). Xiufu Tuanhe Xingong Weihe Meiyou Zhengyi [Why the restoration of the Tuanhe temple is not controversial]. *Zhongguo Shangbao* [*China Business News*]. Retrieved from http://global.factiva.com.

Zhexuejia gua le. (2014, June 10). Retrieved from http://www.weibo.com/1215029183/B8jJP3t7I?type=comment.

ZHTB. (2010, May 27). Xuannao de Zhong Cai Wusheng De Baimiao: Xie Zai Yuanmingyuan Lijie 150 Zhounian Zhiji [Noisy colouring, silent lines: Written during the 150th anniversary of the destruction of the Yuanmingyuan]. *Zhongguo Hangtian Bao* [*China Aviation News*]. Retrieved from http://global.factiva.com.

Zijia Yuanzi Li Xiongwei. (2013, December 7). Retrieved from http://www.weibo.com/3873998774/AmbdebhZU.

ZJCB. (2010, July 10). Jinian Yuanmingyuan Lijie 150 Zhounian You Jiang Zhengwen Huodong Juban [To commemorate the 150th anniversary of the Yuanmingyuan calamity an essay writing contest will be held]. *Zhongguo Jiancai Bao* [*China Building Materials Daily*]. Retrieved from http://global.factiva.com.

ZQB. (2009, October 27). Yuanmingyuan Wenwu Mo Di You Duoshao Mohu Jidai Qingxi [Assessing the Yuanmingyuan cultural relics and the need to be clear how many there are]. *Zhongguo Qingnian Bao* [*China Youth Daily*]. Retrieved from http://zqb.cyol.com.

ZQZX. (2010, October 20). Yuanmingyuan Linan 150 Zhounian: Keyi Kuanshu Dan bu Neng Yiwang [The 150th anniversary of the destruction of the Yuanmingyuan: Possible to forgive but not to forget]. *Zhongqing Zaixian* [*Youth Daily Online*]. Retrieved from http://zqb.cyol.com.

Zui, H. (2010, November 6). Weile Wangque de Jiyi [For forgotten memories]. *Wo de Sohu* [*Sohu Blog*]. Retrieved from http://guguzgz.blog.sohu.com.

ZXS. (2010, February 26). Taiwan Zhanchu Yong Yan Diaosu de Yuanmingyuan shi Er Shou Shou [Taiwan exhibit uses salt statues of Yuanmingyuan's twelve zodiac animals]. *Zhongguo Xinwenshe* [*China News Service*]. Retrieved from http://global.factiva.com.

ZZX. (2002, December 13). Beijing Yuanmingyuan Bainian Daxiu Zhengshi Qidong [Beijing old summer palace's one hundred year official overhaul launched]. *Zhongyangshe Zhongwen Xinwen* [*Central News Agency*]. Retrieved from http://global.factiva.com.

ZZX. (2010, January 19). Shangkou Sayan? Yuanmingyuan Mengnan 150 Zhounian Ban Huodong Zaopi [Salt in the wound? The 150th anniversary activities of the destruction of the Yuanmingyuan meets with criticism]. *Zhongyangshe Zhongwen Xinwen* [*Central News Agency*]. Retrieved from http://global.factiva.com.

CHAPTER 4

Aggressive Nationalism: The Legacy of Japanese Imperialism

This chapter provides our second case study of aggressive nationalism which relates to the legacy of Japanese imperialism. Stretching back to the early 1890s, Japan's record of exploitation and murder in China is considerable and remains a highly incendiary issue amongst the Chinese public, one which is sporadically and easily ignited by the CCP. As with Yuanmingyuan, the party enflames public opinion by issuing reminders of Japan's imperialist past in the state-controlled media or via high-level official statements. This is usually done during diplomatic fallouts in which Japan is perceived and portrayed to be acting as though it was still an aggressive colonial power. As we will see below, topics of dispute between the two nations include assertions of Japanese sovereignty over the disputed Diaoyu Islands, revisions to Japanese history textbooks deemed as whitewashing Japan's war history and visits by Japanese politicians to the Yasukuni Shrine.

As well as issuing strategically timed reminders about Japanese imperialism, the party has also attempted to incite public animosity through its media exposure of events occurring during disputes with Japan. So, for example, following the 2010 collision between a Chinese fishing trawler and two Japanese coast guard vessels near the Diaoyu Islands, Beijing gave prominent media coverage to a series of right-wing, anti-Chinese protests in Japan that supported Japanese sovereignty over Diaoyu, knowing full well the likely impact this would have on the viewing Chinese public. As anticipated, this precipitated widespread popular calls to stage anti-Japanese public demonstrations which the CCP duly

R. Weatherley and Q. Zhang, *History and Nationalist Legitimacy in Contemporary China*, DOI 10.1057/978-1-137-47947-1_4

allowed to go ahead, albeit only for a short period of time. The party has also facilitated anti-Japanese demonstrations in other ways. We will see later how transport was provided to protestors during the 2005 demonstrations sparked by, amongst other things, proposals to grant Japan a permanent seat on the UNSC.

But as with the Yuanmingyuan debate, China's nationalists have not always rallied obediently behind the CCP, with some people raising issues that seriously question the legitimacy of the ruling party. The most common criticism is that the CCP is too tentative in its dealings with Japan on key aspects of national sovereignty, such as Diaoyu. Just as accusations of CCP spinelessness are frequent, so too are unfavourable comparisons with the ineffective late Qing Dynasty still widely despised in China for failing to ward off foreign imperialism. By contrast, tough leaders such as Russia's Vladimir Putin emit lavish praise and envy. Some critics have used the Japan debate to conveniently broaden the scope of their discontent to include other alleged CCP failings, primarily those relating to modern-day socio-economic grievances such as high unemployment, the spiralling cost of living and official corruption. Critics have also accused the party of being no better than Japan when it comes to atrocities committed against the Chinese people, citing the suffering inflicted during Maoist campaigns such as the Great Leap Forward and the Cultural Revolution. In addition, the CCP is accused of being just as culpable as Japan of brainwashing its people with the official line and whitewashing history.

JAPANESE IMPERIALISM IN CHINA

The history of Japanese imperialism in China stretches back to the early 1890s when Japan's Meiji government began to construct an extensive territorial empire in Asia, including parts of northern China and all of Taiwan. In September 1894 the First Sino-Japanese War broke out, triggered by Japan's invasion of Korea and replacement of the Korean emperor with a pro-Japanese administration. As one of the Qing Dynasty's most loyal tributary states, China felt obliged to defend Korea and this precipitated a naval battle between China and Japan on the Yalu River, bordering China and Korea. Defeat for China was sudden and shocking. Within five weeks the entire Beiyang Fleet had been destroyed, opening the way for Japan to capture Lushunkou (Port Arthur) and massacre thousands of civilians. By March 1895, Japan had invaded Shandong Province and Manchuria, wresting control of important sea lanes to Beijing. In response, a beleaguered China sued for peace (Fairbank and Goldman 2006, pp. 220–221).

The post-war prize for Japan was the still controversial Treaty of Shimonoseki which required China to cede the entire Liaodong Peninsula (including Lushunkou) and Taiwan to Japan. China was also obliged to open up some of its key cities to trade with Japan such as Chongqing, Suzhou and Hangzhou (Paine 2003). This completed what many PRC citizens consider to be China's biggest setback during the Century of Humiliation in light of Japan's former status as a "culturally inferior" vassal state. Although it was not long before the European allies forced Japan to withdraw from Liaodong (to be replaced by Russia), the Japanese presence in China continued to expand. This was particularly the case after Japan's landmark victory in the 1904–1905 Russo-Japanese War which was fought exclusively on Chinese soil but without any authorisation from the Qing nor any ability to prevent China from being used as a battleground (Mitter 2004, p. 34).

Japan's full-scale colonisation of China began on 18 September 1931 following the Mukden Incident, a staged event in which a Japanese-controlled railway in Shenyang was bombed by Japan but conveniently blamed on Chinese insurgents. Thousands of Japanese troops poured into China and quickly occupied Manchuria, establishing the puppet state of Manchukuo and installing China's last emperor, Puyi as the official head of state. This led to an influx of over one million Japanese into the region, turning it into the industrial heartland of Japan's ever-expanding empire. The crossing of the Luguo (or Marco Polo) Bridge in Beijing following an exchange of fire between Japanese and Chinese troops (referred to as the Marco Polo Incident) signalled the start of the Second Sino-Japanese War in July 1937 and within a few months Japan had captured the Chinese capital of Nanjing, killing over 300,000 Chinese citizens in December 1937 and January 1938 in what became known as the Nanjing Massacre or the Rape of Nanjing (Ebrey 1996, p. 285). The number of Chinese casualties covering the duration of the entire eight year war is difficult to quantify, although Western historians put the figure at around 20 million. In addition, as Sneider (2013, p. 42) notes, 'the battles that stretched from the north of China to the jungles of Burma made tens of thousands of Chinese into refugees and shattered the economic and political structure of China, literally ripping the country apart'.

The list of Japanese atrocities in China is long and harrowing. In addition to mass killings (including "competition killings" carried out by Japanese officers), Japan's war crimes included human experimentation. The infamous Unit 731 set up by Shiro Ishii (under the direct orders of Emperor Hirohito) subjected its victims to vivisection and amputations without anaesthesia and biological and chemical warfare, causing thousands of cases of bubonic plague, cholera and anthrax (Barenblatt 2004). Perhaps most controversial of all was the mass sexual enslavement of Chinese girls and women (so-called comfort women) by the Japanese military, often resulting in rape and murder (Yoshimi 2000). Japan's failure to dispose of all the chemical weapons abandoned in China after 1945 and subsequent denials that coercion was used against comfort women and claims that the number of Chinese citizens murdered in Nanjing has been exaggerated by Chinese historians has sparked uproar and violence on PRC streets.

THE CCP'S CONTRADICTORY POSITION ON JAPAN

Turning now to the CCP's attitude towards Japan since 1949 and more specifically the official depiction of Japanese imperialism in China, like the Yuanmingyuan incident, Japan's imperialist legacy was not at the forefront of the party's nationalist message under Mao, notwithstanding the fierce anti-Japanese platform upon which the communist revolution was founded (Johnson 1962). Indeed, if anything, the CCP's approach was often quite moderate, avoiding any direct references to Japan's wartime past and presenting a conciliatory face. As Zhou Enlai generously commented to a group of Japanese Diet members in 1954, 'the history of the past 60 years of Sino-Japanese relations was not good. However, it is a thing of the past and we must turn it into a thing of the past. This is because friendship exists between the peoples of China and Japan' (Reilly 2012, p. 55). Instead, as we will see in more detail in the next chapter, rather than focussing its propaganda efforts on Japan, the Mao regime concentrated on denigrating the political record and ideology of Chang Kai-shek and the KMT as part of its quest for domestic legitimacy in the newly established PRC.

The main reason that Japan evaded official censure under Mao was due to its geopolitical importance to the PRC. During the Mao era of international isolation and intermittent hostility from America and the USSR, China needed Japan in a diplomatic sense and specifically sought out recognition by Japan as one of its key foreign policy objectives. This also involved shelving any demands for war reparations and even welcoming the strengthening of the Japanese military (Reilly 2012, p. 55). In 1972, China realised this objective with the formal establishment of Sino-Japanese diplomatic relations, but as part of this process China was obliged to continue downplaying Japanese war atrocities in China, no matter how unpleasant this may have felt. Mitter (2003, p. 118) notes that in the pursuit of diplomatic ties 'the need to appease Japanese sensibilities meant that it was simply not tactful to recall the horrors of the war in detail'.

China's "historical amnesia" continued into the formative years of the post-Mao era under Deng Xiaoping given the importance attached to securing Japanese aid and cementing economic ties with the then second largest economy in the world. As Sneider (2013, p. 44) points out, 'Japanese assistance was crucial to the early stages of Chinese economic recovery and growth following the disastrous years of the Cultural Revolution'. Even Jiang Zemin, who is generally thought to harbour an intense dislike of Japan, set aside these prejudices, particularly in the wake of the 1989 Tiananmen military crackdown when, with the notable exception of Japan, most the international community turned against the PRC, (Reilly 2012, p. 55). Jiang was equally restrained during his controversial visit to Tokyo in 1998 and the year before at the official reopening of the Beijing Memorial Hall of the War of Resistance Against Japan when his inscription referred to the promotion of Chinese national spirit and rejuvenation of the Chinese nation, but studiously avoided any antagonistic, anti-Japanese language (Wang 2008, p. 795).

At the same, however, official attitudes towards Japanese imperialism began to harden during the early 1980s. As the Cold War thawed and China's diplomatic reliance on Japan simultaneously diminished, political space was created for a more critical attitude of Japan's war record in particular and Japan's imperialist legacy in China in general. This process intensified as the US-Japan security alliance became increasingly perceived as a potential threat to China's quest for great power status in the region.

The first obvious sign of a more reproachful chinese stance towards Japan came in 1982 when the media systematically attacked the Tokyo administration for reportedly authorising revisions to Japanese history textbooks which glossed over Japan's wartime history in China.

Continued ill feeling on this issue, together with a carelessly timed visit to the Yasukuni Shrine by then Prime Minister Nakasone's on 15 August, 1985 (marking 40 years since the end of the Second Sino-Japanese War) triggered the first spontaneous public protest against Japan in the post-1949 era (Reilly 2012, p. 56). At around the same time, the Nanjing Massacre Memorial Hall was completed and has since been renovated several times, most recently in 2007 to coincide with the 70th anniversary of the start of the war. The museum contains a graphically descriptive narrative of the events of the war, with eye-watering images of slaughter and depravity carried out by the Japanese military. The aim is not just to remind visitors of the terror inflicted on China by Japan during the eight year war of resistance, but also of China's longer history of humiliation at the hands of the Japanese stretching back to the late nineteenth century.

Two years after the Nanjing Massacre Memorial Hall opened its doors to the public, so too did the Beijing Memorial Hall of the War of Resistance Against Japan, located close to the Luguo Bridge, the site of the Marco Polo Bridge incident. The opening date of July 1987 marked 50 years since the Second Sino-Japanese War began and a third renovation was completed in 2005 to commemorate 60 years since the war ended. As with the Nanjing Massacre Memorial Hall, the narrative on japan is graphic and unforgiving, the photography is brutal and uncompromising and the message to the Chinese public is clear—never forget Japan's

humiliation of China.

The inception of the Patriotic Education Campaign intensified China's critical focus on Japan. We noted in Chap. 1 how of the 40 sites designated as patriotic education bases commemorating external wars and conflicts involving China, 20 were established to commemorate the Second Sino-Japanese War, including of course the Nanjing Massacre Memorial Hall and the Memorial Hall of the War of Resistance Against Japan. For some years, the latter hosted an exhibition and film highlighting Chinese resistance to Japanese aggression during the war. Further north in Manchuria, other patriotic education bases recognise the First Sino-Japanese War the Russo-Japanese War and the Mukden Incident. As with the ruins of Yuanmingyuan, the public are encouraged to visit these bases and contemplate the trauma of China's recent past.

Chinese history textbooks have increased their focus on Japanese war crimes as part of the Patriotic Education Campaign, specifically the

1991 'General Outline on Strengthening Education in Modern and Contemporary History and National Conditions'. According Wu Zeying (2012, pp. 43–44) the 1995 edition of China's secondary school modern history textbooks contained considerably more detail on Japanese war crimes than the 1985 edition. Particular emphasis was placed on the Nanjing Massacre and the ruthless activities of Unit 731, together with a number of vivid photographs to force the point home.

In recent years, the CCP propaganda apparatus has been heavily involved in the production of a plethora of films and TV dramas about the brutality of Japanese imperialism in China (Hays Gries et al. 2016, p. 2). In the build-up to the 70th anniversary of the end of the Second Sino-Japanese War in August 2015, no fewer than 10 new films, 12 TV dramas, 20 documentaries and 183 war-themed stage performances were released in China (International Business Times 2015), although some chinese viewers complained about the excessively violent and salacious nature of some of these productions (Washington Times 2015). The public are not just passively exposed to state-approved anti-Japanese hostility. They are also given the chance take part in active resistance. Annie Nie (2013) shows in her study of anti-Japanese themed computer games and the correlation with state nationalism how a number of the games are based on the Second Sino-Japanese War, enabling Chinese users to engage in vicarious vengeance against Japan.

The party also keeps Japan firmly in the public's consciousness by issuing periodic reminders of Japan's imperialist legacy in China. For example, on 2 September 2016 (the day before the 71st anniversary of Japan's surrender to China) the People's Daily Weibo account featured this detailed catalogue of Japanese atrocities committed against the Chinese people:

> We cannot forget these historical facts - during Japan's invasion of China it committed crimes such as: (i) carrying out large-scale massacres, causing as many as 35 million casualties among Chinese servicemen and civilians; (ii) carrying out biological warfare, chemical warfare and using poisonous gases, and conducting experiments on live human beings; (iii) forcibly drafting Chinese women as sex slaves and euphemistically calling them 'comfort women'; (iv) damaging and sabotaging China's water resources, forests, industry, agriculture and transport links. (RMRB 2016)

Ironically as we will see later, this quotation has since been used against the CCP by its critics.

CONTEMPORARY FLASHPOINTS
Diaoyu Islands

As with Yuanmingyuan, the party is quick to evoke the memory of Japanese imperialism in response to a contemporary flashpoint or an issue of contention between the two nations. One of the biggest and most well-documented is the dispute over sovereignty claims to the Diaoyu Islands. On the face of it, the islands are innocuous, comprising little more than a collection of eight uninhabited rocky outcroppings situated between Okinawa and Taiwan, which also claims the islands as its own. However, the islands have significant material and symbolic value to China. Their material value derives from their location in and around busy shipping lanes, plentiful fishing grounds and potentially rich oil reserves. Their symbolic value derives from a desire by China to assert its growing status and influence in the Asia-Pacific region and to put Japan "back in its box" by reclaiming a territory from a former colonial power with such a wretched history of violence and oppression in the Chinese motherland.

By way of background, aside from a 1945–1972 period of administration by the USA as part of the Ryukyu Islands, the Diaoyu have been controlled by Japan since the 1895 Treaty of Shimonoseki and it is the wording of this Treaty (or perhaps the intention of the wording) that has caused so much disagreement between the two nations. The Treaty ceded control to Japan of Taiwan and all islands 'appertaining or belonging to Japan'. China has insisted since the late 1970s (once evidence of oil reserves became apparent) that the intention of the Treaty wording did not include the Diaoyu Islands as part of the deal, pointing instead to a decision made by the then Japanese Interior Minister Yamagata Aritomo in 1885 that the Diaoyu should not be incorporated into the Japanese empire (Lee 2002). China (and Taiwan) also assert that the Treaty of Shimonoseki was subsequently nullified by the 1951 Treaty of San Francisco signed between Japan and the allied powers, pursuant to which Japan relinquished sovereignty over Taiwan and the islands 'appertaining or belonging to Japan'.

The Japanese response is that the islands were not under the control of any nation in 1895 (known otherwise as "terra nullius") and that China expressed no objection to the Diaoyu being placed under US administration in 1945 as part of the occupation of the Ryukyu. Nor did China protest in 1972 when the USA ended its occupation of the Ryukyu Islands and by implication the Diaoyu Islands, following which the US it handed everything back to Japan.

Against this historical backdrop, the CCP perceives Japan's control over the islands as a persistent reminder of the humiliation inflicted on China by imperial Japan. The islands are seen as a product of Japan's imperial conquest of China and this perception is made very apparent in the party's official narrative on the islands issue dispute, carefully designed for public consumption. In a State Council White Paper devoted entirely to the issue entitled 'Diaoyu Dao: An Inherent Territory of China', the authors set out China's interpretation of the ownership of the islands, making frequent references to Japan's imperialist history in China and drawing pointed comparisons between Japan past and present (IOSC 2012). An article on the islands published in the China Daily (2012) is equally indignant, accusing Japan of 'waging wars of aggression and enslaving the Asian people', as well as 'whitewashing its historical crimes with a wrong approach to history'. The article concludes that 'a country that dares to challenge historical facts is dishonest and extremely danger-ous'. There is even a People's Daily website dedicated to enlisting public support for the recovery of the islands called 'No Concessions on Diaoyu Islands' which states that Japanese attitudes to China are no different today than they were prior to 1945 (People's Daily 2016). Visitors to the website are encouraged to plant a Chinese flag on an image of the islands 'in protest at Japan's imperialist past'. Tens of millions have done so.

Beyond the official anti-Japanese rhetoric, there have been a number of anti-Japanese public protests over the islands, some of which were clearly incited by the CCP. The first major protest took place (albeit not in mainland China) after the forced military eviction in September 1970 of a group of Taiwanese journalists who had landed on one of the islands and erected the national flag of Taiwan. Large-scale anti-Japanese demonstrations took place in Hong Kong, Taiwan and among Chinese expatriates living in America. However, Beijing remained silent on the issue and following the normalisation of Sino-Japanese relations in 1972, the two governments agreed to temporarily sideline the dispute and con-centrate on consolidating political and socio-economic ties (Hays Gries 2004, p. 122).

1996 Lighthouse Incident

Although there were a handful of minor protests over Diaoyu during the 1980s and one in 1990 (Strecker-Downs and Saunders 1998–1999, pp. 127–131), the next significant expression of public discontent occurred in September 1996 after a group of Japanese nationalists from the right-wing Japan Youth Federation had landed on the islands a few months earlier and erected a makeshift, solar-powered lighthouse as a symbol of Japanese sovereignty (Dzurek 1996). This was followed by an open and robust reaffirmation of Japanese rights over the islands by then Foreign Minister Ikeda Yukihiko, which was taken by Beijing as evidence that Tokyo had been behind the incident all along (Strecker-Downs and Saunders 1998–1999, p. 133). China responded by asserting its own historical rights over the islands and reminding Japan of its record of oppression in China. This included a front-page editorial in the People's Daily which declared that 'whoever expects the 1.2 billion Chinese people to give up even an inch of their territory is only daydreaming' (Strecker-Downs and Saunders 1998–1999, p. 133). In addition, a number of high-level military periodicals attacked the alleged resurgence of Japanese militarism and claimed that Japan's actions over Diaoyu were part of a wider conspiracy to contain China and control the Asia-Pacific rim (Beukel 2011, p. 13).

This war of words between Beijing and Tokyo sparked a wave of anti-Japanese demonstrations in both Hong Kong and Taiwan, which intensified after the Hong Kong national David Chan drowned while trying to land on one of the islands as a gesture of support for Chinese sovereignty claims (Hays Gries 2004, p. 122). However, any attempts to organise equivalent protests on the streets of the PRC were quickly suppressed by the authorities in order to preserve Sino-Japanese relations and prevent any anti-Japanese voices turning into anti-CCP voices. So, for example, the government hastily deleted more than 200 messages posted on university electronic bulletin boards calling for mass anti-Japanese rallies. Control was tightened over university computer systems in general and the content of all scholarly works relating to the islands was closely vetted by party censors. Outspoken anti-Japanese activists were "escorted" out of Beijing in the build-up to the anniversary of the Mukden Incident in order to circumvent the potential for demonstrations outside the Japanese embassy. In addition, all provincial governments were instructed to curtail any signs of public dissent (Strecker-Downs and Saunders 1998–1999, p. 136).

Notwithstanding these efforts to muzzle public protest over the lighthouse incident, the CCP failed to prevent the expression of public discontent being articulated in print, on the internet and through other channels, including the establishment of a website called 'Defend

Diaoyu' which has been very active in recent years. Moreover, as we will see in the next section, not all of this discontent was supportive of the CCP and revealed the first real signs of what Hays Gries (2004, p. 122) calls 'a dynamic discourse that challenged the Communist Party's control over nationalism'.

2010 Trawler Incident

A more recent Diaoyu-related incident was the now infamous collision on 7 September 2010 between a Chinese fishing trawler and two Japanese coast guard vessels that were sailing very close to the Diaoyu Islands. The arrest of the captain of the trawler, Zhan Qixiong, initially brought a muted response from Beijing in the expectation of an early release without any diplomatic complications. But when Zhan's detention was extended on 19 September in order that he could be tried under Japanese law, the CCP took a more affirmative stance by cancelling all bilateral exchanges, arresting four Japanese citizens working in China for allegedly filming Chinese military sites and restricting the export of rare earth materials to Japan (Weiss 2014, p. 165).

Beijing was also infuriated by the frequent and very public Japanese assertions of sovereignty over the islands and by perceived attempts to drag America into the dispute so that it would side with Japan. This led to a series of official statements clearly designed to incite public opposition to Japan. For example, the People's Daily reported a "private" conversation in which Vice-Foreign Minister Wang Guangya threatened Japanese Ambassador Uichiro Niwa that if Captain Zhan was not released 'Japan shall suffer all the consequences that arise' (People's Daily 2010a). In addition, the Chinese media deliberately exaggerated the level of public anger over the trawler incident during September 2010, with Xinhua suggesting (incorrectly) that 'hundreds of Chinese gathered outside Japanese diplomatic residences across the country on Saturday [18 September] to protest Japan's seizure of the captain as sirens wailed to mark the 79th anniversary of Japan's invasion' (Xinhuanet 2010). The People's Daily claimed that 'millions of Chinese people vented their anger online on Monday [20 September] after Japan extended its detention of a Chinese fishing trawler captain, calling for a boycott of Japanese goods and asking the Chinese government to take stronger measures' (People's Daily 2010b). This approach continued even after Zhan was released without charge on 24 September, mainly because Tokyo refused to give compensation or issue an apology. In particular, the CCP authorised extensive media coverage of a series of right-wing protests that had taken place throughout Japan supporting Japanese claims to the islands and criticising China for its abrasive attitude and unwarranted claims to the islands (Weiss 2014, p. 179).

All of this triggered public demonstrations against Japan in more than 20 second and third tier Chinese cities, including Xian, Chongqing and Chengdu. Protest banners and chanted slogans derided Japan for its imperialist past and accused it of continuing to act like an oppressive imperialist power. Although the demonstrations were eventually quelled by the Chinese authorities, the fact that they were allowed to be staged in the first place, together with clear signs of encouragement in the build-up to the demonstrations, suggests a strong degree of complicity and support for the cause of the demonstrators. As Shi Yinhong from Beijing's Renmin University commented, 'if the government very consciously opposed or didn't want these demonstrations, if they resolutely didn't want them, then there would be nothing' (Weiss 2014, p. 180). Official statements even supported the demonstrators once they had taken to the streets. Foreign Ministry spokesman Ma Zhaoxu insisted that 'it is understandable that some people expressed their outrage against the recent erroneous words and deeds on the Japanese side' (Weiss 2014).

2012 Nationalisation Incident

Anti-Japanese demonstrations erupted again in 2012, only this time the protests were more widespread and more violent. The trigger was the so-called nationalisation of the islands by the Japanese government. In April 2012, the Governor of Tokyo, Shintaro Ishihara, a renowned nationalist and China hawk, announced his plan to purchase three of the islands from their private owner (the only islands not already owned by the Japanese government) so that he could develop facilities on them. Claiming that the Japanese government had failed to adequately protect the territory in the face of growing Chinese assertiveness, Ishihara launched a public donation campaign to raise money for the proposed purchase. This proved to be extremely popular and within a short space of time Ishihara raised over one billion yen (Weiss 2014, p. 194).

In an effort to circumvent Ishihara's controversial plan, Prime Minister Noda announced that the government was intending to buy the three islands, insisting that this was being done so that Tokyo could administer the islands more peacefully and to safeguard Sino-Japanese relations in light of the Ishihara initiative. But this was not how the announcement was received in Beijing. Firstly, the timing of the statement was deemed to be at best unfortunate and at worst provocative. Noda made his announcement on 7 July, coinciding with the 75th anniversary of Japan's full-scale invasion of China and prompting reminders of Japanese wartime atrocities in China. Secondly, the move was seen as a barely concealed way of strengthening Japanese control over the islands when the more obvious course of action from the Chinese perspective would be to simply block Ishihara's bid. Thirdly, Tokyo was accused of breaching the gentleman's agreement between China and Japan that discussions about sovereignty over the islands should be carried out behind closed doors, not in the full glare of the world's media. As with the trawler incident, Tokyo was charged with internationalising the issue in an effort to garner support from the USA and other overseas allies (Weiss 2014, pp. 194–196).

As well as openly chastising Japan for its actions, the CCP provided indirect support for grassroots nationalist protest against Japan. For example, on 12 August a boat containing 14 activists (including one from mainland China) was allowed to sail from Hong Kong to the islands in what was a partially successful attempt to land there—five of the crew swam to the islands carrying two PRC flags and one Taiwanese flag before being arrested by the Japan Coast Guard. This was the first time Beijing had not intervened to stop a Chinese protest boat headed for the Diaoyu. Moreover, the voyage was given widespread attention by the Chinese media, with CCTV providing live coverage of the landing which took place on 15 August to coincide with the 67th anniversary of Japan's defeat in the Second World War. Although the Japanese government quickly complied with Beijing's demands to release and deport the arrested activists, more than 150 Japanese activists, parliamentarians and local assembly members set sail for the islands and on 19 August, ten of the crew (five of whom were local assembly members) were allowed to swim ashore to plant Japanese flags (Weiss 2014, pp. 199–201).

The media publicity given to the Chinese voyage and the provocative response by Japan triggered a wave of anti-Japanese demonstrations across more than 30 Chinese cities, including Beijing, Shanghai and Guangzhou, all of which went unopposed by the CCP. Although most of the protests passed away without incident under close supervision by local police units, there was some sporadic violence. This was most notable in Shenzhen where marchers chanting "smash Japanese imperialism" burned flags of Japan, overturned Japanese cars (including a police car), vandalised Japanese-style restaurants and department stores selling Japanese goods and attempted to storm a government building, demanding that the CCP declared war on Japan and retake the islands by force.

Further demonstrations broke out during the weekend of 25–26 August following joint military exercises between Japan and America near to the islands. However, the most significant demonstrations took place in September after the decision by the Noda administration to purchase the three islands for just over two billion yen, despite a personal letter from Hu Jintao to Noda imploring him not to do so. Spurred on by official pronouncements such as Xinhua's accusation that 'Japan has ignobly engaged in double-dealing with China on the islands' and Premier Wen Jiabao's statement that China would make 'absolutely no concession on issues concerning its sovereignty and territorial integrity', protestors took to the streets in over 180 cities, culminating on 18 September (the 81st anniversary of the Mukden Incident) in widespread violence. In Qingdao, several Japanese factories and a Toyota Motor dealership were set on fire. Japanese nationals were verbally and physically harassed in Shanghai. A Panasonic factory was set ablaze in Shandong, and in Xian protestors seriously assaulted the owner of a Toyota car. Although the demonstrations went initially unopposed by the authorities, security forces were called into stop the protests once the violence started to erupt.

History Textbooks, Comfort Women and Other Issues

It is not just differences over the Diaoyu Islands that have triggered accusations of continuing Japanese imperialism and public anger on Chinese streets. A number of other issues have sparked uproar, all of which can be traced directly to Japan's imperialist legacy in China. One such issue is the sporadic Japanese state approval given to the publication of history textbooks which are alleged to have whitewashed key aspects of Japan's militarist past. The most recent instance of this was Tokyo's reauthorisation in early 2005 of the 'New History Textbook' written by the Japanese Society for History Textbook Reform. According to its critics, including CCP researchers, the textbook covers up Japanese war crimes against China committed during the First and Second Sino-Japanese Wars and ignores controversies surrounding the then Prime Minister Koizumi's visits to the Yasukuni Shrine. With the 60th anniversary of the end of the Second World War fast approaching, the timing of Tokyo's approval of the textbook was particularly infuriating and was given broad coverage by the Chinese media. So too was the fact that the textbook had been roundly condemned by the Japan Teachers' Union when it was first published in 2001, with less than half a per cent of Japanese high schools using the textbook for teaching purposes. However, the book was a commercial success, selling over 600,000 copies by June 2004 (Asahi Shimbun 2004).

One of the topics allegedly covered up in the textbook is the full extent of the Nanjing Massacre, with doubts being raised about the accuracy of Chinese claims that 300,000 people were killed during the incident (Wang 2012, pp. 208–209). Japanese public officials have added fuel to this controversy. In May 1994, Justice Minister Shigeto Nagano dismissed the Nanjing Massacre as a complete fabrication (Japan Times 2012). So too did a group of more than 100 ruling Liberal Democrat Party politicians in June 2007, accusing Beijing of using the incident as nothing more than a 'political advertisement' (Nishiyama 2007). Other high-profile denials have come from Shintaro Ishihara, Takashi Kawamura (Mayor of Nagoya) and Naoki Hyakuta, Governor of NHK (Japan's public broadcasting company) who stated that 'in 1938, Chiang Kai-shek tried to publicise Japan's responsibility for the Nanking Massacre, but the nations of the world [League of Nations] ignored him. Why? Because it never happened' (BBC 2014).

The downplaying of the role of Chinese comfort women has been another thorn of contention in Sino-Japanese relations, particularly when the Japanese historian Ikuhiko Hata (2007) published a detailed article for the Society of the Dissemination of Historical Fact in which he accused China of grossly exaggerating the number of comfort women used by Japan during the occupation of China and insisted that none of them were forcibly recruited by the Japanese military. A number of Japanese politicians have agreed with this position, arguing that the testimonies of former comfort women are inconsistent and unreliable. For example, the Mayor of Osaka, Toru Hashitomo, claimed that 'there is no evidence that people called comfort women were taken away by violence or threat by the [Japanese] military' (Morris-Suzuki 2012). Bitter memories of the past have also been rekindled by the CCP whenever there are reports of large groups of Japanese businessmen travelling to China as "sex tourists" (BBC 2003).

Simmering tensions over these ongoing issues of contention, together with a proposal by the so-called G4 that Japan be granted a permanent seat on UNSC, culminated in widespread protests across China in April 2005. As with the 2010 and 2012 demonstrations, the protestors vandalised Japanese cars, restaurants and department stores, but what differentiated this from the later two demonstrations was the level of support given by the CCP. For the first time in its history, the party authorised the establishment of an online public signature campaign in opposition to Japan's admission to the UNSC, with a number of official websites following suit, including Xinhua.net. In addition, not only were the demonstrations implicitly supported (arguably encouraged) by the CCP who were, of course, entirely hostile to the G4 proposal, but in Beijing transport was provided to take students and other protestors to and from the Japanese embassy and ambassador's residence where they were permitted to March, throw missiles and shout insults and slogans, although as Weiss (2014, p. 134) notes many students declined offers of transportation, most likely as a form of protest against the authorities. Of particular note were public comments by Chinese Premier Wen Jiabao linking the CCP's opposition to the G4 proposal to Japan's apparent refusal to own up to its imperialist past:

> Only a country that respects history, takes responsibility for its past, and wins over the trust of the people of Asia and the world at large can take greater responsibility in the international community.

SELECTIVE NATIONALISM

The CCP's adoption of aggressive nationalism on the subject of Japan is unmistakeable—pointed references to the shameful legacy of Japanese imperialism in China, strongly worded parallels drawn between Japan's past and present following a perceived act of deliberate provocation by Tokyo, condemnatory media coverage of anti-China protests by the Japanese right. But as noted earlier in the chapter, the party does not always assume an aggressive posture towards Japan on issues of national significance. The Mao era saw a notable degree of restraint from Beijing because of the importance attached to securing diplomatic relations with its former enemy. The early post-Mao era continued with this approach given that the requirement for aid and trade with Japan was so fundamental to the credibility and success economic reform process. Maintaining diplomatic and economic ties with Tokyo has remained paramount for the CCP leadership which explains, for example, the rather muted official response to the 1996 lighthouse incident and the strenuous curtailment of prospective forms of public protest about this incident. It also explains the party's decision to rapidly shut down a fledgling internet petition set up by nationalists in August 2004 who objected to the use of Japanese bullet train technology for the development of a high-speed rail network in China.

But just as there are political ends behind Beijing's need to tread carefully on the question of Japan's imperialist past, so there are political ends (albeit different) behind an intermittent willingness to resuscitate the bitter memories of the pre-war era in what might best be described as a selective exercise of aggressive nationalism For example, the very real prospect in 2005 that Japan might be granted a permanent seat on the UNSC explains not only the sudden increase in unfavourable Chinese media coverage of Japanese wartime attrocities but also the Chinese practial assistance given to anti-Japanese protestors in Beijing who wanted to march past the Japanese embassy, and the careful relaxation of controls over petition signing and other forms of public protest against the Japan's accession. Beijing was reluctant to actively veto the G4 proposal given the international fallout this might evoke. Consequently, it in effect stage-managed a nationwide show of angry public dissent against Japan which it then used as the reason why it was unable to support the proposal. As Weiss (2014, p. 138) explains:

> By allowing grassroots mobilization against Japan's bid, including a signature campaign and protest marches, Chinese officials could point to visible evidence that popular pressure required a tough stance, demonstrating the strength of Chinese resolve and effectively tying the government's hands.

In addition to this, the party was keen to be perceived by its populace as standing up for Chinese national interests, for faithfully representing the strident voice of the people in opposition to Japan's admission to the UNSC, based largely on the grounds of Japan's reprehensible history. In noting the scale of the demonstrations that were taking place at the time, Chinese Foreign Ministry spokesman Liu Jianchao stated how 'this one again demonstrates that the Japanese side should adopt a responsible attitude toward historical issues, so as to win the trust of the people of Asian countries, including China' (Weiss 2014, pp. 139–140).

The quest for nationalist legitimacy also explains Beijing's muscular approach to the 2010 and 2012 Diaoyu incidents during which the party played a key role in inciting public anger and then allowing open protest against Japan to play out. As with 2005, the CCP worked hard to position itself as the mouthpiece of public anger on Japan.

Dissenting Voices

The level of anti-Japanese feeling in the PRC is unmistakeable as demonstrated by the scores of street protests that have taken place during the last 10 years or so. But as with the Yuanmingyuan debate, not every anti-Japanese protestor is pro-CCP or believes that the CCP is doing a good job of representing the nation's interests. Quite the opposite. A number have come out against the CCP on several different counts.

Weak on National Issues

Starting with the Diaoyu Islands dispute, we noted earlier how the Chinese authorities quickly suppressed any fledgling anti-Japanese public demonstrations that threatened to emerge in the wake of the 1996 lighthouse incident but were unable to prevent other expressions of anger towards Japan on-line or in print. Another example of this was the hastily written sequel to 'China Can Say No' (noted in Chap. 2), entitled 'China Can Still Say No' published shortly after the lighthouse incident (Song Qiang et al. 1996). Hays Gries (2004, pp. 122–123) notes how the book aimed to present an anti-Japanese perspective, mainly because many people had objected to the apparently inadequate anti-Japanese position presented in 'China Can Say No', with some observers asking 'why were you so polite to Japan?' and 'don't you see that Japan is even more wicked than America?'. Consequently, the authors of 'China Can Still Say No' did not hold back, insisting that 'Chinese "hatred of Japan" is not necessarily a bad thing'. They also portrayed the dispute over Diaoyu as part of a much wider, historic confrontation between China and Japan for control of the Asia-Pacific region: 'to the majority of contemporary Chinese, the mission of containing Japan has already begun; the final battle of the Western Pacific—Protecting Diaoyu—has already become imminent'. More subtle, but no less significant were criticisms of the CCP for failing to stand up to Japan, not just over Diaoyu but on other issues of importance. This is apparent in the claim that 'China has been too warm and accommodating towards Japan'. In general, the authors implored the CCP to take a more forceful stance, implying that the party's attempts to stifle anti-Japanese protests from taking place in China was actually evidence of its lack of patriotism (Hays Gries 2004, p. 123).

A more forceful criticism of alleged CCP subservience towards Japan appeared in a book entitled 'Be Vigilant Against Japanese Militarism!' published in 1997 and contains an entire chapter on the Diaoyu crisis. Like 'China Can Still Say No', the book positions the Diaoyu dispute within the wider context of an impending Japan threat, insisting that China should not give any ground whatsoever to its erstwhile enemy across the East China Sea. Their message to CCP policy makers is blunt: 'no Chinese should be willing or dare to relinquish sovereignty over Chinese territory, leaving a name to be cursed for generations' (Zi and Xiao 1997, p. 78). If the party does not take a firm line in standing up to Japan, they imply that the Chinese people should and will revolt.

Strecker-Downs and Saunders (1998–1999, p. 137) provide other examples of public dissent against the government in the wake of the lighthouse incident. While the dispute was actually taking place, over 37,000 letters written by Chinese citizens, together with petitions containing more than 150,000 signatures, were mailed to the People's Daily and the People's Liberation Army Daily, insisting that the CCP should take a more aggressive defence of Chinese sovereignty claims to the islands. Students from various universities in Beijing told TV and newspaper reporters that the CCP's foreign policy on Japan was hopelessly weak, expressing sympathy and support for the demonstrations which took place in Hong Kong and Taiwan. Whilst some students refrained from protesting due to concerns about personal safety, others were less cautious, blaming the party's lack of assertiveness on Japan on the structure of China's communist political system (Becker 1996, p. 8).

But it was not just the party's alleged timidity towards Japan that drew criticism from some quarters. So too did the rapid suppression of any public protest over the incident, which appeared to fly directly in the face of the party's anti-Japanese propaganda following the inception of the Patriotic Education Campaign. As Strecker-Downs and Saunders (1998–1999, p. 136) conclude 'the Chinese leadership's efforts to quell domestic unrest and downplay the dispute again hurt the regime's nationalist credentials'.

The more recent public protests over Diaoyu, particularly in 2012, incited even sterner criticisms of the CCP as weak on national issues. Some criticisms have been quite subtle. For example, across many cities where anti-Japanese demonstrations took place, marchers carried pictures of Mao Zedong, perceived (rightly or wrongly) to be more forceful on the question of national sovereignty than successive post-Mao administrations. However, other protestors were more blunt and to the point. According to one demonstrator in Beijing who was quoted in the Associated Press (2012), 'Mao Zedong was tough. He never backed down when it came to the national interests. Our current government is spineless. If Mao were alive, we would have already attacked Japan'. Another protestor is quoted as saying 'our government has been spineless on many things—Diaoyu being one of them. The diplomatic protests are meaningless when they are not backed with actions. The government has behaved the same year after year, making the public more nostalgic about Mao' (Associated Press 2012). As we will see in Chapter. 5, the conviction that Mao would have been tougher on Japan over Diaoyu does not sit altogether comfortably with those critics who have suggested that Mao was too familiar with Japan and thanked Japanese officials on several occasions after 1949 for weakening the KMT military during the Second Sino-Japanese War thus allowing the CCP to triumph during the Chinese Civil War.

In addition to very public accusations of CCP weakness following the 2012 Diaoyu crisis, similar accusations were made in private. As part of their research on public opinion expressed on Weibo, Miao Feng and Elaine Yuan (2014) identified a number of critical netizen voices in the wake of the incident. One netizen sarcastically congratulated the CCP for its failure to prevent the purchase of three of the islands by Tokyo: 'how generous of the Chinese government: offering the Japanese imperial army the Diaoyu islands on both hands. Don't blame Japan for calling us coward!' (Feng and Yuan 2014, p. 127). Another insisted that the party should have responded much more assertively on the issue, warning that 'if we don't "return the fire," we would be in a very passive position on the Diaoyu islands and would exhaust the solidarity of the people. If we fight back determinedly, we can deflate Japan's aggression and create a new balance' (Feng and Yuan 2014, p. 126). One particularly damning criticism claimed that the current government was no more assertive than the late Qing government, widely loathed amongst Chinese nationalists as ineffective in the face of encroaching foreign powers. Instead, the netizen commented that the CCP would do better to follow the example of more robust leaders like Vladimir Putin:

> If our leaders were (tough) like the Russian President Putin, would it still be like this today? Our government is no better than that of the late Qing Dynasty The Japanese made arrests on our territorial waters but we didn't respond. Someone sold out our country. (Feng and Yuan 2014, p. 127)

Further attacks on the party's alleged passivity over Diaoyu arise just about every time a claim to sovereignty over the islands appears in the national press. After a robustly worded People's Daily commentary on 3 May 2016 entitled 'Refuting Japan's Deceptive Talk on the Diaoyu Island Issue', one netizen known as Qiankunpaozhu (2016) wrote that:

> As an ordinary and honest Chinese person, I just want to tell the Chinese government: you have a big pile of excuses, but the law is known to all. You claim the islands belong to you, but you refuse to land on those islands. Instead you let the other powers occupy the islands, and you only issue protestations. This is a weak and impotent party, with soldiers who are only good at talking. You cannot beat the gangsters and cannot deceive the people. With the judgement day approaching, what other tricks can you play?

Another scathing condemnation of the party came after a fleet of Chinese ships were reported to have sailed near to Diaoyu, but without actually landing on the islands:

> Why do I always feel China is very passive? If you say the Diaoyu Islands belong to China, why are you behaving like thieves? Many problems have been caused by China's own weakness! There is no courage to say (the right) things and do (the right) things. (Duanjian 2016)

Further fury against the party followed the landmark decision by the Hague against China in the South China Sea arbitration case on 13 July 2016:

> Nothing happened after NATO bombed our embassy [in 1999]. The situation relating to the Diaoyu Island is exactly the same. Now it is South China Sea. Are we always being bullied because we have always been weak? What more can we do apart from protesting or strongly protesting? If it

goes on like this for ever and we never resist even when we are bullied on our doorstep, this will make us lose confidence in the ruling party. Does it matter if we just kill them? Kill them! (Danaomen Guniang 945 2016)

But it is not just the Diaoyu islands protests that led to accusations of CCP weakness. Similar accusations were levelled against the party during the 2005 protests against Japan's application for full membership of the UNSC. One of the most assertive comments came from this protestor who drew unflattering parallels with China's weakness under the CCP and its weakness under the Qing:

To this day, the government has not taken a clear stance opposing Japan's permanent membership. If the Chinese government doesn't veto Japan's entry into the UNSC, this government will be no different than the Qing government. If the government doesn't veto Japan's permanent membership, we will know in our hearts that the government is weak and useless. How can the government continue to rule and hold its head up, losing face for the Chinese people! What ability can it have to reunify with Taiwan'. (Weiss 2014, p. 141)

Broader CCP Failings

As with the Yuanmingyuan debate, critics of the party on Japan-related issues have often broadened the scope of their censorious narrative to encompass other apparent CCP failings such as an inability to deal with modern-day socio-economic dislocations deriving from the CCP's own policies. In particular, there is a feeling that if the party cannot deal properly with domestic problems such as adequate housing, unemployment and public safety, how can it ever deal adequately with the defence of Chinese national interests against Japan. Expressing the hopelessness felt by many people in China, combined with the widespread dismay at the party's ineffectual stance over Diaoyu, one netizen asked:

Can you protect your house from being torn down by force? Can you save your job? Can you protect yourself from being run over by a car driven by Li Gang's son? If not, how can you protect the Diaoyu islands? (Feng and Yuan 2014, p. 132)

The reference to Li Gang's son is especially significant given the implicit criticism of the CCP. By way of background, Li Gang was Deputy Director of the Public Security Bureau in Baoding (Hebei Province). In what became a widely publicised incident, his son Li Qiming, ran over two pedestrians in a drink-driving car accident, calling out 'my dad is Li Gang' when security guards tried to detain him in the belief that his father's position would give him immunity from prosecution. It did not, but the incident still provoked uproar across China and the name Li Gang has become synonymous with CCP privilege and abuses of political power.

Another combined expression of discontent over socio-economic issues and Diaoyu is as follows:

> Classic ways to lose your life in China: eating toxic food, falling from the bridge, burned on the bus, and drowned on a rainy day. The rest of us could all die from anger over the Diaoyu islands dispute! (Feng and Yuan 2014, p. 132)

Critics have also used the so-called city inspectors (known in Chinese as the chengguan) as a vehicle for criticising the party on matters of domestic concern, often linking this to inassertiveness over Diaoyu. Established by the CCP throughout China to tackle local low-level crime, the chengguan has become a symbol of CCP corruption and the abusive exercise of power. For example, there is repeated condemnation of chengguan heavy handedness in requisitioning land on behalf of the state for redevelopment. One netizen ironically compared the powerlessness of the citizen in this context with the powerlessness of the CCP in the context of Diaoyu:

> When it comes to land use, the party has always dealt with us little guys by tabling the dispute and siding with developers. Now in the dispute over the Diaoyu islands, the party was shocked to realize that it had become the little guy itself, Japan was tabling the dispute and going right ahead with the development. Summon the city inspectors to destroy Japan by force. (Feng and Yuan 2014, p. 132)

Other netizens have suggested (again ironically) that the CCP would be better advised directing the energies and resources of the chengguan away from fire-fighting at home and towards the capturing of the

Diaoyu. Feibuguoqianshan (2016) suggests that the party should 'select personnel to form a chengguan force which should then land on the Diaoyu Islands and dismantle illegal Japanese structures'. Another critic broadened the scope of the international task that could be apportioned to the chengguan: 'we could solve China's territorial issues simply by setting up city inspector bureaus in Sansha, the Diaoyu islands, and Taiwan. It is that simple. Whoever armed the city inspectors controls the world' (Feng and Yuan 2014, p. 132).

Aside from the role of much-hated chengguan, there is also a feeling that the party's hubristic approach on Diaoyu is a diversionary tactic to deflect public attention away from problems at home. According to Yiluqianxingyilupin (2016) 'using the Diaoyu Islands to divert attention from domestic issues? This tactic is too old and out-dated!'. Similarly, Tanshaokafei (2016) insists that high-sounding official proclamations about Diaoyu is 'just pretence intended to divert domestic attention. If you [the CCP] are capable, then attack. Do you dare to show your sword?'.

CCP Double Standards

Another approach favoured by critics of the CCP is to take issue with official statements about Japanese atrocities in China by claiming that that the party's record is no better in this regard. We noted earlier the September 2016 People's Daily Weibo posting which contained a four point categorisation of alleged abuses committed by imperialist Japan against the Chinese population. Whilst many Weibo users echoed the party's sentiments, expressed often with a high degree of anger and the occasional expletive, a significant number turned their anger on the CCP, accusing them of double standards. For example, one blogger known as Licaidaxuejulebu (2016) offered an equivalent list of human rights abuses allegedly committed by the CCP against its own people:

> We should not forget these historical facts—since the Yellow Russians' [the CCP] came to power in China, they have committed crimes such as: (i) causing large-scale famine which led to approximately 35 million casualties among Chinese people; (ii) enforcing family planning warfare, milk powder warfare, vaccine warfare and conducting experiments on live babies; (iii) cunningly recruiting Chinese women as sex slaves whilst euphemistically calling them an 'art troupe'; (iv) damaging and sabotaging China's water resources, forests, industry, agriculture and transport links.

Another blogger known as Xiangyizhihenxian (2016) went even further than Licaidaxuejulebu by suggesting that the CCP is actually more culpable than Japan in terms of atrocities against China:

> It is undeniable that the Japanese killed Chinese people, but the number of people they killed was not necessarily more numerous than those killed by the red regime [the CCP]. Moreover, the Japanese did not destroy China's cultural relics which had accumulated over thousands of years, they did not massacre and persecute intellectuals and they did not turn schools into useless places just for show. But our party did all these things and this broke the spine of our nation.

A more general statement was made by Carp in Sea 111 (2016) in a posting entitled 'Selective Blindness': 'look at what you [the CCP] yourselves have done to the people since 1921. If you cannot look at history honestly, then you are not qualified to preach about history'. Other critics focus on specific campaigns that caused suffering in China. Referring to the Great Leap Forward, Qiandengweideng (2016) asks 'when will you [the CCP] reflect on the three year Great Famine in which 30 million people starved to death?'. Xiaohuihui97925 (2016) asserted that 'Mao starved over 20 million people with a single mistake. This is comparable to what the Japanese did, not even counting the Cultural Revolution. Those you starved are looking at you now'. A less biting, but no less historically significant observation comes from Shuicaogongshi (2016) who criticises the CCP for conveniently ignoring the war crimes committed by imperial Russia in Manchuria, in particular the so-called Sixty-Four Villages East of the River Incident referring to a massacre of thousands of Chinese citizens that took place in 1900.

A similar netizen outburst followed the publication of a Global Times Weibo posting in February 2015 entitled 'Old Japan Was Good at Brainwashing With Textbooks' (HQSB 2015a). The posting expressed outrage at the Japanese government for authorising the deletion of references to comfort women from a history textbook published by the Suken Shuppan publishing company. The posting asserted that Japan had not changed its brainwashing of the Japanese people since the Second World War when the government 'used textbooks to train youths of the militarist state', pointedly concluding that 'in Japan, changing textbooks usually has deeper levels of meaning'. Tempers became particularly frayed after the Japanese foreign ministry's efforts in January 2015 to persuade US publishers to remove all references to comfort women from American high school textbooks (Guardian 2015).

Although the posting was sympathetically received by many netizens, others such as Nanfangxiansheng (2015) accused the party of double standards: 'the CCP has always brainwashed the people. Does it have no shame?'. Similar accusations came from Yanhuaxiansanyue (2015) who asserted that 'the CCP has inherited the true essence of Japanese militarists and has far exceeded the Japanese militarists when it comes to brainwashing people with textbooks'. PchyGuo (2015) noted that 'although Japan's actions are repulsive, I hope our country can reflect on itself, too'. The most emphatic attack on the CCP came from Guzhouyiye56 (2015):

> China has not taken any countermeasures against Japan!!! China can only standby idly whilst Japan refuses to admit to its history of aggression and even blames China!! The CCP always promotes patriotism, but it only ever issues 'strong condemnations' when humiliated by others. In the end China still tries shamelessly to develop economic and diplomatic relations with Japan!! Do you regard all Chinese as fools! Is it possible for you be tough even just once???

FROM AGGRESSION TO CONSENSUS

In the last two chapters, we have seen clear signs of an aggressive mode of state-formulated nationalism grounded in China's history of exploitation at the hands of foreign imperialist powers. Frequent reminders via government-controlled media channels, formal white papers and other official pronouncements have kept the memory of such exploitation firmly in the Chinese consciousness. Say the word "Japan" to a Chinese friend, associate or even just a passer-by and the response is unlikely to be positive and more likely to be somewhere on the scale between indifference, contempt and outright hostility. Certainly, opinion polls in China have shown that there is still a strong association between contemporary Japan and the militarist Japan of the past, as noted in Chapter. 2. The mention of Yuanmingyuan is less likely to give rise to public vitriol on such a consistent and predictable basis, but a level of anger towards Britain and France is still apparent, especially in the context of any Anglo-French criticism of China's current human rights practise.

But ongoing public enmity towards Japan and other former imperialist nations does not automatically translate into support for the CCP and its self-professed nationalist achievements. Dissent against the party is not uncommon, with accusations ranging from whitewashing Chinese history to mismanaging China's socio-economic reforms. Worse of all, the party is accused of being timid in the face of foreign pressure, no more willing or able to stand up for Chinese interests than the ill-fated Qing dynasty during the final throes of the imperial period.

We will examine the wider impact of these dissenting views in Chap. 7, assessing the extent to which such views may have an impact on government policy-making and agenda-setting. The next two substantive chapters will change direction as we focus on a more consensual form of state nationalism, based on a revised view of the Republican era under the KMT and a more positive portrayal of the KMT's participation in the Second Sino-Japanese War.

REFERENCES

Associated Press. (2012, September 20). *In protests, Mao holds subtle message for Beijing.* Retrieved from https://web.archive.org/web/20120922030630/http://www.cbsnews.com/8301-505245_162-57516907/in-protests-mao-holds-subtle-messages-for-beijing/.

Barenblatt, D. (2004). *A plague upon humanity: The secret genocide of axis Japan's germ warfare operation.* New York: HarperCollins.

BBC. (2003, September 28). *China hotel 'Orgy' sparks fury.* Retrieved from http://news.bbc.co.uk/1/hi/world/asia-pacific/3146514.stm.

BBC. (2014, February 4). *Governor of Japan broadcaster NHK denies Nanjing Massacre.* Retrieved from http://www.bbc.co.uk/news/world-asia-26029614.

Becker, J. (1996, September 26). Students in Beijing 'Too scared' to protest. *South China Morning Post*, p. 8.

Beukel, E. (2011). *Popular nationalism in China and the Sino-Japanese relationship.* Copenhagen: Danish Institute for International Studies.

Carp in the Sea 111. (2016, September 2). Retrieved from http://www.weibo.com/2803301701/E6nUanO21?refer_flag=1001030103_&type=comment.

China Daily. (2012, October 15). *Evidence shows Diaoyu Dao is China's territory.* Retrieved from http://www.chinadaily.com.cn/opinion/2012-10/15/content_15816504.htm.

Danaomen Guniang 945. (2016, July 13). Retrieved from http://www.weibo.com/3989349805/DEAy953iU.

Duanjian, A. (2016, June 16). Retrieved from http://www.weibo.com/5072544526/DAtbn5dCq.

Dzurek, D. (1996, October 18). *The Senkaku/Diaoyu islands dispute.* Retrieved from http://www-ibru.dur.ac.uk/resources/docs/senkaku.html.

Ebrey, P. (1996). *Cambridge illustrated history of China.* Cambridge: Cambridge University Press.

Fairbank, J., & Goldman, M. (2006). *China: A new history.* Cambridge, MA: Harvard University Press.

Feibuguoqianshan. (2016, August 8). Retrieved from http://www.weibo.com/1974576991/E2C9jk6p7.

Feng, M., & Yuan, E. (2014). Public opinion on Weibo: The case of the Diaoyu islands dispute. In T. Hollihan (Ed.), *The dispute over the Diaoyu/Senkaku islands: How media narratives shape public opinion and challenge the global order* (pp. 119–140). New York: Palgrave.

Guardian. (2015, January 15). *Japan urges US publisher to remove comfort women from textbooks.* Retrieved from https://www.theguardian.com/world/2015/jan/15/japan-urges-us-publisher-delete-references-comfort-women.

Guzhouyiye56. (2015, February 3). Retrieved from http://www.weibo.com/1974576991/C2E81iymW.

Hata, I. (2007). No organized or forced recruitment: Misconceptions about comfort women and the Japanese military. *Society for the Dissemination of Historical Fact*, 1–20. Retrieved from http://www.sdh-fact.com/CL02_1/31_S4.pdf.

Hays Gries, P. (2004). *China's new nationalism: Pride, politics and diplomacy.* California: University of California Press.

Hays Gries, P., Steiger, D., & Wang, T. (2016). Popular nationalism and China's Japan policy: The Diaoyu islands protests, 2012–2013. *Journal of Contemporary China, 98*(25), 264–276.

HQSB. (2015a, February 3). *Jiu Riben Shanchang Yong Jiaokeshu 'Xinao'* [Old Japan was good at 'Brainwashing' with textbooks]. *Huanqiu Shibao* [Global Times]. Retrieved from http://www.weibo.com/1974576991/C2E81iymW.

International Business Times. (2015, August 19). *China: Behind the scenes of a second world war anti-Japanese propaganda TV series.* Retrieved from http://www.ibtimes.co.uk/china-behind-scenes-second-world-war-anti-japanese-propaganda-tv-series-1516025.

IOSC. (2012). *Diaoyu Dao: The inherent territory of China.* Beijing: Information Office of the State Council. Retrieved from http://english.gov.cn/archive/white_paper/2014/08/23/content_281474983043212.htm.

Japan Times. (2012, February 23). *Nagoya mayor won't budge on Nanjing remark.* Retrieved from http://www.japantimes.co.jp/news/2012/02/23/national/nagoya-mayor-wont-budge-on-nanjing-remark/#.V9FxHsv2aUk.

Johnson, C. (1962). *Peasant nationalism and communist power: The emergence of revolutionary China, 1937–1945*. Stanford: Stanford University Press.

Lee, S. (2002). Territorial disputes among Japan Taiwan and China concerning the Senkaku Islands. *Boundary and Territory Briefing*, *3*(7), 1–37.

Licaidaxuejulebu. (2016, September 2). Retrieved from http://www.weibo. com/2803301701/E6nUanO21?refer_flag=1001030103_&type=comment.

Mitter, R. (2003). Old ghosts new memories: China's changing war history in the era of post-mao politics. *Journal of Contemporary History*, *38*(1), 117–131.

Mitter, R. (2004). *A bitter revolution: China's struggle with the modern world*. Oxford: Oxford University Press.

Morris-Suzuki, T. (2012, December 6). Japan's paradoxical shift to the right. *Inside Story*. Retrieved from http://insidestory.org.au/japans-paradoxical-shift-to-the-right.

Nanfangxiansheng. (2015). Retrieved from http://www.weibo. com/1974576991/C2E81iymW.

Nie, H. (2013). Gaming nationalism, and ideological work in contemporary China: Online games based on the war of resistance against Japan. *Journal of Contemporary China*, *22*(81), 499–517.

Nishiyama, G. (2007, June 19). Japan ruling MPs call Nanjing massacre fabrication. *Reuters*. Retrieved from http://in.reuters.com/article/idININdia-30380820070619.

Paine, S. (2003). *The Sino-Japanese war of 1894–1895: Perception, power, and primacy*. Cambridge, MA: Cambridge University Press.

PchyGuo. (2015, February 3). Retrieved from http://www.weibo. com/1974576991/C2E81iymW.

People's Daily. (2010a, September 21). *Illegal detention of Chinese trawler's captain harms Chinese public's trust in Japan*. Retrieved from http://en.people. cn/90001/90776/90883/7146535.html.

People's Daily. (2010b, September 21). *Public outrage flares up again over Japan's detention of Chinese trawler captain*. Retrieved from http:// en.people.cn/90001/90776/90883/7146526.html.

People's Daily. (2016). *No concession on Diaoyu islands*. Retrieved from http:// en.people.cn/102775/206053/.

Qiandengweideng. (2016, September 2). Retrieved from http://www.weibo. com/2803301701/E6nUanO21?refer_flag=1001030103_&type=comment.

Qiankunpaozhu. (2016, May 3). Retrieved from http://www.weibo. com/5519817701/DtMd1mGFR.

Reilly, J. (2012). *Strong society, smart state: The rise of public opinion and China's Japan policy*. New York: Columbia University Press.

RMRB. (2016, September 2). Retrieved from http://www.weibo. com/2803301701/E6nUanO21?refer_flag=1001030103_&type=comment.

Shimbun, A. (2004, July 20). Retrieved from http://www.asahi. com/2004senkyo/localnews/TKY200407040200.html.

Shuicaogongshi. (2016, September 2). Retrieved from http://www.weibo. com/2803301701/E6nUanO21?refer_flag=1001030103_&type=comment.

Sneider, D. (2013). Textbooks and patriotic education: Wartime memory formation in China and Japan. *Asia Pacific Review*, *20*(1), 33–54.

Song, Q., et al. (Eds.). (1996). *Zhongguo Keyi Shuo Bu: Lengzhanhou Shidai de Zhengzhi yu Qinggan Jueze* [China can say no: Political and emotional choices in the post-cold war era]. Beijing: Zhonghua Gongshang Lianhe Chubanshe.

Strecker-Downs, E., & Saunders, P. (1998–1999). Legitimacy and the limits of nationalism: China and the Diaoyu islands. *International Security*, *23*(3), 114–146.

Tanshaokafei. (2016, August 8). Retrieved from http://www.weibo. com/1974576991/E2C9jk6p7.

Wang, Z. (2008). National humiliation, history education, and the politics of historical memory: Patriotic education campaign in China. *International Studies Quarterly*, *52*(4), 783–806.

Wang, Z. (2012). *Never forget national humiliation: Historical memory in Chinese politics and foreign relations*. New York: Columbia University Press.

Washington Times. (2015, May 21). *China's bizarre anti-Japanese TV and movie kitsch backfires*. Retrieved from http://www.washingtontimes.com/ news/2015/may/21/inside-china-anti-japanese-tv-propaganda-dramas-ba/.

Weiss, J. (2014). *Powerful patriots: Nationalist protest in China's foreign relations*. New York: Oxford University Press.

Wu, Z. (2012). *The effects of patriotic education on Chinese youths' perceptions of Japan*. Mphil Thesis, Lingnan University.

Xiangyizhihenxian. (2016, September 2). Retrieved from http://www.weibo. com/2803301701/E6nUanO21?refer_flag=1001030103_&type=comment.

Xiaohuihui97925. (2016, September 2). Retrieved from http://www.weibo. com/2803301701/E6nUanO21?refer_flag=1001030103_&type=comment.

Xinhuanet. (2010, September 19). *Japan extends detention of Chinese skipper to September 29*. Retrieved from http://news.xinhuanet.com/english2010/ world/2010-09/19/c_13519964.htm.

Yanhuaxiansanyue. (2015, February 3). Retrieved from http://www.weibo. com/1974576991/C2E81iymW.

Yiluqianxingyilupin. (2016, August 8). Retrieved from http://www.weibo. com/1974576991/E2C9jk6p7.

Yoshimi, Y. (2000). *Comfort women: Sexual slavery in the Japanese military during world war II*. New York: Columbia University Press.

Zi, S., & Xiao, S. (1997). *Shi Jingti Riben Diguo Zhuyi!* [Be vigilant against Japanese militarism!]. Beijing: Jincheng Press.

CHAPTER 5

Consensual Nationalism: The KMT and the Second Sino-Japanese War

The Second Sino-Japanese War is a deeply traumatic event in the history of modern China. The Nanjing Massacre, the sexual exploitation of Chinese women and the widespread use of chemical and biological weapons is never far from Chinese minds, thanks in the main to the concerted propaganda efforts of the CCP. This chapter also looks at that terrible eight year period for China, but from a completely different perspective. Here we examine how, as part of a consensual mode of nationalism, the party has revised the history of the war to highlight the integral role played by the KMT in defeating Japan, a role that for many years was barely mentioned in the PRC. The wider focus is on cultivating common historical ties between the CCP and its erstwhile enemy, with the long-term objective being peaceful reunification with Taiwan.

The party's reassessment of the Second Sino-Japanese War actually began back in the 1980s as senior KMT generals, who had been denigrated or simply ignored by the Mao regime, were posthumously honoured as national heroes for their participation in the war. In addition, a number of high-profile KMT-led battles were made into popular films, often portraying the KMT in a more favourable light than was previously acceptable in Mao-era war films. Museums commemorating the war and the KMT's role in it began to spring up throughout the country. Again, the depiction of the KMT was more positive than before.

Although the public were already becoming curious about this sympathetic re-evaluation of the war and the KMT, popular interest really took off after 2000 with the election of the pro-independence Chen Shuibian

© The Author(s) 2017   117
R. Weatherley and Q. Zhang, *History and Nationalist Legitimacy in Contemporary China*, DOI 10.1057/978-1-137-47947-1_5

as President of Taiwan. This served to unite the anti-independence CCP and KMT in a marriage of political convenience. As the CCP became even more hospitable towards the KMT and its role in the war, greater political space was created for an open and energetic public debate on the war period. The media began searching the country for surviving KMT veterans to interview about their experiences of the war. Some of those who were found became overnight heroes, as millions of people learned about their courage for the very first time. Innovative individuals established and paid for their own personal projects to commemorate the war by filming documentaries or by building their own war museums. Some people organised a commemorative tour of the memorial sites in Burma where their long-lost KMT relatives had fought and died with no recognition by the state. Others have formed civil organisations who hold informal funeral rituals inside the PRC at locations where KMT soldiers are thought to have fought and died.

But in acknowledging the KMT's war effort in an attempt to bolster its nationalist legitimacy, the CCP has taken something of a gamble and, as we will see in this chapter, that gamble may well have backfired. Having relaxed the parameters of permissible debate on this topic, the CCP is now struggling to keep control of the debate. Alongside strong expressions of national pride for the victory over Japan is a growing sympathy towards the KMT veterans who fought in the war. But with this sympathy has come antipathy towards the CCP who are accused of persecuting KMT soldiers after 1949, of rewriting the history of the war for its own propaganda purposes and of betraying the nation by avoiding armed conflict with Japan, leaving the KMT to fight the war on its own and at times even attacking the KMT. In light of this backlash, we argue that instead of bolstering the party's nationalist legitimacy, the official reappraisal of the KMT's role in the war may well be damaging that legitimacy.

TOWARDS A CONSENSUAL PARTY LINE

Under the Mao regime, the history of modern China was officially portrayed as a momentous battle between the CCP and the KMT, almost at the complete expense of the Second Sino-Japanese War. The focus at this time was much less on China's military struggle with Japan and much more on the CCP's class struggle against the KMT, with particular emphasis on the polar opposite visions of Mao Zedong (good) and

Chiang Kai-shek (bad). What little official commentary there was on the war depicted the CCP as the sole pioneers of the military effort (Mao 1954). No mention was made of any positive role played by the KMT for fear of contradicting the established party line and detracting from the gleaming image of the CCP as China's national saviour (Mitter and Moore 2011). By and large, the official position was that 'Chiang Kai-shek's troops were led by corrupt generals who were ill-trained and ineffective' (Mitter 2003, p. 119).

During the mid-1980s, the CCP modified its official historiography in two inter-related ways. Firstly, it elevated the status of the Second Sino-Japanese War and secondly it downgraded its attacks on the KMT's role in that war. Dealing first with the elevation of the war, one of the key reasons for this derived from the changing international climate. We noted in the previous chapter that during the Mao era of international isolation and intermittent hostility from America and the USSR, Beijing specifically sought out official recognition by Japan as one of its key foreign policy objectives, and in 1972 it realised that objective with the formal establishment of diplomatic ties. As part of the process of détente with Japan, China was diplomatically obliged to downplay Japanese war atrocities, no matter how unpleasant this may have felt. However, as the Cold War thawed and China's need to rely on Japan diminished, the way opened up for a much more critical attitude of Japan's war record. This intensified as the US-Japan security alliance increasingly became perceived as a potential threat to China's national security interests.

The downgrading of attacks on the KMT's war contribution was part of a wider effort by the CCP to improve relations with its former nemesis, with the long-term objective being the reunification with Taiwan. For the sake of clarity, reunification had always been at the very top of the CCP's political agenda. But after the Mao years of aggressive posturing and occasional military assaults (e.g. the shelling of the Quemoy and Matsu islands in 1958), the Deng regime opted for a calmer approach to reunification through dialogue and cooperation with the KMT. A more positive assessment of the KMT's role in the Second Sino-Japanese War was integral to this more conciliatory approach, part of what Coble (2007, p. 402) describes as an 'attempt by Beijing to lure Taiwan into an agreement for unification'. Gradually, the historic struggle between the CCP and the KMT began to take second stage to a new narrative that emphasised unity between the two parties in the face of Japanese aggression (Mitter 2007).

One way that this more positive attitude manifested itself was through the official recognition of high-profile KMT generals who had fought in the war against Japan. For example, Zhang Zizhong, the most senior general to die in the war, was posthumously awarded the title of revolutionary martyr in 1982 (Waldron 1996). Li Zongren, later Vice-President of Taiwan, was also recognised by the CCP for the leading role he played in the 1938 Battle of Taierzhuang in Shandong, the first major Chinese victory of the Second Sino-Japanese War (Li 1979). In fact, both Zhang and Li were estranged from Chiang Kai-shek. Although Zhang participated in the 1927–1928 Northern Expedition, he never recognised the Chiang regime that came to power as a result of that campaign and repeatedly tried to displace it. Li was also a long-time political opponent of Chiang, and after fleeing to the USA at the end of the civil war, Li returned to China in 1965 in support of Zhou Enlai amidst much fanfare (Bonavia 1995). Zhang and Li's opposition to Chiang explains why they were singled out for praise and recognition by the CCP. Chiang was still "public enemy number one" in China at this time, so there was little risk to the CCP in acknowledging Chiang's enemies as the party's friends. Nevertheless, the recognition of Zhang and Li still represented a significant change in official attitude towards the KMT and its role in the war against Japan.

Other indications that the party was taking a more positive position towards the KMT's war effort included the release of several war films which portrayed the KMT in a favourable light, most notably 'The Great Battle of Taierzhuang' released in 1986 (Mitter 2003). This contrasted sharply to earlier war films such as 'Landmine Warfare' (1962), 'Tunnel Warfare' (1965) and 'Little Soldier Zhang Ga' (1963) which largely ignored the KMT. The CCP also authorised the construction of a number of museums commemorating the war. As noted in Chap. 1, these included the Nanjing Massacre Memorial Hall built in 1985 and Memorial Hall of the War of Resistance Against Japan which opened in Beijing in 1987 to mark 50 years since the war began (Mitter 2000). Both museums depict the KMT in a more positive light than was previously acceptable, particularly the Beijing Memorial Hall which acknowledges the role played by the KMT in the key battlegrounds of Taierzhuang, Taiyuan and Wuhan. Zhang Zizhong, Li Zongren and other lesser-known KMT generals are commended, the KMT is praised for its participation in Burma and there is even a large KMT flag in one of the main halls right next to a picture of Zhou Enlai.

Chinese history textbooks also began to change their story about the KMT for the better. As we saw in the previous chapter, Wu Zeying (2012, pp. 45–46) has noted how the 1995 edition of China's secondary school modern history textbook emphasised cooperation between the KMT and the CCP, whereas in earlier editions, even as recent as 1985, 'many paragraphs were used to condemn the KMT for collaborating with, or not resisting, the Japanese Army'. Wu puts this down to an improvement in relations between the two political parties for purposes of national unification. Daniel Sneider (2013, p. 45) has also identified a more flattering portrayal of the KMT war effort in Chinese history books. In the 1995 'Illustrated History of China's War of Resistance Against Japan,' the authors describe the war as 'a nationwide war against aggression' during which 'the troops of the Kuomintang [KMT] and the Communist Party fought against Japanese invaders sometimes each on their own, while at other times in coordination'.

During the mid-1990s, as relations between the CCP and KMT became strained, particularly during the Taiwan Strait missile crisis of 1995–1996, Beijing took a few steps back from its KMT charm offensive. China's national news administration even went as far as instructing the mass media to refrain from praising the KMT's war effort and to place a greater emphasis on the supremacy of the CCP's role (Chang 2001). However, the election of Chen Shuibian as President of Taiwan in 2000 precipitated an abrupt recovery in CCP–KMT relations. As head of the long-time opposition DPP and an ardent advocate of formal independence from China, Chen's election was seen by the CCP as a direct threat to China's national security (Zhao 2006). In an effort to isolate the DPP and its pro-independence Pan-Green camp which included the Taiwan Solidarity Union, the CCP adopted a two-pronged strategy comprising military pressure on the DPP and peace offensives towards the KMT, itself an opponent of formal independence. Specifically, the CCP sought to engage Taiwan's anti-independence Pan-Blue camp, which included not just the KMT, but also its splinter parties the People First Party and the New Party (Zhao 2003). The objective was to create a united front with the Pan-Blue camp against the new Chen administration.

As part of this process, Beijing invited a number of Pan-Blue politicians to China, including more than one-third of the 221 member Legislative Yuan during the first year of the Chen incumbency (Zhao 2003). The most high-profile visit was made in 2005 by KMT Chairman Lian Zhan just before the 60th anniversary of the end of the war against

Japan. Lian's visit was widely reported by the Chinese media and the coverage was largely upbeat. President Hu Jintao reinforced this positive reception shortly after the visit when he acknowledged the important role played by the KMT in the war against Japan: 'resistance forces under the leadership of the KMT and the CCP were engaged in operations against Japanese aggressors on frontal battlefields and in the enemy's rear respectively, forming a strategic common front against the enemy' (Xinhuanet 2005). This remarkably frank assessment of the KMT's role in the war was a significant departure from the CCP's conventional line and represented a high point in CCP–KMT relations.

Other key concessions made during 2005 included the decision to lift an earlier ban on the 1994 war film 'Iron and Blood at the Kunlun Pass' about a series of struggles between KMT forces and the Japanese army during 1939–1940 for control of the Kunlun Pass. This was a strategically important position in Guangxi Province. The film had been banned because it starred KMT generals who later fought against the CCP in the Chinese Civil War, but it now appeared on the recommended list issued by the Central Propaganda Department and the State Administration of Radio, Film and Television (YZZK 2005a).

The KMT's wartime cooperation with the CCP quickly became an oft-repeated theme. A novel called 'Drawing Sword' written by Du Liang (2005) was published to critical claim and was later made into an award-winning television series. As well as highlighting the heroic experiences of a CCP general during the Second Sino-Japanese War, the Civil War and the Korean War, it also depicted KMT forces as being patriotic allies to the CCP in their common cause to defeat the Japanese.

TAKING NATIONALISM AS THE KEY LINK

The knock-on effect inside China of reassessing the KMT's war effort has been dramatic to say the least and not altogether what the CCP would have expected or wanted. But before we examine this, it is important to reiterate the legitimising objectives behind the CCP's pursuit of this more open and honest reappraisal. This brings us back to the theme of nationalism. We have seen already how the party has sought to invent itself as a nationalist force after the crisis of economic legitimacy that led to the Tiananmen demonstrations. However, in contrast to the aggressive nationalism identified in the last two chapters, the official position on the KMT and the Second Sino-Japanese War has been more consensual and collaborative, emphasising national unity and a sense of historical commonality with the KMT in an effort to move positively towards reunification with Taiwan (Mitter 2000).

As the Second Sino-Japanese War has become increasingly pre-eminent in China, the significance of China's other wars has rather faded away. This is primarily because of a lack of utility for the party's nationalist purposes. The Chinese Civil War is by definition inappropriate given the party's objective has been to show unity with the KMT not conflict. Nor is the Korean war helpful anymore with its anachronistic emphasis on the victory of socialism. Moreover, according to Diamant (2011), the legacy of the Korean conflict has caused sharp divisions in Chinese public opinion about its necessity and long-term benefit to China. The same public frictions apply to the humiliating 1979 border clash with Vietnam. By contrast, the public's contempt for Japan as a result of the Second Sino-Japanese War remains unwavering, and as such it is a very useful nationalist tool for the CCP.

At the same time, by praising the key role played by the KMT in the Second Sino-Japanese War, the party has taken something of a punt. In years gone by, the party built its nationalist credentials on a strict and unforgiving repudiation of the KMT and this applied in particular to the Second Sino-Japanese War. We saw earlier how KMT troops were portrayed as corrupt and ineffective, whilst the CCP was China's "knight in shining armour", the vanguard of the war effort. So why take the risk of altering the official line so radically? Putting aside issues to do with nationalism and reunification, the CCP elite probably felt confident that it could control the domestic discourse on the KMT's war effort given its pervasive control over the Chinese media. It probably also felt that it could control the KMT, especially after 2000 when the KMT lost power to the DPP for the first time. As the largest political party in the world in charge of one of the most powerful countries in the world, the CCP was in a much stronger position than the KMT, which between 2000 and 2008 was no longer in control of the tiny and diplomatically isolated island of Taiwan. But as we will now see, controlling the public reaction to the growing revelations about the KMT's front-line role in the war has proved to be extremely difficult, if not impossible.

POPULAR INTEREST IN THE WAR

The relaxation of official restrictions on the Second Sino-Japanese War has precipitated a dramatic increase in media reporting of this tortuous period. This was particularly apparent during the 60th anniversary of the war in 2005, with many media outlets sending reporters all over China and even to Burma in pursuit of KMT and CCP war veterans. Commenting on the intense media coverage of this event, the Guangzhou-based Southern Metropolis Daily, itself at the very forefront of the activity, observed how the Chinese media became engaged in a movement to "rescue memories". According to the paper, 'many interviewees were telling their own war experiences publicly for the very first time. Had it not been for the efforts of journalists, their stories would have disappeared when they died' (NFDB 2005).

High-profile TV personalities also became involved. Cui Yongyuan, a popular host who worked for the state-run network CCTV, invested over eight years of his life and over 130 million RMB (significantly some of the donors were Japanese) in what he called a 'verbal history project' of the war. As part of this project, Cui tracked down and interviewed over 3500 people who had experienced the war, including nearly 400 KMT and CCP war veterans. From the mass of information that he accumulated, Cui then produced a 35-part documentary series called 'My Resistance War' (ZXW 2010). The series was first shown on the internet, generating a massive audience response (more than ten million hits within one month). It was then aired simultaneously by 85 TV stations across China and in April 2011 CCTV also started screening it. According to Cui, from the very beginning he did not expect to recoup all of his costs. Instead, he did it because he wanted to record the experiences and emotions of individuals during the war and treated the project as a 'precious emotional investment'.

Other innovative (and self-funded) individuals became engrossed in the national effort to preserve the memory of the Japanese war, most notably Fan Jianchuan, a real estate developer and private collector from Sichuan. In 2006, Fan founded the Jianchuan Museum near Chengdu, a significant part of which commemorates the war against Japan. Fan has also established a number of other smaller museums dedicated to the war (bringing the total to eight) as well as 12 museums which remember the Cultural Revolution. It is thought that Fan has spent more than more than 130 million RMB on his various commemorative projects (China Boom Project 2011).

Similarly, in 2008 Sun Chunlong established the Shenzhen Longyue Charity Foundation which attempts to track down surviving Chinese war veterans, particularly those who fought on the side of the KMT. Sun funded the charity himself following initial scepticism from prospective donors and friends. But as more and more information on the KMT's role in the war became available through official and unofficial sources, Sun found it easier to procure sponsorship money and support and now runs the charity as a full-time job. As Sun explained to the Global Times (2014) 'people began to learn about the history [of the war] and more people came to participate and help us find the veterans'.

Western scholarship of the war has also attracted interest in China, particularly the works of those thinkers who portray the KMT's participation in a positive light. One example of this is Hans van de Ven's book 'War and Nationalism' in China, originally published by Routledge in 2003 and translated into Chinese in 2007 (van de Ven 2007) to critical acclaim within academic circles. The decision to allow the book to be sold in China was significant in itself because it demonstrated a greater official tolerance of what once would have been considered a controversial foreign perspective on the KMT's war effort.

Rana Mitter's 2013 book entitled 'Forgotten Ally' was translated into Chinese and published in China during 2014. The book attracted much scholarly and online attention in China, particularly in the build-up to the 70th anniversary of the end of the war. Even, the Chinese authorities noted its value. In an interview with the author, the People's Daily praised the book as 'filling a gap in history studies in the United Kingdom' (RMRB 2015).

But it is not just translated Western scholarship that is supportive of the KMT's role in the war. We will see shortly how much of China's media coverage has also been laudatory, focusing in particular on the contribution and sacrifices made by the KMT. The public response to this positive media coverage has been twofold: pride in the efforts of KMT soldiers and sympathy for the neglect and persecution that they suffered after the war, most notably during the highly repressive Mao era.

National Pride

Almost every country that participated in the Second World War on the allied side has taken great pride in its war history and China is no different. But what has become increasingly apparent to the Chinese is the genuine lack of international recognition for their forefathers' contribution to the war in fighting the Japanese both at home and abroad. According to Hays Gries (2004) one of the most passionate themes in recent Chinese scholarship is demanding that the world acknowledges and respects China's war accomplishments and this has also become a widespread public assertion. But as the public has learned more and more about the sacrifices made by KMT soldiers during the war, the focal point of national pride has shifted away from the CCP and towards the KMT.

Dealing firstly with China's overseas participation in the war, the achievements of the Chinese Expeditionary Force to Burma (1941–1945) have received considerable attention in the Chinese media, mainly because they provide clear evidence that China was not only defending itself during the war, but was also contributing directly to allied campaigns in foreign lands. Chinese TV stations have produced a number of very popular programmes on the Chinese contribution in Burma, including the CCTV documentary series the 'Chinese Expeditionary Force' (first shown in May 2011) and a popular drama series with the same name. In addition to this, a unique activity was organised in 2010 entitled 'Walk the Path of the Chinese Expeditionary Force'. This brought together for the very first time the relatives of KMT veterans from both China and Taiwan in a tour of the memorial sites along the route of the Expeditionary Force where thousands of Chinese lives were lost at the hands of the Japanese. The event was widely covered by the Chinese media, including the official Xinhua News Agency (XHW 2010) and is reported to have generated huge public interest and nostalgic pride for the efforts of KMT soldiers.

The Global Times (2014) has been particularly vocal in praising the patriotic sacrifices made by KMT soldiers during the Burma campaign. In an interview with You Guangcai, a KMT veteran who fought in Burma, the paper acknowledged that most of the 400,000 soldiers sent to Burma were KMT members, many of whom died there. More significantly, the paper admitted that their contribution in Burma was 'concealed for a long time'. This is attributed to 'the sensitive status of the KMT' which meant that 'they were not acknowledged by either the government or the public on the mainland until recent years'.

In relation to the war at home, the traditional victim narrative, which for years portrayed China as defenceless against Japanese aggression particularly during the Nanjing Massacre, is no longer prevalent. Instead, a narrative of heroism has emerged, with the Chinese public preferring to think of their forefathers as courageous fighters rather than helpless victims of rape and murder. The CCP did provide an earlier version of the victor narrative in which it triumphed over Japan by using the time-honoured Maoist techniques of guerrilla warfare. This was manifested in the release of propaganda films such as 'Tunnel Warfare', 'Landmine Warfare' and 'Little Soldier Zhang Ga'. These were light comedies depicting the communists as clever guerrillas who always prevailed over the foolish Japanese invaders. But as more information on the war became available, it became harder for people to believe that the war was won through guerrilla warfare alone. Instead, the large-scale conventional battles fought by the KMT in Taierzhuang and elsewhere provided a much more potent and believable discourse of resistance and heroism and one upon which the Chinese public have increasingly seized.

Regional pride is also an important ingredient in the growing popularity of China's war history. In those places that were major KMT battlefields during the war, local people, including local officials, have expressed great respect for their forefathers' heroism, whether they were communists or nationalists. According to Asia Weekly, (YZZK 2005b) people in Nanjing refer to their city as the 'capital of the Republic', whilst residents of Chongqing call their city China's 'wartime capital'. In Yunan, there is an increasingly palpable sense of pride in the history of the KMT-led Chinese Expeditionary Force and in Guangxi many people praise the heroism of Li Zongren's forces.

Sympathy for KMT Veterans

Increased interest in the war is also apparent through expressions of public sympathy for KMT war veterans. We noted earlier the frenetic media activity that took place in 2005 as reporters travelled far and wide to interview participants in the war. In addition to this, China's three major online news portals, Sina, Sohu and Netease, opened special web pages dedicated exclusively to the war veterans and created special email accounts to solicit information from the public about any surviving veterans (NFDB 2007).

As part of this nationwide campaign, the local media in Chongqing unearthed Yang Yangzheng, a KMT veteran born in 1914. Unbeknown to all, Yang had participated in the Defence of the Sihang Warehouse, a historic seven-day battle that took place during late October 1937 and signalled the end of the KMT's military resistance to Japan in Shanghai (Wakeman 1996). The defenders at Sihang, who shortly afterwards were heralded throughout China as the Eight Hundred Heroes (there were actually only 423 of them!), are thought to have stood firm in the face of relentless Japanese attacks and provided cover for hundreds of retreating KMT troops. Although their efforts did not prevent Japan from taking Shanghai, their bravery is thought to have greatly boosted Chinese morale at this difficult time.

As public interest in Yang's story grew, a Shanghainese newspaper paid for the 91-year-old (who lost his left eye at Sihang) to travel by train back to Shanghai in July 2005 so that he could visit the scene of the battle for the very first time since it had taken place. His visit attracted massive media attention and a number of news outlets from across the country sent reporters to Shanghai to cover the event (CQCB 2005). Pictures of the frail Yang being helped to the now renovated warehouse by family members were posted on the internet and aroused immense public sympathy. So too did Yang's death in December 2010, with the Chongqing Evening News lamenting that 'the last of the Eight Hundred Heroes has been lost' (CQWB 2010).

But Yang was not the last. Just days before his death, another surviving Sihang participant emerged, Yang Genkui born in 1921 in Sichuan. Known only to the people in his village, Yang revealed his full identity during a visit to the Jianchuan Museum (YCWB 2011). As with Yang Yangzheng (no relation), Yang Genkui's story was seized upon by the Chinese media, disseminated across China and quickly captured the imagination of the entire country. What was particularly striking about Yang's experience was the harsh treatment meted out to him after the CCP came to power in 1949. Although Yang tried his best to conceal his earlier membership of the KMT, rumours inevitably spilled out and he suffered repeated persecution during the numerous political campaigns that characterised the Mao era (YCWB 2011). To add insult to injury, when Yang asked local officials whether he was entitled to a war veteran's pension or free medical care on seeing Yang Yangzheng gain recognition, he was told in no uncertain terms to 'go to Taiwan to ask the Kuomintang [party] for benefits' (Epoch Times 2011). When news of this terse response was made public, it is thought to have caused uproar amongst internet users. Sections of the Chinese media also came out in sympathy with Yang and although journalists and broadcasters are unable to criticise the party overtly due to censorship issues, the underlying feeling of disapproval was tangible. As one reporter from the Guangzhou-based Yangcheng Evening News wrote 'the veterans are fading away, but the glory of the whole generation of resistance war veterans will never fade. It is time to put a carnation into the veterans' hands, which used to hold guns' (YCWB 2011).

In fact, the authorities in China have not completely ignored the heroics of those who fought in Sihang. In 1983, the grave of KMT general Xie Jinyuan, a leading figure in the battle, was transferred to the prestigious Wanguo Public Museum in Shanghai alongside other Chinese patriots (RMW 2005). Then in 2005 China Telecom released a collection of themed telephone cards, one of which featured Xie Jinyuan next to the Sihang Warehouse. However, anecdotal evidence suggests that this response was deemed inadequate by the Chinese public, to the point of being insulting.

Public sympathy for KMT war veterans has not been limited to the dramatic events of Sihang. In 2007 the Hong Kong-based (and Beijing-backed) Phoenix TV screened a documentary about Wu Dehou, one of the KMT officers who was chiefly responsible for Japan's humiliating defeat at Taierzhuang. The documentary shows how after 1949 Wu's leading role at Taierzhuang was completely overlooked, as the Mao regime preferred instead to concentrate on his former membership of the KMT. This ensured that Wu spent more than ten years in prison and suffered many more years of discrimination (FHW 2007). The highly emotive documentary was posted online in China in 2010 and was widely circulated on the Chinese internet and on the Sina Weibo microblogging site where it was retweeted more than 3400 times in just a few days. One angry viewer noted that 'Wu experienced all the hardships and sufferings one can imagine in his lifetime, but he never betrayed the country and never complained! We should never forget such people and should never again repay their virtue with evil!!' (GZRB 2010).

Also in 2010, a Shenzhen-based private studio made a documentary entitled 'Finding the Major', which tells the story of former KMT army major Zhao Zhenying, who was responsible for the security operation for the ceremony marking Japan's surrender to China on 9 September 1945. According to media reports on the story, during the Cultural Revolution, Zhao was jailed as a counter-revolutionary and his wife was forced to divorce him (ZQB 2010).

KMT veteran You Guangcai also suffered during the Cultural Revolution simply because he fought for the "wrong" side. According to the Global Times (2014), not only was You's wife forced to divorce him and to remarry, but after doing so his daughter had to adopt the family name of her new stepfather in order to avoid any association with her natural father. You's daughter (Du Heng) recalled that 'when her father came to school to visit her, the father introduced himself as "Du's uncle" to avoid troubles that might pass onto her during that time of political unrest'.

Those who did not survive the war have also been the focus of sympathy from the Chinese public, sometimes via Taiwan. In December 2008 the Taiwanese United Daily News reported that tombs containing Chinese prisoners of war had been discovered in Papua New Guinea. The prisoners, including some of the Eight Hundred Heroes, had been taken there by the Japanese to carry out hard labour and had either died of exhaustion or been executed. The tombs were found by an Australian pilot who had contacted the Chinese embassy in Papua New Guinea, but the embassy reportedly showed no interest in the findings (LHB 2008). When a Beijing-based web user reposted the original press report on the internet, the public reaction was explosive. Within just two weeks, over 100,000 people signed an online petition urging the Chinese authorities to take the soldiers' remains back to China for proper burials. Some people even organised a committee to plan the retrieval of the remains. This spurred both the Chinese and Taiwanese governments into action. The Chinese Foreign Ministry sent embassy officials to Papua New Guinea to inspect the tombs (LHB 2009a) showing just how effective public opinion can sometimes be in the PRC. Not to be outdone, the Taiwanese Ministry of National Defence did likewise, "inviting" the soldiers' spirits to the National Revolutionary Martyrs' Shrine in Taibei (LHB 2009b). In March 2009, the Ministry of Foreign Affairs (2009) in China pledged that the remains of Chinese soldiers would be returned to China, stating that 'the Chinese government takes seriously the remains of Chinese soldiers in Papua New Guinea during the Anti-Japanese War. Solemn commemoration will be held in their honour. At present, the preparation is under way'. However, we are some years on, and this still does not appear to have happened.

Ritualised Remembrance

One notable manifestation of public sympathy for KMT war veterans has been the emergence of informal rituals which are conducted to commemorate the memory and sacrifice of lesser-known KMT soldiers who perished during the war. According to the ongoing PhD research of Lin Zhenru (2017) carried out in Hunan Province, the rituals usually take place at locations where, according to accumulated local knowledge, KMT soldiers are believed to have fought and died. These are often in desolate areas such as overgrown fields, hillsides or discarded wasteland. This enhances the symbolism of the occasion because it is thought to represent the fate of the dead KMT soldiers, largely forgotten by Chinese history books. Contrast this to the memory of CCP soldiers who died during the war which is flamboyantly recognised by, for example, the 38 metre high Monument to the People's Heroes at the south side of Tiananmen Square.

According to Lin, the rituals performed for the KMT soldiers are very similar to traditional Chinese funeral rites and include the reading of a funeral oration by a pre-ordained master of ceremonies, the burning of incense and paper money, the offering of symbolic gifts such as fruit and vegetables and a period of silent reflection and kneeling. Some participants or volunteers (sometimes referred to as mourners) wear t-shirts bearing the flag of the KMT (blue sky and white sun) or Taiwan (blue sky, white sun and red background). Others are more discretely dressed for fear of being noticed or arrested. Makeshift banners are often prepared and erected honouring the KMT war dead.

Lin highlights one occasion when, on hearing that a farmer had stumbled across the debris of a KMT gravestone on a hill near Changsha, around 100 volunteers came together to organise a Sending the Martyrs Home ritual at the site of the gravestone, deliberately held on 15 August 2015 to coincide with the 70th anniversary of the Japanese surrender. Having extensively researched local archives that were available to them, the volunteers discovered that at least eight of the KMT soldiers who had died by the hillside were from Hangzhou in Zhejiang Province. They then managed to locate and invite eight relatives of these dead soldiers to attend the ritual where they were presented with eight boxes of soil from the hill to represent the ashes of their dead ancestors. Each of the boxes was covered with the Taiwan national flag, and the eight attendees were asked to take the boxes back to a public graveyard in Hangzhou and spread the soil around the area. According to Lin (2017, p. 6), this kind of ritual challenges the political marginality of KMT soldiers in at least two ways. 'First they are no longer restless ghosts that are politically marginalized because of the national flags on their "bodies". Second, because of the ritual, they are now ancestors who can be worshipped and brought home by their offspring'.

The organisers of these rituals come from all over China. They are usually middle aged, originating from poorer areas but often becoming people of means (e.g. entrepreneurs or white-collar state employees). As such, they can afford to devote time and money to these ritualistic projects. Some are relatives of late KMT soldiers or KMT officials who did not actually fight in the war. Others are just sympathisers with the KMT cause. Most are inhospitable towards the CCP regime. The organisers communicate with each other on the internet or via WeChat (the Chinese equivalent of Snapchat), and there are certain requirements that must be met before qualifying as a volunteer. Many express sadness at their forgotten ancestors. As one volunteer put it 'these heroes have been dead for 70 years, but nobody has come to worship or even light incense. The whole nation should be mourning for them. We should inform more people about our authentic history and honor the true martyrs fairly' (Lin 2017, p. 3).

CCP Under Fire

We noted earlier the immense popular sympathy generated by Yang Genkui, particularly in relation to his harsh treatment after 1949. But the public disquiet at this uncomfortable truth for the CCP is not limited to Yang's case. In an article entitled 'Let the Resistance War Veterans Shed No More Tears' published by the Beijing-based Century Weekly magazine, historian Zhang Lifan praised charitable individuals and Chinese NGOs for caring for Chinese war veterans and questioned the continuing neglect by the CCP of KMT veterans. Zhang also noted that most KMT war veterans were treated very poorly after 1949. One example were the veterans of the Burma Expeditionary Force who received no financial or social welfare assistance from the state and were instead forced to rely on charitable donations or money from friends and relatives. In 2010, when the government gave a one-off cash payment of 3000 RMB to veterans living in rural areas to mark the 65th anniversary of the victory over Japan, no non-communist veterans were included. Concluding his article, Zhang insisted that all governments, including the CCP, were obliged to look after their war veterans:

> Whether it is from the perspective of peaceful reunification or of the united front policy, the political wisdom of the mainland authorities is being tested on how to set an example for the society and gain trust from the people. (XSZK 2011)

Zhang's criticism of the CCP is plain to see and as the public has discovered more about the KMT's leading role in the war against Japan, criticism of the party has become more widespread and more vocal, particularly online. Three accusations have been levelled at the CCP: firstly, that the party persecuted KMT war veterans, many of whom are now national heroes, secondly that it deliberately distorted the history of the war to portray itself as the sole pioneers of the war effort and thirdly that it betrayed the nation by letting the KMT fight the Japanese without much support and even ordering its troops to shoot at KMT soldiers.

Persecuting National Heroes

The rise in public sympathy for the plight of KMT war veterans has been nothing short of astonishing, but as stories have emerged about the persecution suffered by many of them after 1949, this sympathy has turned into antipathy towards those who were responsible for the persecution: the CCP. In addition to Zhang's exhortations, another writer, the Sichuan-based Ran Yunfei, has spoken out. In an article written for Asia Weekly, Ran (2010) insisted that countless KMT veterans, including many who did not even fight in the civil war against the CCP, were punished, incarcerated or executed during the Mao era. Ran has also accused the CCP of having no respect for those KMT soldiers who gave their lives for China in the war against Japan, noting as evidence the numerous KMT war cemeteries that were destroyed by Red Guards during the hysteria of the Cultural Revolution. Using highly emotive language, Ran lamented that 'whenever I think of the remains of the loyal soldiers that lie exposed in the wilderness and cannot rest in peace, I feel as if endless darkness is pressing into my chest'.

We saw earlier how the story of the Taierzhuang war hero Wu Dehou moved many people to tears when it was posted online in China in 2010. But with these tears came anger and disdain for the CCP at the treatment inflicted on Wu in later years. One internet user asked 'how can our national hero be treated like this?' (RMW 2010a). Another expressed himself in more forthright terms: 'a grandfather who should have enjoyed honour was subjected to all this hardship. Please think it over. Who forced him to go through all this?' (RMW 2010a).

Anger at CCP mistreatment of KMT veterans has also come from the organisers the commemorative rituals noted earlier. One female volunteer known only as Ms Wintersweet recalls the persecution suffered by her parents because her father had been a doctor in the KMT military prior to 1949: 'during the Cultural Revolution, the Red Guards rushed into our house and forced my parents [on] to the streets for humiliation. After my mother committed suicide, I hated my father'. Ms Wintersweet also suffered due of her father's KMT affiliation because she was prevented from getting an education. One question that she constantly asked her father at the time was 'why did the KMT anti-revolutionists not defeat the Japanese?'. However, on learning about the pivotal role of the KMT from her father during the last few days of his life in 2012, she turned her anger towards the CCP and became a volunteer. Another volunteer from a poor peasant family in Shanxi Province, known only as Mr Eagle, recalls how his father and grandfather were victimised after 1949 because of their affiliation with the KMT. He concludes in no uncertain terms that 'our miserable condition was caused by the Communist Party. It is impossible for the CCP and me to live under the same sky' (Lin 2017, p. 8).

Distorting History

An even more serious accusation made against at the CCP is that it has intentionally distorted the true history of the war to favour its own role and negate the role played by the KMT. According to Ran Yunfei (2010), at least 95% of Chinese people throughout the world are unaware of what really happened during the war and Ran leaves no doubt where he thinks the blame for this lies:

> The reason is that the CCP authorities' cover-up, distortion and filtering have blurred the true history of the war of resistance against Japan, a war led by the nationalist government for the Chinese nation. The version of history known to many mainland Chinese people has been distorted by the CCP authorities and has been turned upside-down.

In contrast to his criticism of the party, Ran is wholly supportive of the exhaustive efforts to shed light on the war made by Cui Yongyuan, producer of the documentary 'My Resistance War'. He also praises the Sichuanese private collector Fan Jianchuan, founder of the Jinchuan Museum. But both Cui and Fan have been hindered by 'ideological shackles', Ran argues, particularly Fan who, in order to prevent the Jianchuan Museum from being closed down, was obliged by the Chinese authorities to build a much bigger museum commending the CCP's wartime performance.

Ran has not been alone in accusing the CCP of distorting the history of the war to beautify the party's image. In a blog entry entitled 'Those Who Abuse History Will Eventually Be Forsaken By History', Beijing-based author Cheng Xingzhi (2010) criticised CCP propaganda films such as 'Tunnel Warfare' and 'Landmine Warfare' for grossly exaggerating the CCP's wartime performance, representing a cruel war as 'stupid child's play' and insulting people's intelligence. According to Cheng, these films were 'fabricated for certain state goals' in order to create a 'fake ideological mirage' and Cheng suggested that the party will continue to block the truth because:

> If the lies concern the political destiny of a certain political force, if the lies concern whether some people can continue to make illicit gains, then any search for historical truth will meet with desperate resistance from the manufacturers and defenders of those lies.

Further accusations of truth distortion followed the 70th anniversary of the end of the war in September 2015. A Zhejiang-based blogger known only as Jiang Hao Rocky insisted that 'it is not scary if someone does not know the truth. What is scary is that they [the CCP] are still distorting history and continuing to cover up the truth' (BBC 2015). According to one blogger from Hunan, part of the blame for the alleged continued distortion of the truth lies with the general public themselves: 'those who have been brainwashed would never like to accept the facts and would not even have the courage to find out about the truth. They have been behaving like slaves for too long' (BBC 2015).

Betraying the Nation

In addition to the growing accusation that it has played down the KMT's war effort and inflated its own, the CCP has faced a much more serious allegation, that of treachery to the Chinese nation. Chinese scholars such as the CASS historian Yang Kuisong (2010) have revealed that Mao wanted the CCP to avoid major military conflict with Japan and to focus instead on domestic expansion. Based upon such revelations, an increasingly common claim is that the party never really intended to fight the Japanese. Instead, it kept out of the war as much as it could and allowed the KMT to overextend itself. The thinking was that once the war against Japan was over, a more rested, better organised CCP would be in a much stronger position to defeat a war-weary KMT.

One exponent of this line is the exiled dissident Xin Haonian. In his book 'Which is the New China' based on materials published inside China, Xin (1999) argues that Mao and the CCP followed a 'traitorous path' during the war against Japan, putting up a deceptive pretence of resistance, whilst in reality pursuing an agenda of domestic expansion. According to Xin, although Mao claimed to be the only true leader of the Chinese resistance, he never actually directed any military action against the Japanese. On the contrary, the telegrams he sent to his commanders in the field either ordered communist forces not to fight the Japanese or instructed them to point their guns at their supposed KMT allies.

Accusations of CCP treachery during the war are not limited to overseas dissidents. After an extensive survey of party documents and the memoirs of CCP generals, the historian Xie Youtian (2002) claimed that the CCP had no interest in fighting the Japanese from the moment Japan invaded Manchuria in 1931 and simply left the KMT to it, whilst sometimes even launching attacks on the KMT. In this way 'the armed forces of the Chinese nationalists had to fight two enemies at the same time: the Japanese army and the CCP forces led by Mao Zedong'. From this Xie concluded angrily that Mao and the CCP 'sold out the Chinese nation':

> For the CCP, a group with a vested interest, Mao was a great man with great achievements. But for the Chinese nation, which has thousands of years of history, he was a great sinner!

As with much of the critical discourse on the war, accusations of CCP betrayal are especially prevalent on the internet. Writing on the Caixin website, the veteran economist Mao Yushi (2011) compared Mao unfavourably to Stalin. The author noted that for all the mass executions ordered by Stalin, there was no denying that he was at the very forefront of the Soviet war effort against Germany. By contrast, 'at the crucial moment of life and death for the Chinese nation, Mao Zedong did not fight the Japanese but focused on his selfish calculations, preparing to reap the harvest after victory was won'. The article provoked a strong backlash from the pro-Mao internet camp (see shortly) and was later removed from the Caixin website, but not before it was reposted on the China Report Weekly website and widely circulated throughout the country.

Another focus of online criticism is Mao's alleged expressions of gratitude to Japan for weakening the KMT during the war, thereby helping the CCP seize power. Indeed, the text of Mao's purported remarks is so prevalent on the internet that the Chinese authorities felt it necessary to defend Mao in the media. In 2008, the Beijing Daily (BJRB 2008) invited Central Party School professor Li Donglang to answer a reader's question on Mao's remarks. Li admitted that Mao had thanked the Japanese on various occasions, but said that Mao was just being 'humorous' and what he really meant was that the Japanese invasion had helped 'awaken' the Chinese people. However, an article published in the Shanghai-based Wenhui Book Review (WDZ 2011) quoted the CASS historian Zhang Zhenkun as saying that the Japanese invasion created the conditions for the communist victory and that Mao's words of gratitude should be interpreted as a genuine expression of his gratitude. Those poorly chosen words 'revealed Mao's true emotions and were not off-hand remarks or displays of humour'.

THE PARTY COMES OUT FIGHTING

As one might expect, the CCP has not simply stood by and listened mutely to criticism of its role during the war against Japan and its subsequent treatment of former KMT soldiers. In response to internet criticism of Wu Dehou's maltreatment by the CCP, the People's Network website (RMW 2010a) published an article defending the party's imprisonment of Wu, insisting that it was proportionate to Wu's alleged crime during the civil war when he purportedly helped to prevent the defection of his superior officer to the communist side:

> From the perspective of historical materialism, sentencing Wu Dehou to 10 years' imprisonment is exactly because the CCP took into account that Wu had been an anti-Japanese hero. This sentence provides concrete evidence that the CCP is true to the facts and is very magnanimous.

The article also rounded on sections of the Chinese media for their 'one-sided and selective reporting' which 'distorted the facts, negated the party's history, sullied the party's image and led to dissatisfaction towards the CCP among the audiences'. This response from the mouthpiece of the CCP shows the increasing party concerns about the way the Chinese media is handling KMT war-related stories and the corrosive impact that this is having on the CCP's credibility.

Adding his voice to the party backlash has been Xu Yan (2010) of Beijing's PLA National Defence University. In article in the People's Daily, Xu roundly condemned the alleged tendency of some people to exaggerate the KMT's participation in the war, identifying this as part of a wider effort by 'hostile forces at home and abroad' to destabilise the CCP. As Xu put it 'their purpose is to undermine the legitimacy of China's revolutionary wars and the struggle to found a New China through praising and beautifying the reactionary old forces that were overthrown by the people's revolution'.

Maoist websites have also come out all guns blazing. An article in Utopia insisted that 'we can no longer treat lightly or turn a blind eye to these savage attacks from anti-Mao and anti-communist elements', calling on all levels of the party and government in China to 'attach a high level of importance to this issue'. The article suggested that those in authority should use all the resources at their disposal to publicise the details of the many communists who died during the war. In addition, it implored other pro-Mao web-users, or 'patriotic netizens', to join the effort to 'fight back and expose the shameless slander and lies of anti-Mao, anti-communist elements' and to help restore the CCP's reputation as 'the mainstay of the resistance' (WZX 2010).

Official concerns about the growth of anti-CCP feeling over the war against Japan have been reflected in intermittent changes to Beijing's official narrative. We noted earlier Hu Jintao's laudatory speech in 2005 when he acknowledged the front-line role played by the KMT. But this admission was not repeated in 2010 on the 65th anniversary of the end of the war. Indeed, the KMT's contribution was barely mentioned in the People's Daily editorial marking the anniversary (RMW 2010b). Instead, the positive focus fell squarely on the CCP:

> At the critical moment of national survival or subjugation, the CCP blew the first bugle call for counter-attacking the external enemy. In that magnificent and mighty war, the CCP was the mainstay with its firm will and exemplary actions. The most fundamental reason why the Chinese people were able to work a great miracle in the defeat of a powerful country by a weak country was because the CCP represented the will of all the Chinese

people, led and pushed forward the great war of resistance against Japan, represented the hopes of all the people who wanted to save the nation from subjugation and ensure its survival, and became the vanguard of the nation.

The author of the editorial also attributed the CCP's later defeat of the KMT in the civil war to its purportedly integral role in the defeat of Japan: 'it was precisely on the basis of the victory of the war of resistance against Japan that the CCP led the Chinese people to victory in the new democratic revolution, set up the People's Republic of China and realised the greatest and deepest social transformation in the history of China' (RMRB 2010).

This sharp turn in the official narrative against the KMT compelled the KMT government in Taiwan to issue strong statements rejecting the CCP's claim. The then Taiwanese president Ma Yingjiu insisted that the People's Daily editorial deviated shamelessly from the truth, noting that Hu Jintao's 2005 statement was much closer to what really happened. The Taiwan Ministry of National Defence at that time also blasted the CCP's attempt to take all the credit for the victory at the expense of the real champions of the war effort, the KMT (China Post 2010).

The reason for this partial return to the orthodox CCP line was two-fold. Firstly and most obviously, the party was (and continues to be) worried about the rise in public feeling against it over the war. Given the difficulty in controlling internet dissent in particular, the CCP started looking for ways to smother the gathering public momentum against it and one such way was to revert to the old orthodoxy. Secondly, the party no longer needed the KMT as much as it did before. Following successive presidential victories for Ma Yingjiu in 2008 and 2012, there was less of a perceived requirement for the party to side with the KMT. As yet, the election of the DPP's Cai Yingwen as President in January 2016 has not precipitated a return to the CCP–KMT marriage of political convenience that occurred after 2000, but Cai's intermittent criticisms of the CCP over its alleged denial of the KMT's role during the war might well bring this about. Cai was especially critical of Lian Zhan's attendance at the 2015 China Victory Day parade in Tiananmen Square to mark the 70th anniversary of the end of the war. She noted that, in light of the PRC's refusal to rule out military action against Taiwan, Lian's decision to attend the military parade was 'not in accordance with the feelings of Taiwanese and could send the wrong message to the international community' (Taipei Times 2015).

A particularly vehement official backlash against war-related critics of the CCP arose during 2015 in the build-up to the 70th anniversary of the end of the war. This was primarily in response to claims made in a number of blogs, including those contained in the verified Weibo accounts of celebrities with large numbers of online followers (known colloquially as big Vs) that CCP soldiers killed only fraction of the number of Japanese soldiers compared to the number killed by the KMT. This included a tweet from the writer and historian Zhang Yihe (daughter of Zhang Bojun, Minister of Communications in the early 1950s) that only 851 Japanese soldiers were killed by the CCP, as opposed to 318,883 killed by the KMT and 126,607 killed by the Soviet Red Army. Zhang's post went viral and was retweeted tens of thousands of times.

In response to Zhang's claims (and similar claims made by other bloggers), in the Global Times an article entitled 'Vilifying the CCP Again! But How Brainless Must You Be to Believe in this Rumour?' responded angrily on its official Weibo account that 'as the 70th anniversary of the victory in the War of Resistance against Japan nears, a new round of mudslinging against the Communist army's record of resistance is running rampant and the rumours have become ever more shameless, shocking and stupid' (HQSB 2015). Likewise, the semi-monthly CCP journal Red Flag Manuscripts (HQWG 2015) run by Seek Truth magazine, dismissed the allegations as nothing more than 'a sensational rumour' stating that:

> The commemoration of the 70th anniversary of the victory in the War of Resistance is an opportunity to once again show (our determination) to bury historical grievances and strive together for the regeneration of the Chinese nation. But some public intellectuals and big Vs, in an attempt to damage the legitimacy of the CCP's rule, have been fabricating and spreading a large number of rumours vilifying the CCP's resistance effort behind enemy lines. This will only result in raking up historical grievances and once again tear open the divide between social classes. We have to pay great attention to this and launch a resolute counterattack against it!

The People's Liberation Army Daily also joined in the counter-attack publishing an article which criticised those who 'spread rumours that the Communist Party only lost one general in the anti-Japanese war and only killed 851 Japanese soldiers, using this to negate the Communist Party's role as the mainstay of the resistance, and even negating the legitimacy of

Communist Party rule'. By contrast, the article praised what it described as the 'online positive energy' of pro-CCP netizens who criticised negative comments made about the CCP's war record against Japan. But if anything, these angry rebuttals provided evidence of the scale and seriousness of the anti-CCP attacks in relation to the war (JFJB 2015).

THE STRATEGY BACKFIRES?

We have identified in this chapter a cautious movement towards an official party line which finally recognises the pivotal role played by the KMT in defeating Japan during the Second Sino-Japanese War. The posthumous rehabilitation of certain KMT generals, the screening of war films which acknowledge the contribution of the KMT and the laudatory statements coming out of Beijing, particularly during the 2005 visit of Lian Zhan, are just some examples of an increasingly positive re-evaluation of the KMT's war effort. More recent instances include President Xi Jinping's praise for the combined military forces of the CCP and the KMT (including the Eight Hundred Heroes at Sihang) as a 'prominent example of how the Chinese people would not succumb to force and are willing to give their lives for their country' (RMRB 2014). Xi reiterated this praise during his face-to-face meeting in Beijing with Lian shortly before the 70th anniversary commemorations when he noted that 'both the front line and the battlefield behind enemy lines closely coordinated with each other and made important contributions to the victory' (Xinhuanet 2015). The rationale for these generous words and conciliatory deeds is part of a more consensual official approach towards relations with the KMT, with the peaceful reunification of Taiwan as its core objective. This has also served the CCP's nationalist purposes, with the party presenting itself as flexible and tolerant, seeking to represent national unity and harmony across the Taiwan Straits.

The evidence suggests, however, that as with aggressive nationalism, attempts to bolster the party's legitimacy in this more consensual manner are not proving altogether successful. By opening up the parameters of permissible debate, the party has left itself vulnerable to criticism from its detractors. The public response has ranged from anger and derision at the poor treatment of KMT veterans after 1949, accusations of a CCP cover-up over the true history of the war and allegations that the party betrayed the nation by failing to adequately support the KMT in fighting the Japanese and by ordering communist soldiers to fire on their nationalist counterparts rather than support them in ousting the enemy.

In the next chapter, we will see how the rehabilitation of the KMT has widened to include a more sanguine interpretation of the Republican era and the contribution of the KMT during that era. As with Second Sino-Japanese War the CCP's rationale for doing so is linked to consensual nationalism and the desire to present itself as the party of national unity based on shared historical experiences with the Republic and the KMT. Again, however, much of the public response has questioned rather than acknowledged the party's role during and after this period as well as its own nationalist credibility.

References

BBC. (2015, November 5). *South China sea: US defence chief Ash Carter Wades into row.* Retrieved from http://www.bbc.co.uk/news/world-asia-34737051.

BJRB. (2008, December 15). *Zhengque Lijie Mao Zedong Pinglun Riben de Yijuhua* [The correct understanding of a remark made by Mao Zedong on Japan]. *Beijing Ribao* [Beijing Daily]. Retrieved from http://www.bjd.com.cn/gdjc/200812/t20081215_495586.htm.

Bonavia, D. (1995). *China's warlords.* New York: Oxford University Press.

Chang, J. (2001). The politics of commemoration: A comparative analysis of the fiftieth-anniversary commemoration in mainland China and Taiwan of the victory in the anti-Japanese war. In D. Lary & S. MacKinnon (Eds.), *Scars of war: The impact of warfare on Modern China* (pp. 136–161). Vancouver: University of British Columbia Press.

Cheng, X. (2010, September 11). *Xiedu Lishi de Ren zhong Jiang Hui bei Lishi Tuoqi* [Those who abuse history will eventually be forsaken by history]. *Zhongguo Xuanju yu Zhili* [China Elections and Governance]. Retrieved from http://www.chinaelections.org/NewsInfo.asp?NewsID=186779.

China Boom Project. (2011, July 16). *The legacy of property provides stability.* Retrieved from http://chinaboom.asiasociety.org/period/emancipation/0/110.

China Post. (2010, September 5). *Ma stresses ROC's role in victory over Japan.* Retrieved from http://www.chinapost.com.tw/taiwan/national/national-news/2010/09/05/271398/Ma-stresses.htm.

Coble, P. (2007). China's 'New remembering' of the anti-Japanese war of resistance, 1937–1945. *China Quarterly, 190,* 394–410.

CQCB. (2005, July 5). *Kangri Laobing Yang Yangzheng Chongfan Laozhanchang Shanghai Sihang Cangku* [Anti-Japanese veteran Yang Yangzheng returns to the old battlefield at the Shanghai Sihang warehouse]. *Chongqing Chenbao* [Chongqing Morning News]. Retrieved from http://news.163.com/05/0705/08/1NSS96I60001127G.html.

CQWB. (2010, December 17). *Babai Zhuangshi Zuihou Laobing Yang Yangzheng Zou le* [Yang Yangzheng, the last of the eight hundred heroes, passed away yesterday]. *Chongqing Wanbao* [Chongqing Evening News]. Retrieved from http://www.cqwb.com.cn/NewsFiles/201012/17/20100017120000412114.shtml.

Diamant, N. (2011). Conspicuous silence: Veterans and the depoliticization of war memory in China. *Modern Asian Studies, 45*(2), 431–461.

Du, L. (2005). *Liang jian* [Drawing sword]. Beijing: Jiefangjun Wenyi Chubanshe.

Epoch Times. (2011, February 2). *Last Chinese war hero suffers destitution and insult*. Retrieved from http://www.theepochtimes.com/n3/1502745-last-chinese-war-hero-suffers-destitution-and-insult/full/.

FHW. (2007, June 19). *Fenghuang Dujia: Lengnuan Rensheng zhi "Laobing bu Si" shang* [Phoenix TV exclusive: Life story tale of 'Old soldiers never die']. *Fenghuang Wang* [Phoenix TV Network]. Retrieved from http://phtv.ifeng.com/phinfo/200706/0614_45_135240.shtml.

Global Times. (2014, September 14). As KMT veterans receive newfound respect, others gauge political winds. Retrieved from http://www.globaltimes.cn/content/881379.shtml.

GZRB. (2010, August 18). *Laobing Shipin Gandong Wangluo* [Video of a veteran moves internet users]. *Guangzhou Ribao* [Guangzhou Daily]. Retrieved from http://gzdaily.dayoo.com/html/2010-08/18/content_1072442.htm.

Haonian, X. (1999). *Shui shi Xin Zhongguo* [Which is the new China]. Blue Sky Publishing House. Retrieved from http://www.huanghuagang.org/new-china/index-eNewChina.html.

Hays Gries, P. (2004). *China's new nationalism: Pride, politics and diplomacy*. California: University of California Press.

HQSB. (2015). *You Hei Zhonggong! Ke Ni Dei Duo mei Naozi Cai Hui Xin Zhege Yaoyan a?* [Vilifying the CCP again! But how brainless must you be to believe in this rumour?]. *Huanqiu Shibao* [Times]. Retrieved from http://www.weibo.com/1974576991/CpI1ujKTV.

HQWG. (2015, July 14). *Cong Yize Songren Tingwen de Yaoyan Shuoqi* [About a sensational rumour]. *Hongqi Wengao* [Red Flag Manuscripts]. Retrieved from http://www.qstheory.cn/dukan/hqwg/2015-07/24/c_1116028754.htm.

JFJB. (2015, September 11). *Shengli Ri, Wangluo Zheng Nengliang Ye Shoudao Jianyue* [On victory day, online positive energy also under inspection]. *Jiefangjun Bao* [People's Liberation Army Daily]. Retrieved from http://www.81.cn/jmywyl/2015-09/11/content_6676456.htm.

LHB. (2008, December 22). *Ba Niu Yiyu Guojun Huangzhong Qiangu Ku* [Over 1,000 desolate tombs of nationalist soldiers found in the foreign land of Papua New Guinea]. *Lianhe Bao* [United Daily News]. Retrieved from http://mag.udn.com/mag/world/storypage.jsp?f_ART_ID=182327.

LHB. (2009a, February 6). *Dalu Wangyou Ni Fu Ba Niu, Ying Kangri Zhanshi Yihai* [Mainland netizens plan to go to Papua New Guinea to retrieve remains of anti-Japanese soldiers]. *Lianhe Bao* [United Daily News]. Retrieved from http://mag.udn.com/mag/world/storypage.jsp?f_ART_ID=182335&pno=7.

LHB. (2009b, March 8). *Ba Niu Guojun Yingling, Hun Gui Zhonglieci* [Papua New Guinea national army soldiers' souls enshrined in martyrs' shrine]. *Lianhe Bao* [United Daily News]. Retrieved from http://mag.udn.com/mag/world/storypage.jsp?f_MAIN_ID=409&f_SUB_ID=4051&f_ART_ID=182325.

Li, Z. (1979). *The memoirs of Li Tsung-jen, Te-kong Tong and Li Tsung-jen.* Boulder: Westview.

Lin, Z. (2017). *Ritualized remembrance in post-socialist China* (Unpublished paper).

Mao, Y. (2011, May 3). *Ba Mao Zedong Huanyuan Cheng Ren: Du 'Hong Taiyang de Yunluo'* [Restore Mao Zedong as a human being: A review of the 'Fall of the Red Sun']. *Zhongguo Baodao Zhoukan* [China Report Weekly]. Retrieved from http://www.china-week.com/html/5972.htm.

Mao, Z. (1954). *The policies, measures, and perspectives of combating Japanese invasion.* Beijing: Foreign Languages Press.

Mitter, R. (2000). Behind the scenes at the museum: Nationalism, history and memory in the Beijing war of resistance museum, 1987–1997. *China Quarterly, 161,* 279–293.

Mitter, R. (2003). Old Ghosts, new memories: China's changing war history in the era of post-Mao politics. *Journal of Contemporary History, 38*(1), 117–131.

Mitter, R. (2007). China's "Good war": Voices, locations and generations in the interpretations of the war of resistance to Japan. In S. Jager & R. Mitter (Eds.), *Ruptured histories: War, memory, and the post-cold war in Asia* (pp. 172–191). Cambridge, MA: Harvard University Press.

Mitter, R., & Moore, A. (2011). China in world war II, 1937–1945: Experience, memory, and legacy. *Modern Asian Studies, 45*(2), 225–240.

NFDB. (2005, September 1). Yichang Qiangjiu Jiyi de Meiti Yundong: Gaomidu Huanyuan Kangzhan Lishi [A media movement to rescue memories: Intensively restoring the history of the war of resistance]. *Nanfang Dushibao* [Southern Metropolis Daily]. Retrieved from http://news.sina.com.cn/c/2005-09-01/09566837675s.shtml.

NFDB. (2007, November 7). *Nandu Tuichu "Xunfang Kangzhan Laobing" Shuxie Laobing Chuanqi* [Southern metropolis daily publishes 'Finding veterans from war of resistance series', Penning the legends of veterans]. *Nanfang Dushibao* [Southern Metropolis Daily]. Retrieved from http://nd.oeeee.com/special/book/comment/200711/t20071107_602217.shtml.

Ran, Y. (2010, September 19). *Qirong "Guoshang" Qingshi Jin Cheng Hui?* [How can the history of the 'National martyrs' be allowed to turn into dust?].

Yazhou Zhoukan [Asia Weekly]. Retrieved from http://www.yzzk.com/cfm/
Content_Archive.cfm?Channel=tt&Path=2254381392/37tt1.cfm.

RMRB. (2010, September 3). *Mingji Lishi, Kaichuang Weilai - Jinian Zhongguo Renmin Kangri Zhanzheng ji Shijie Fan-Faxisi Zhanzheng Liushiwu Zhounian* [Remember the history, open up the future - commemorating the 65th anniversary of the victory of the war of resistance against Japan by the Chinese people and the world anti-fascist war]. *Renmin Ribao* [People's Daily]. Retrieved from http://opinion.people.com.cn/GB/40604/12621793.html.

RMRB. (2014, September 4). *Zai Jinian Zhongguo Renmin Kangri Zhanzheng ji Shijie Fan-Faxisi Zhanzheng Shengli 69 Zhounian Zuotanhui shang de Jianghua, 2014 Nian 9 Yue 3 Ri* [Speech at seminar marking the 69th anniversary of the victory of the war of resistance against Japan by the Chinese people and the world anti-fascist war, 3 September, 2014]. *Renmin Ribao* [People's Daily]. Retrieved from http://cpc.people.com.cn/n/2014/0904/c64094-25599907.html.

RMRB. (2015, May 29). *Waiguoren Yanli de Zhongguo Kangzhan: Zhongguo Kangzhan Gongji Juda er Dute - Fang Niujin Daxue Lishi Jiaoshou Lana Mite* [China's resistance war in a foreigner's eyes: China's achievements in the resistance war are huge and unique - An interview with Oxford university history professor Rana Mitter]. *Renmin Ribao* [People's Daily]. Retrieved from http://dangshi.people.com.cn/n/2015/0529/c85037-27074882.html.

RMW. (2005, 20 April). *Kangri Jiangling Xie Jinyuan* [Anti-Japanese general Xie Jinyuan]. *Renmin Wang* [People's Network]. Retrieved from http://politics.people.com.cn/GB/8198/46867/46884/3336338.html.

RMW. (2010a, August 18). *Renmin Shiping: Tantan dui Guomindang Junguan Wu Dehou de Baodao* [On the media coverage of KMT officer Wu Dehou]. *Renmin Wang* [People's Network]. Retrieved from http://sn.people.com.cn/GB/190202/190236/12474874.html.

RMW. (2010b, September 3). *Mingji Lishi, Kaichuang Weilai: Jinian Zhongguo Renmin Kangri Zhanzheng Ji Shijie Fan Fanxisi Zhanzheng Shengli Liushiwu Zhounian* [Remember history, open up the future: Commemorating the 65th anniversary of the victory of the war of resistance against Japan by the Chinese people and the world anti-fascist war]. *Renmin Wang* [People's Network]. Retrieved from http://opinion.people.com.cn/GB/40604/12621793.html.

Sneider, D. (2013). Textbooks and Patriotic Education: Wartime memory formation in China and Japan. *Asia Pacific Review, 20*(1), 33–54.

Taipei Times. (2015, August 31). *Lien flies to China amid controversy*. Retrieved from http://www.taipeitimes.com/News/front/archives/2015/08/31/2003626584/2.

van de Ven, H. (2007). *Zhongguo de Minzu Zhuyi he Zhanzheng: 1925–1945* [War and nationalism in China: 1925–1945]. Beijing: SDX Joint Publishing Company.

Wakeman, F. (1996). *The Shanghai badlands: War terrorism and urban crime, 1937–1941*. Cambridge: Cambridge University Press.

Waldron, A. (1996). China's new remembering of world war II: The case of Zhang Zizhong. *Modern Asian Studies, 30*(4), 945–978.

WDZ. (2011, February 25). '*Zhongjian Didai*' *de Geming Gaosu Ni: Zhonggong Heyi Bisheng*? [Revolution in the 'Intermediate zone' tells you: Why was the CCP bound to be victorious?]. *Wenhui Book Review* [Wenhui Dushu Zhoubao]. Retrieved from http://dszb.whdszb.com/whdszb/html/2011-02/25/content_76243.htm.

Wu Z. (2012). *The effects of patriotic education on Chinese youths' perceptions of Japan*. Mphil Thesis, Lingnan University.

WZX. (2010, September 3). *Kangri Zhanzheng de Lishi bu Rong Cuangai* [The history of the war against Japan brooks no falsification]. *Wuyou Zhi Xiang* [Utopia]. Retrieved from http://www.wyzxsx.com/Article/Class14/201009/177109.html.

XHW. (2010, May 20). *Er Zhan Laobing Houdai Qicheng Chongzou "Zhongguo Yuanzhengjun Zhi Lu"* [Offspring of world war two veterans begin walking the 'Path of the Chinese expeditionary force']. *Xinhua Wang* [Xinhua Network]. Retrieved from http://news.xinhuanet.com/2010-05/20/c_12124738.htm.

Xie, Y. (2002). *Zhonggong Zhuangda Zhimi: Bei Yangai de Zhongguo Kangri Zhanzheng Zhenxiang* [The mystery over the rise of the CCP: The concealed truth of China's war of resistance against Japan]. Mirror Books. Retrieved from http://blog.dwnews.com/post-144134.html.

Xinhuanet. (2005, September 3). *Speech at a meeting marking the 60th anniversary of the victory of the Chinese people's war of resistance against Japanese aggression and the world anti-fascist war*. Retrieved from http://news.xinhuanet.com/english/2005-09/03/content_3438224.htm.

Xinhuanet. (2015, September 1). Xi stresses Mainland-Taiwan unity for war anniversary. Retrieved from http://news.xinhuanet.com/english/2015-09/01/c_134577112.htm.

XSZK. (2011, April 11). *Rang Kangzhan Laobing bu Zai Liulei* [Let the resistance war veterans shed no more tears]. *Xinshiji Zhoukan* [Century Weekly]. Retrieved from http://magazine.caing.com/2011-04-08/100246206.html.

Xu, Y. (2010, March 26). *Xu Yan Shaojiang: Wang Shang Dui Guomindang Kangzhan You Zhongduo bu shi Chuixu* [Colonel Xu Yan: There is a lot of untrue praise for the KMT's wartime performance]. *Renmin Wang* [People's Network]. Retrieved from http://military.people.com.cn/GB/1076/52984/11227767.html.

Yang, K. (2010). '*Zhongjian Didai*' *de Geming: Guoji Dabeijing Xia Kan Zhonggong Chenggong Zhidao* [Revolution in the 'Intermediate zone': The CCP's path to success seen within the broad international context]. Taiyuan: Shanxi People's Publishing House.

YCWB. (2011, January 22). *Women bu Pa Siwang, Women Pa bei Yiwang - Guilai de Zhuangshi Yang Genkui* [We are not afraid of death, we are afraid of being forgotten - returning hero Yang Genkui]. *Yangcheng Wanbao* [Yangcheng Evening Daily]. Retrieved from http://www.ycwb.com/epaper/ycwb/html/2011-01/22/content_1024559.htm.

YZZK. (2005a, August 28). *Zhonggong Jinian Kangzhan Guojun Huo Kending* [The CCP's commemoration of the nationalist army's war effort recognised]. *Yazhou Zhoukan* [Asia Weekly]. Retrieved from http://www.yzzk.com/cfm/Content_Archive.cfm?Channel=ae&Path=2268386452/35ae4.cfm.

YZZK. (2005b, August 28). *Wei Jiang Jieshi Pingfan, Zhonggong Kangzhan Shiguan Weimiao Bianhua* [Chiang Kai-shek rehabilitated, subtle changes in the CCP's view of second world war history]. *Yazhou Zhoukan,* [Asia Weekly]. Retrieved from http://www.yzzk.com/cfm/Content_Archive.cfm?Channel=ac&Path=2268386452/35ae1a.cfm.

Zhao, S. (2003). Beijing's wait-and-see policy toward Taiwan: An uncertain future. *East Asia, 20*(3), 39–60.

Zhao, S. (2006). Conflict prevention across the Taiwan strait and the making of China's anti-secession law. *Asian Perspective, 30*(1), 79–94.

ZQB. (2010, September 8). *Laobing Guilai* [The veteran returns]. *Zhongguo Qingnian Bao* [China Youth Daily]. Retrieved from http://zqb.cyol.com/content/2010-09/08/content_3408656.htm.

ZXW. (2010, September 11). *Cui Yongyuan Chengqing 'Wo de Kangzhan' Tou 130 million Yuan Chen Mei Xiang Shouhui Chengben* [Yongyuan clarifies that investment for 'My war of resistance' was 130 million yuan, says he did not intend to recoup the costs]. *Zhongguo Xinwen Wang* [China News Network]. Retrieved from http://www.chinanews.com/yl/2010/09-11/2527046.shtml.

CHAPTER 6

Consensual Nationalism: The Republican Era and the Rise of Republican Fever

The last ten years or so has seen the emergence in China of a phenomenon known as Republican fever This refers to an increasing groundswell of popular interest in and support for Republican China. Those infused with Republican fever believe that the Republic was much more vibrant, open and successful than previously propagated by the overwhelmingly negative CCP narrative. One widespread claim is that the Republic enjoyed a surprisingly high level of academic and media freedom and that notable progress was made in spreading democratic thinking and building democratic institutions. Proponents also praise the economic and diplomatic achievements made during the period and suggest that Chiang Kai-shek's KMT rather than Mao's CCP ended the Century of Humiliation. Ultimately, supporters associate themselves with an alternative Republican national identity, expressing an affinity for Taiwan, the KMT and the system of multiparty democracy and human rights practised in Taiwan, but not in the PRC.

Whilst there is no clear evidence to suggest that Republican fever was deliberately initiated by the CCP, the party did set the trend in motion by allowing greater room for public discussion of the Republican era. There are at least two reasons for this upon which we elaborate later in the chapter. The first reason can be traced back to the introduction of economic reform in the early 1980s when Deng Xiaoping actively encouraged Chinese scholars to present a positive image of the Republican economy and entrepreneurial spirit in order to enhance the credibility of the new reforms and incentivise PRC entrepreneurs to

© The Author(s) 2017

R. Weatherley and Q. Zhang, *History and Nationalist Legitimacy in Contemporary China*, DOI 10.1057/978-1-137-47947-1_6

continue where their Republican predecessors had left off several decades earlier.

The second reason relates to the party's quest for nationalist legitimacy and, in particular, what we referred to in the previous chapter as a consensual form of nationalist legitimacy rather than the more abrasive form discussed in Chaps. 3 and 4. By relaxing the previously stringent controls on discussing the Republic, as it has done on the KMT's role in the Second Sino-Japanese War, the CCP has attempted to present itself as a key partner in a pro-reunification, patriotic front with the KMT, a more modern and open-minded communist party with the interests of the nation at the very fore.

But as with each of the other case studies that we have discussed in this book, the CCP is finding that the debate it has initiated is increasingly turning against it. Just as academic, media and democratic freedoms during the Republic are applauded by exponents of the Republican fever, so the absence of such freedoms in the PRC is lamented. As the apparent strength and potential of the Republican economy has come to light, so there is a discernible feeling that the economy might have developed more quickly without the CCP. Just as the diplomatic achievements of the Republic are increasingly recognised, so doubts are being raised about the CCP's self-proclaimed success in safeguarding Chinese sovereignty after 1949. As more and more Chinese people have come to identify themselves with the legacy of the Republic and Taiwan, so they have come to distance themselves from the PRC and everything it stands for. Once again, the double-edged nature of Chinese nationalism is apparent, as a debate which was expected to bolster CCP legitimacy may well be detracting from it.

POST-MAO INTEREST IN THE REPUBLIC

We saw in the previous chapter how the KMT's role in the Second Sino-Japanese War received little official attention during the Mao era and what attention it did receive was overwhelmingly derisory. Republican China received more attention under Mao, but again it was negative. According to the exaggerated party line, the Republican economy was on the verge of collapse after inefficient governmental handling and corruption led to massive unemployment, gross underproduction and unprecedented high levels of inflation. Chinese society was portrayed as impoverished, fragmented and disenfranchised and the KMT as impotent in the face of warlordism and highly oppressive under the auspices of the ruthlessly dictatorial and fascistic Chiang Kai-shek. "Old China", it was argued, was ripe for liberation and this duly came with the victory of the CCP in 1949. Put simply, the CCP saved China from impending disaster under the KMT.

Academic Research

The political ascent of Deng Xiaoping in the late 1970s did not lead to an immediate repudiation of this grim official depiction of the Republic and the KMT. However, the relaxation of political controls that accompanied Deng's rise did create sufficient political breathing space for a re-evaluation of the era. This was initially apparent within academic circles as archival materials from Taiwan and further abroad became increasingly available to PRC historians, who for years had been starved of anything meaningful to research about the Republic. One particular area of activity focused on discovering what had happened to certain high-profile KMT figures who had been mentioned in PRC history books, but then vanished without a trace from the written page. Hu Hanmin (1879–1936) is one such example. Head of the KMT's Legislative Yuan in Nanjing from 1927–1931 and an important ally of Sun Yat-sen, Hu's career up until about February 1931 was closely documented in PRC history texts. It was at this point that Hu was placed under house arrest following disagreements with Chiang over the drafting of the new provisional constitution. Intrigued by Hu's subsequent absence from PRC texts despite living for another five years, historian Chen Hongmin set about completing the picture as part of his postgraduate dissertation at Nanjing University which he wrote during the early 1980s. Chen's research showed that Hu had been airbrushed from the CCP's official historiography after 1931 because he consistently maintained an anti-communist political stance. But Chen rightly noted that Hu was equally opposed to the Chiang Kai-shek regime and to Japan's military aggression, a fact that was conveniently ignored by the CCP. Chen (2011) later argued that party censors had acted unfairly and that Hu should be posthumously credited for his staunch anti-Japanese position.

Chen's thesis met with stiff opposition from the more orthodox members of Nanjing University's party apparatus who insisted that his reassessment of the "rightist" Hu Hanmin was excessively and unacceptably positive. However, other academics at Nanjing supported Chen's stance and his dissertation eventually passed and even received positive reviews from some quarters. More than three decades on and Chen is now a highly respected senior historian whose work, on Hu is well-regarded and who now heads up Zhejiang University's Modern History Institute and Centre on Chiang Kai-shek and Modern China.

Another early post-Mao researcher on the Republic was Yang Shubiao of Hangzhou University In the early 1980s Yang took the bold step of founding the PRC's first ever university module on the study of Chiang Kai-shek which sought to evaluate Chiang's political legacy independently of the established CCP line. Shortly after founding the course, Yang was targeted by the October 1983 Campaign Against Spiritual Pollution, a movement orchestrated by Deng Liqun (head of the Propaganda Department) who was strongly opposed to allegedly liberal and anti-Marxist trends amongst certain Chinese intellectuals (Mackerras 1984; Saich 1984) . Yang was accused of conspiring to usurp the official verdict on Chiang's "reactionary crimes" and replace it with a "revisionist" alternative. Although Yang was formally criticised for his alleged errors, those who investigated him acknowledged that the under-lining tone of his module was patriotic. This allowed Yang to continue his teaching and research into the Republican era (Ye 2010) and by 1989 Yang had completed the first biography of Chiang Kai-shek to be published in the PRC (Yang 1989).

The environment for PRC scholarly research into the Republic has since become increasingly relaxed with Jeremy Taylor (2009) describing the field as 'decidedly fashionable' in the PRC, whilst Zhang Li (2011) writing in the Taiwan-based CNA Newsworld noted how the history of the Republic has evolved from a 'dangerous subject' into a 'prominent subject'. According to Wang Chaoguang (2008) of CASS, the Republic has become the most dynamic and productive field in Chinese history studies. Indeed, in 2011 CASS compiled and published a landmark 36 volume history of the Republic, bringing together decades of research by several generations of mainland historians (Li 2011).

Yet, the Republic remains a sensitive subject and one that is prone to sporadic official censure. In 2002, the CASS historian Yang Tianshi published a book entitled 'Chiang's Secret Files and the Truth about Chiang Kai-shek' based on excerpts from Chiang's diaries. Within a few weeks, an anonymous open letter appeared on the internet accusing Yang of elevating Chiang, a 'war criminal and a traitor', to the status of a national hero, thereby directly challenging the authority of the CCP.

Yang (2003) was then required to write a detailed report in response to these accusations in which he denied calling Chiang a hero, pointing out that he had actually been quite critical of Chiang in his book. The CASS authorities looked into the allegations made against Yang and concluded in their report to central government that Yang's book was a piece of 'solid academic work'. In the end, no action was taken against Yang (JJGB 2010).

Popular Culture

In addition to scholarly interest in the Republican era, a broader public interest has been apparent since the early 1980s. This is partly because of the Republic's chronological proximity to the present, making it more relevant to everyday life in the PRC. But it is also because of the scarcely believable official narrative on the period which was espoused for so long by the CCP. Whilst KMT figures such as Chiang were well-known during the Mao era of the PRC, they were only known by their derisory ideological labels such as "counter-revolutionary" or "national traitor". Similarly negative labels were applied to the Republic. But as Deng moved to ease domestic political tensions, a public demand emerged for TV programmes, books and magazine articles offering a less politicised assessment of the era. This led to the landmark screening in 1984 of a Hong Kong television drama entitled 'The Bund' based on the criminal activities of the 1920s Shanghai triads, which quickly became a hit with the viewing Chinese public (XGL 2008).

At around this time, a number of books began to appear on Chinese bookshelves in what was known as Republican exposé. These were cheaply produced and low-quality books which focused on two aspects of the Republican era: the criminal underworld (leading on from the popularity of 'The Bund') and the lives of notorious historical figures such as spy chiefs and military officers from the KMT's Whampoa Military Academy. The book titles were often sensationalist, such as 'Dai Li: King of Spies', 'Chen Guofu: The KMT Godfather' and 'Chiang Kai-shek and the Three Heroes of Whampoa'. The books portrayed the Republic as a period characterised by corruption, internecine gangland warfare and high-level assassinations (XGL 2008). So at this early stage, there was no obvious contradiction of the CCP's official narrative on the era, nor was there any implied challenge to the party's incumbency or record in power.

THE EMERGENCE OF THE FEVER

We noted previously how the election of Chen Shuibian as Taiwan's President in 2000 helped to thaw CCP–KMT relations. This, together with the deaths in 2001 of KMT General Zhang Xueliang (instigator of the 1936 Xian Incident) and in 2003 of Soong May-ling (Madame Chiang Kai-shek), served to intensify the mainland Chinese interest in the Republican era that had been actively discouraged by the CCP during the 1990s when relations between the two parties were tense. In 2006 references to a new phenomenon called Republican fever began to appear in the PRC media. According to Zhou Weijun (2008), writing in the Southern Metropolis Daily, Republican fever emerged following the successful launch of a series of scholarly and non-specialist books on the Republic including titles such as 'The Bad Temper of History' and 'Waves Under the Pen'. What differentiated these books from earlier publications was the more optimistic portrayal of the Republic. Whereas previously the emphasis had been on the allegedly shady, dangerous and corrupt features of the Republic, these new books depicted an era of diversity, sophistication and unrealised potential, as we will discuss in more detail shortly.

Publishers quickly saw the market potential in this area and started releasing Republic-themed books in droves. In 2007, the China Youth Daily reported that one bookshop in Beijing had over 700 books on its shelves whose titles contained the characters Minguo, short for Republic of China (ZQB 2007). Given that many of the books previously written on the Republic did not have these characters in their titles, this was a significant number and an indication of how the political climate was more appropriate for the release of such books.

But Republican fever is not the exclusive domain of the publishing industry. As an article in the Guangzhou-based News Weekly pointed out, since the year 2000 a large number of Republican-based period dramas have been screened on Chinese TV to massive popular appeal (XZK 2010). One such drama was called 'The Grand Mansion Gate' based on the real life experience of the family who owned the renowned Chinese pharmaceutical company Tongrentang. Another was entitled 'Like Mist, Like Rain and Like Wind', a love story set in 1930s Shanghai. Some of these dramas followed the conventional CCP view of Republican society as oppressive. Others have adhered to the model set out in 'The Bund' by focusing on the chaos and corruption of the Republican era. But, taken as a whole, the image of Republican society as represented in these dramas has become much more diverse, colourful and modern. Furthermore, viewers are often attracted to the unique elegance of the styles and temperament which subtly combined Chinese traditions with Western influences.

The temperature of the Republican fever rose even higher in 2011, as the PRC marked the centenary of the 1911 Revolution. This saw a significant shift in the focus of public interest from culture towards political issues, as the constitutionalist and democratic ideals of Republican revolutionaries became hot topics for discussion in the media. Reviewing the popular interest in the Republican era, Xie Yong, a professor of Chinese literature at Xiamen University noted that 'initially, public interest in the Republican era focused on education. Later people started taking an interest in culture. In the past few years, the public have also developed a strong interest in [Republican era] politics' (SZTB 2012).

The internet has also been a source for popular support for Republican fever. Douban.com, one of China's largest social networking sites, hosts a number of Republican interest groups, with topics of discussion ranging from history and politics to art and literature. Some of the groups have thousands of members, including an internet group formed in memory of the liberal intellectual Hu Shi (http://www.douban.com/group/hushi/), another called Republican Style (http://www.douban.com/group/roc_style/) and one called Republican Years (http://www.douban.com/group/138111/). Supporters of the Republic are also active on Renren.com and Weibo. They often use the flags of the Republic and the KMT as their profile pictures and have the KMT emblem as part of their online monikers, all of which is in open defiance of official Chinese web censors.

Using the Past to Serve the Present

Economic Rationale

The official toleration of a more relaxed political environment that has allowed Republican fever to emerge can be linked in part to the early post-Mao implementation of economic reform. In an effort to legitimise its radical change in economic direction, the Deng Xiaoping regime actively encouraged PRC historians to embark on a positive reassessment of the Republic's record on the economy. One reason for this was to demonstrate to the bourgeoning number of PRC entrepreneurs that they could learn something useful from the business practices and entrepreneurial acumen of Republican entrepreneurs (Wright 1993, p. 214). Similarly, Marie-Claire Bergere (1989, p. 5) suggested that Chinese leaders were trying to exploit the 'progressive and cosmopolitan force' produced by the bourgeois phenomenon in Republican China, which was 'full of useful lessons' for the new Chinese reform era. Bergere (2000, p. 55) also suggests that PRC entrepreneurs may feel inspired to take up where their Republican predecessors had left off several decades earlier:

> There was a growing feeling that Deng Xiaoping and the reformists were taking up the job that had been left unfinished in 1949. The Republican era was more and more perceived as the starting point of a forceful modernization drive, as a time of economic and cultural innovation and creativity to which contemporaries should turn for inspiration.

According to Li Huaiyin (2013), the party was so keen on encouraging historians to carry out research on the Republican economy that they provided them with generous grants. This was so that they might adopt a modernisation narrative which would prove the historical and logical necessities of the capitalist transformation of the post-Mao Chinese economy and its integration into the world economy.

The role of the Republic era in legitimising Deng's reforms was also reflected in the changes that underwent government policy. For example, when the party decided during the early 1990s to restore Shanghai's former position as an international commercial centre, its semi-colonial, imperialist past suddenly changed from being a political liability to an economic role model to which the rest of the country should aspire. On visiting Shanghai in February 1991 to assess the then Mayor Zhu Rongji's report on the proposed development of Pudong, Deng stated in very clear terms that 'Shanghai used to be a financial centre where currencies could be freely traded. In the future it should be like this, too. If China is to attain an international standing in the field of finance, it must depend on Shanghai first and foremost' (Huang 1994, p. 5). In light of this, as Lu Hanchao (2002) has pointed out, 'nostalgia about pre-1949 Shanghai was tolerated [by the CCP] and to some extent even encouraged and promoted'.

Nationalist Rationale

A second reason for the toleration and sometimes encouragement of a public debate on the Republic brings us back to the CCP's quest for nationalist legitimacy. In the previous chapter we examined the consensual nationalism underpinning the party's positive re-evaluation of the KMT's role in the Second Sino-Japanese War. In particular, we highlighted the wider CCP focus on Chinese national unity and historical commonality with the KMT as part of a positive move towards reunification with Taiwan. The forbearance of a more sympathetic analysis of other aspects of the Republican era and the KMT's record during that era is an integral part of this consensual nationalist approach in which the party has sought to present itself as flexible, tolerant and with the national interest as its core interest.

The emergence of Republican fever also provides an example of the post-Mao utilisation of the Maoist principle of using the past to serve the present. This refers to the expedient interpretation (or reinterpretation) of Chinese history—in this case, the history of the Republic—to serve the political purposes of the incumbent regime—in this case, the legitimation of successive post-Mao regimes. As part of this process, the post-Mao CCP has given its historians more freedom than ever before to discuss the Republic and in an environment when disagreement within the party leadership is tolerated. Consequently, as Jonathan Unger (1993, p. 7) has pointed out, although Chinese thinkers still operate under significant political constraints, they can now choose to serve their preferred patron or "political master" and follow the political perspectives associated with that individual or political faction. Moreover, within these loosened constraints, many scholars have even been able to publish their own views. But as Unger (1993, p. 8) further points out, this use of the past to serve the present is not without risks, potentially acting as a double-edged sword which sometimes undermines CCP-sponsored interpretations of history or sabotages the party's latest political line. This, in turn, can challenge the authority and legitimacy of the CCP, which is exactly what is happening within the context of the Republican era, as we will now see.

RIGHTS AND FREEDOMS DURING THE REPUBLIC

Academic Excellence

One of the most commonplace claims made by those infused with Republican fever is that intellectual scholarship during the Republic was remarkably sophisticated, much more so than previously thought and much more so than PRC levels of scholarship. This point was endorsed by the historian Tang Xiaobing (2008) of Shanghai's East China Normal

University. Writing in the Guangzhou-based Southern Window magazine, Tang identifies numerous best-selling books and periodicals published in recent years about the democratic principles championed by Republican era intellectuals, primarily as a reaction to some of the undemocratic features of contemporary China. In particular, Tang identifies a growing aversion towards China's 'authoritarian political culture and rising tide of consumerism and cynicism'. According to Tang, this also explains why modern-day Chinese intellectuals tend to identify themselves with their liberal-minded counterparts from the Republic (e.g. Hu Shi), whilst left-wing intellectuals associated with the current regime (e.g. the CCP founding members Chen Duxiu and Li Dazhao) are often ignored or even criticised.

This nostalgia for liberal-minded Republican intellectuals is linked to a desire amongst contemporary intellectuals to 'inherit their spiritual legacy' according to Tang, as well as a wish to re-establish the concepts of democracy, freedom and human rights that were openly discussed by many Republican intellectuals and intermittently practised during Republican era. Indeed, the legacy of Republican liberals and their 'unfinished mission of enlightenment' has become the starting point for many modern-day Chinese thinkers who want to resurrect and take forward this enlightenment, in Tang's view. Here again, we can detect implicit criticism of the CCP.

In an article published on the People's Daily website, historian Zhang Lifan (2010) suggested that post-49 Chinese intellectuals are some considerable distance behind their Republican era predecessors in terms of the quality of their scholarship:

> A large number of great masters emerged in the first half of the twentieth century, but during the sixty years of the PRC we have only seen them leave us and no new masters have appeared. It is quite regrettable. The questions we are discussing now have all been discussed by them [Republican intellectuals] over half a century ago. We have still not surpassed them, nor have we reached their intellectual heights.

Sun Yu, Dean of the School of Liberal Arts at the Renmin University and author of the book 'In the Republic' is particularly forthright in contrasting the standards of modern-day intellectuals with their Republican predecessors. According to Sun (2008), 'the academic brilliance created by Republican intellectuals in very difficult times puts present-day intellectuals to shame'. Xie Yong (2010), a specialist in Chinese literature at Xiamen University, asserts that China's most prominent intellectuals either emerged during the Republican era or received their education during that era, especially in the field of humanities and literature when 'it was definitely better before 1949'. Xie's reference to humanities and literature is significant because, although he does not say so directly, Xie is probably taking a swipe at the CCP whose record of suppressing "cultural intellectuals" is ill-famed during the Mao era (e.g. the Anti-Rightist Campaign and the Cultural Revolution) and to a lesser extent in the post-Mao era (e.g. the Campaign Against Spiritual Pollution and the 1986 Campaign Against Bourgeois Liberalisation).

Xie further claims that even in the realm of natural sciences where the CCP has been much less intrusive in the work of intellectuals, life was better in the Republic. Xie cites and agrees with Qian Xuesen, the founder of China's space programme, in saying that China has failed to produce a single high-calibre scientist since 1949. Xie also notes that each of the ethnic Chinese scientists to have won the Nobel Prize were educated during the Republican era, not in the PRC (Xie 2010). Xie's implied criticism of the CCP is unmistakable.

In 2012, the veteran Chinese journalist Deng Kangyan produced a ten-episode documentary series on Republican era intellectuals such as Hu Shi, Cai Yuanpei and Liang Shuming and held related exhibitions in various cities across China that were well attended by members of the public (ZQB 2012). The documentaries heaped praise on the quality of scholarship produced by these thinkers. In an interview with News Weekly, Deng praised them for 'combining the knowledge, learning and science of civilisation of both the East and the West', comparing them with the founding fathers of ancient Chinese philosophy such as Confucius and Mencius. In a subtle dig at their later PRC counterparts, Deng pointedly stated that 'Republican era scholars were undoubtedly the only people in the last millennium who could be compared with the scholars of the Hundred Schools of Thought during the Spring and Autumn period and the Warring States period' (XZK 2012).

The Education System

The admiration for Republican intellectuals has also led to praise for the education system that produced them and this has simultaneously given rise to doubts about the quality of education after 1949. In his article published on the Phoenix TV website entitled 'What We Can Learn from Republican era Education?', Gansu-based writer Xue Linrong (2010) asserts that the contemporary Chinese education system has a long way to go before it can reach the level attained during the Republic. According to Xue, the KMT was genuinely committed to improving education standards, as manifested by the financial investments that it made, such as unusually high pay for teaching staff. Even during the socio-economic chaos that beset China during the Second Sino-Japanese War, free education was available in KMT-controlled areas.

Zhang Lifan broadly agrees with Xue. According to Zhang (2010), there are at least two reasons why so many reputable intellectuals were produced during the Republican era. Firstly, people at that time received a solid educational grounding in both traditional Chinese culture and Western ideas, encouraging a more diverse and open-minded intellectual development. Secondly, the education system was characterised by a free and inclusive academic atmosphere which was highly conducive to scholarly excellence, something not experienced after 1949.

Other commentators praise the large amount of money that KMT spent on education. In an article in the Yangcheng Evening News, the author Liao Baoping suggested that the only sector on which the KMT spent more money than it did on education was on defence during the Second Sino-Japanese War. According to Liao, Chinese scientists who played a key part in developing nuclear bombs and man-made satellites in the post-1949 era, such as Qian Ji, Deng Jiaxian, and the Nobel prize laureates Li Zhengdao and Yang Zhenning, all benefited from KMT-funded education during the Republic. Liao concluded from this that in a country where so much importance was attached to education, even when the state was under grave military threat, 'there was no reason why some great masters could not be produced' .

University Education

Much of the praise for the Republican education system focuses on the quality of its universities. In his article in Southern People Weekly commemorating the centennial of Beijing's Qinghua University (founded towards the very end of the Qing dynasty), Zhang Lifan (2011) insisted that 'the Chinese higher education institutions that rose in the first half of the twentieth century were steeped in European and American influences and enjoyed academic freedom'. Aiming a direct attack on the

CCP, Zhang argued that the same is not true for the post-1949 university sector. According to Zhang, the PRC's university reforms of 1952 were an 'unprecedented educational disaster' mainly because the Western-oriented education system was replaced by the Soviet model which was designed to produce "instruments" that would work for the system at the expense of independent thinking.

The post-Mao era has fared little better, in Zhang's opinion. Although the Soviet model has gradually been phased out with the ascent of Deng Xiaoping, Chinese universities are still under CCP control and are increasingly subject to commercial pressure. Zhang concluded with a rather damning observation that on losing the independent spirit and freedom of thought that characterised the Republican era, China lost the potential to have great thinkers: 'once the independent and free thinking spirit disappeared from the campus, we can only lament that there will be no more great masters after they left us'.

Zhang's positive assessment of the Republican university system is shared by other thinkers. In an article published in Beijing News, Hebei scholar Xie Zhihao (2008) noted that many contemporary Chinese intellectuals, especially education historians, have great respect for the way in which university education flourished in Republican times. Xie, author of several volumes on the history of the Chinese university system, claimed that this was in stark contrast to the widespread disdain for the current university system which is riddled with academic corruption and political and commercial interference: 'contemporary Chinese universities are such a let-down. Republican universities, no matter how unsatisfactory, at least maintained a minimum standard of education'.

During 2010 the Phoenix TV website published an online special report about the post-imperial history of the Chinese university system (FHW 2010). The report was extremely complimentary about Republican universities, describing them as having an 'independent character and free spirit'. By contrast, universities during the Mao era were described as being forced to endure 'collective reformation and ideological unification'. Things were not much better after the death of Mao, according to the report. Due to political and commercial pressure, universities have become 'floating duckweed without roots and instruments without souls'.

For some commentators, idealism and a sense of mission was the key to the success of Republican era universities. Yue Nan, author of a bestselling book about intellectuals during wartime in Republican China said at a seminar in Nanjing in 2013 that Republican era intellectuals were strongly compelled by a sense a responsibility to dedicate themselves to China's cultural and educational development. This, combined with their strong background in both traditional and Western learning and the tolerant academic environment, contributed to the development of 'great masters' in elite universities during the Republic (XHRB 2013).

Primary and Secondary School Education

The quality of primary and to a lesser extent secondary school education during the Republic has also attracted some very positive attention in the PRC. In 2005, the Shanghai Scientific and Technological Literature Publishing House (SSTLPH), which is affiliated to Shanghai Library, reprinted three sets of primary school textbooks that were widely used during the Republican era. They were the Commercial Press National Language Textbooks (1917), the World Press National Language Textbooks (1930) and the Enlightenment National Language Textbooks (1932). Sales were lukewarm for the first three years after the reprint, but saw a sharp rise in 2008 (JHSB 2010). The Enlightenment National Language Textbooks (written by prominent author and publisher Ye Shengtao and illustrated by the painter and cartoonist Feng Zikai) were especially popular with consumers and by the end of 2010 they had been reprinted five times. Two other publishing houses (one illegally) also reprinted these textbooks and sensing the market potential of this genre, numerous other publishers began to reprint Republican primary school textbooks (NFDB 2011).

Zhao Ju (head of the SSTLPH) puts forward two reasons for this increased interest in Republican era primary school textbooks. Firstly, he argues that it reflects the growing public enthusiasm for the teaching of traditional Chinese ethics in plain Chinese, something which was commonplace in the Republic. Secondly and more significantly, it demonstrates the increasing public dissatisfaction with modern-day Chinese textbooks which, according to Zhao, are filled with partisan political content but are deficient in traditional culture and modern civic values (JHSB 2010).

The state-controlled Beijing Daily also acknowledged the increased popularity of Republican era school textbooks, both at primary and secondary school level. An article published in November 2015 noted that over 100 Republican era school textbooks were republished during the previous eight years or so and although the number subsided a little by late 2013, these textbooks continued to be published during 2015 (BJRB 2015).

The widely published and popular historian of Republican China, Fu Guoyong (2010) carried out a detailed review of primary school textbooks published during the Republican era compared to those published in the PRC. Fu found that whilst PRC textbooks have focused heavily on ideology, Republican era schoolchildren were taught about government, elections, citizenship, international law and world affairs. Fu concluded that Republican primary school textbooks are an important spiritual legacy of the Chinese nation and that contemporary Chinese thinkers are duty bound to 'return to that era' and produce quality textbooks for present and future generations.

Republican era rural education has also attracted popular attention in the PRC. In February 2015, the China Youth Daily published a full-page feature on the Simin Primary School, which is located in a rural part of Zhejiang Province. The school is thought to have produced hundreds of distinguished graduates between 1929 and 1949, many of whom later made prominent contributions across a range of disciplines, including culture, education, science, the military, economics and politics. However, after 1949, the numbers of graduates from this school declined markedly. According to Wang Li (2015) the author of the article, the school:

> was like a live specimen showcasing the achievements of rural education during that era. It changed my previous impression that rural education was necessarily 'backward' and that the countryside was necessarily 'isolated' and 'conservative'. Compared with the widespread decline of rural education in contemporary China, it makes people sigh with deep emotion.

Support for the Republican primary education system can even be found within CCP circles, most notably from Hu Deping (2010), son of former General Secretary Hu Yaobang and a senior member of the Chinese People's Political Consultative Conference. Writing in the magazine China Reform, Hu praised Republican era primary school textbooks for openly discussing concepts such as democracy, human rights and freedom. By contrast, Hu observed that 'many of our adults have not received such a basic education. We discarded an education in citizenship that should not have been discarded. This is a profound lesson'.

Media Freedom

Turning to freedom of expression during the Republic, the foreign scholarly consensus has portrayed an era characterised by sweeping restrictions on basic civil rights, particularly in relation to the freedom of publication in the media. Ting Lee-hsia Hsu (1974) has cited a 1930 press law which gave the KMT broad powers of media censorship. This resulted in the forced redaction of sections of newspaper and magazine articles that were critical of the KMT, the subsequent closure of many of these newspapers and magazines and even the arbitrary arrest and sections of execution of some editors and journalists who refused to be silenced by the KMT. Conversely, Frank Dikotter (2008, p. 25) has argued in 'The Age of Openness' that the Republic's media was actually quite autonomous, more so than some European media and much more so than the PRC media: 'even with censorship, often erratic and inconsistent, the opportunities for political expression outside of the ruling party before 1949 by far exceeded anything even remotely possible under emperor or Mao'.

A number of Chinese commentators have posited views that accord with Dikotter's claims. Zhang Ming (2011), a professor of political science at Renmin University, believes that the high point of media freedom in China was from 1911 to 1927 during the experimental period of constitutional democracy known as the Beiyang era. At this time, Zhang notes, there was little if any official censorship of the media. In general, journalists were able to write or say what they wanted. Official censorship of the media did start to creep in after the Northern Expedition brought the KMT to power in 1928 under a single-party authoritarian system of government. In response to this, Zhang continues, some newspapers deliberately left blank spaces where paragraphs or pages had been removed by KMT censors to make it clear to the reading public that some words had been taken out. But this was nothing compared to the censorship that the media has been subjected to since 1949, Zhang argues. In a direct attack on the CCP, Zhang notes that in contrast to the practice of leaving blanks to show that the press had been censored, the press after 1949 'did not even have the courage to leave a blank'.

Notwithstanding the media censorship enforced by the KMT after 1928, Xin Lijian (2011a), president of a private education company called Xinfu Education Group, believes that there was still a considerable degree of media freedom back then. According to Xin, despite its overtly anti-KMT rhetoric, the CCP-controlled Xinhua Daily was still permitted to operate in KMT-controlled areas between 1938 and 1947, relatively free from KMT intervention. This autonomy extended to 'calling on workers and peasants to rise up and overthrow the KMT' and even to 'encouraging the KMT army to turn their guns on the government'. In light of this, Xin praises the media freedom of the Republican era and laments the fact that 'this valuable legacy was cut off in 1949 and has not been reconnected since'.

Other commentators have claimed that Republican era journalists prioritised media freedom and social progress above everything else, thereby setting a good example for their contemporary Chinese counterparts. According to Zhang Chaoyang (2014) of Henan Agricultural University, journalists working during the Republican era 'viewed media freedom as their ideal, followed the principle of truthfulness, persistently defended the position of news and public opinion, facilitated the progress of the whole society and left an indelible mark in China's media history'. Wu Xijuan (2014), a researcher for the journal Today's Mass Media shares this perspective, suggesting that the legacy of Republican era journalists remains relevant today because it 'reminds contemporary media professionals who live in an era full of material desires that they should hold on to their conscience, maintain the spirit of media professionalism and inherit the passion and sense of responsibility of their Republican era predecessors'.

The Democratic Legacy

Closely related to this frank discussion of media freedom during the Republic is a much broader debate about the democratic legacy of the era, particularly the democratic ideas articulated by intellectuals during that period. Once again, there is an overlap with recent Western scholarship. According to Dikotter (2008, p. 7), although China was hardly a model of democracy during the Republican era, 'it was politically more democratic than many comparable regimes in Europe at the time than the People's Republic has been'. Similarly, Orville Schell (2004, p. 118) identifies a 'hidden democratic legacy' during the Republic, boasting a whole host of 'founding father-like intellectuals' such as Liang Qichao, Sun Yat-sen and Hu Shi.

Chinese thinkers are even more enthusiastic about the democratic legacy of the Republic, particularly during the Beiyang era. One such enthusiast is the Tianjin-based media commentator Li Shumin (2005) who argues that Beiyang was unquestionably the most democratic period of China's entire history. In a 2005 article published in the liberal magazine Yanhuang Annuals, Li acknowledged that there were deep flaws in the Beiyang democratic process, but insisted that 'the separation of powers was formally adopted and political power was contained, people's rights and freedoms were to some extent respected and guaranteed, an independent judiciary was established and the freedom of speech was to some extent protected'. For Li, 'the Beiyang era occupies an important position in the history and development of modern democratic politics in China during the twentieth century'. Li concluded pointedly that the CCP has much to learn from this period.

This positive view of Beiyang democracy spread to a much wider public audience, partly (and ironically) because of the release in 2011 of the official PRC film commemorating the 90th anniversary of the founding of the CCP entitled 'Beginning of the Great Revival'. Although the objective of the film was to bolster CCP credibility, what really captured public attention was the depiction of Beiyang as an era of political dynamism. After watching the film, the blogger Yang Hengjun (2011) wrote of his nostalgia at seeing how 'Chinese citizens enjoyed freedom of association, demonstration and protest at a time when many countries in the world were not very free'. Likewise, a widely circulated online post quoted by the artist Chen Danqing at a Republic-themed seminar, commended the film for 'using vivid scenes, brilliant examples and heartwarming details' and listed a number of freedoms enjoyed during the era:

> Newspapers could be owned by private individuals, the media could criticise the government, universities enjoyed academic independence, students could demonstrate in the streets, ordinary people could form secret associations, the police could not arrest people at will, power had boundaries, laws worked, human rights were protected, the poor could make a living and the youth had ideals. (Kuisong et al. 2011)

The political historian Yan Quan of Shanghai University has carried out extensive research in support of the Beiyang parliamentary system. In a newspaper article introducing his book 'Parliamentary Politics in the Early Republic' published in Beijing, Yan (2015) cited several examples of how the Beiyang parliament held the Chinese government to account on defence spending, diplomatic affairs and personnel appointments to high office, agreeing with Hu Shi that the Beiyang parliamentary system was the best model for Chinese democratic politics. Although the parliamentary system had collapsed by 1928, Yan correctly points out that 'during the twentieth century very few countries were able to establish democratic political systems at the first attempt'. As such, the failure of parliamentary politics during Beiyang was not somehow doomed to failure from the outset, but should be more appropriately seen as a 'temporary halt'.

It is not only Beiyang that has received praise from PRC commentators. The single-party system established by Chiang Kai-shek during the Nanjing Decade (1927–1937) has also been more favourably reassessed. Writing in Southern Weekend, the historian Qin Hui (2011) from Qinghua University stated that 'although the Republic did not succeed in building a constitutional political system, it did sow the seeds. The progress of democratisation in contemporary Taiwan cannot be said to have nothing to do with this'. Others have praised Chiang more directly. In a November 2011 blog, Hu Xingdou (2011), an economist at the Beijing Institute of Technology, wrote that 'Chiang Kai-shek was the greatest man in modern China'. As well as leading China to victory in the war against Japan and establishing China's status as a respected international power (see immediately below), Chiang 'formulated a first-rate constitution that was comparable to American and European constitutions'. Xin Lijian has been equally complimentary of Chiang's constitutional achievements, most notably the promulgation of the 1946 Constitution which remains in force today in Taiwan. With this praise has come criticism of the PRC's constitutional record. In an August 2011 blog, Xin (2011b) stated that 'in many respects, our current constitution still falls far behind the 1946 Constitution'. Describing the constitutional process in the PRC as a failure, Xin wrote that 'the civil war overwhelmed the Chinese people's constitutional aspirations and mainland China lost its best opportunity to practise constitutionalism'.

THE REPUBLIC'S NATIONALIST CREDENTIALS

China's International Status

Perhaps the most vociferous claims made by exponents of Republican fever relate to the diplomatic achievements of the Republic and China's rising international status during this time. According to the official PRC view, the encroachment of foreign imperialist powers during the nine-teenth-century Qing Dynasty reduced China to a "semi-colonial soci-ety". It was not until 1949, under the leadership of the CCP, that China was finally liberated from foreign oppression and China's sovereignty was finally restored after the Century of Humiliation. Conspicuous by its absence, however, is any acknowledgement of the diplomatic successes made by the KMT during the Republican period, something which has been duly noted and addressed by Western thinkers. According to William Kirby (1997, p. 458), the Republic 'successfully defended China's status internationally while regaining its full sovereignty inter-nally' as China 'moved from being a ward, if not semi-colony, of the "great powers" to being a great power itself' (Kirby 1997, p. 433).

Some Chinese thinkers are now challenging the PRC orthodoxy. Indeed, such challenges started emerging some years before the emer-gence of Republican fever. Writing in 1997 in Historical Research, one of China's most authoritative history journals, the CASS scholar Wang Jianlang recognised the role played by successive Republican govern-ments in abolishing the unequal treaties that China was forced to sign with imperialist countries under the Qing. According to Wang (1997):

> This was the result of the unrelenting efforts by several generations and several governments, including not only the PRC government which finally completed the feat, but also the Nanjing nationalist government which always claimed to be revolutionaries and the Beijing government which was more ready to make compromises.

In a later journal article, Wang (2012) was even more explicit in praising the Republic's achievements in elevating China's international status:

> Within 30 years, China changed from a country that was repeatedly bul-lied and called a 'quasi-colony' or 'semi-colony' into one of the 'Big Five', which had an important say in world peace and security. It must be said that this was a huge development.

Qin Hui (2012a) an historian at Qinghua University adds his weight to this position. Writing in Southern Weekend, Qin claimed that Republican governments were actually 'quite successful in their diplo-macy and international political activities' and it was during the Republic that China emerged on the world stage. Qin specifically praised the wartime diplomacy of the era when 'China chose the right international alignments and became one of the victorious nations. These were great successes for Republican diplomacy and had a huge significance in enabling China to stand up'. A month later, Qin published another article in Southern Weekend directly refuting the claim that the CCP was solely responsible for freeing China from imperialist subjugation. Qin (2012b) insisted that the unequal treaties were actually abolished in 1942, at which point 'China's sovereignty and independence had undoubtedly been established'.

Another supporter of this position is the veteran liberal economist Mao Yushi (2010) In an article entitled 'When Did the Chinese People Stand Up?' published by the Yanhuang Annuals, Mao suggested that China emerged from its Century of Humiliation not in 1949 as the CCP has consistently maintained, but on defeating Japan in 1945 following which China retrieved Manchuria and Taiwan from Japanese occupation and became a permanent member of the UNSC. According to Mao, 'it was upon winning the War of Resistance that China truly ended its national humiliation and, as Sun Yat-sen had hoped, began to be treated fairly as a nation'. Mao continued, 'this was the goal that the Chinese people had desired after enduring, a 100 years of humiliation'. Mao reiterated this position a few years later:

> Retrieving the three Northeastern provinces and Taiwan, taking back the sovereignty over the foreign concessions in China, becoming a founding member state of the United Nations and a permanent member of the Security Council, eliminating the century-long humiliation, were done by Chiang Kai-shek, and were the results of the Chinese people's arduous eight-year long resistance. (BBC 2015c)

Just as Republican governments have been praised for wresting control of Chinese sovereignty from foreign powers, so questions have been asked about whether the CCP can be credited with any international successes in 1949. In a 2010 speech which was widely circulated on the internet, Qin Hui (2010) asked in a forthright manner 'which unequal treaty was abolished in 1949 and what economic rights, such as customs rights, however big or small, were obtained in 1949? I believe no-one can answer that. Indeed, nothing can be found'. Yan Changhai (2011a), who has also been critical of the party over Yuanmingyuan as we saw in Chap. 3, has accused the CCP of failing to safeguard Chinese sovereignty in the post-revolutionary era. In an August 2011 blog carried by the Phoenix TV website, Yan listed the numerous 'traitorous pacts' that Mao Zedong made with the Soviet Union when signing, amongst other things, the 1950 Treaty of Friendship, Alliance and Mutual Assistance. Under this Treaty, Yan argued, the CCP 'sold out Chinese territories and sovereignty', such as the maintenance of Soviet control over China's Eastern Railway in Manchuria and Port Arthur in Dalian. Referring to the CCP as a collection of vested interest groups, Yan accused them of:

> Pretending that the 'overseas anti-China forces' are the enemy and shamelessly claiming to be the 'protector' of the Chinese nation, so that they can deceive the Chinese people into supporting them. But in fact, they have never really defended the country or the nation. On the contrary, countless facts have proved that they are traitors through and through.

Economic Development

One of the most commonplace official assertions about the Republic relates to the allegedly ruinous state of the Chinese economy. For many years the CCP line held that China's economy under the KMT was in disarray and only after 1949 did China genuinely industrialise its base. Much of the Western scholarship has reinforced this position, but some Western thinkers, most notably Dikotter, have been more positive about the Republic's economic legacy. According to Dikotter (2008, p. 5), economic activity in the Republic was remarkably free from state intervention by comparison with the Qing and CCP regimes. Moreover, the economy 'was steadily growing and thriving, even in the countryside. Human enterprise may have been frustrated by civil war or local officials, but it proliferated, even in the hinterland'. Dikotter (2008, p. 89) also notes that, notwithstanding the slump in the Chinese economy from 1931–1935, it was actually 'much less severe than the Great Depression in the United States and Europe during 1929–1939'.

A number of Chinese commentators have concurred with Dikotter's position. In May 2011, the Guangzhou-based newspaper New Express published a full-page feature rejecting the version of history contained in some PRC school textbooks that the economy was so weak during the Republic that China 'could not even produce matches or nails'. Instead, the article argued that the roots of China's industrialisation can be traced back to the late Qing and that during the Republican period many factories were not only producing matches and nails, but also cars, modern weaponry, gunboats and even aeroplanes (XKB 2011). Yuan Weishi (2010b), who has spoken out on Yuanmingyuan, insists that China enjoyed rapid economic expansion during the Republic, with average industrial growth at 13.8% per annum in the decade after 1912. Xin Lijian (2009b) agrees with this perspective. Describing the Nanjing Decade as a 'golden decade', Xin claims that the KMT oversaw an 'economic miracle' with annual industrial growth rates averaging 9.3% between 1931–1936. From this Xin concludes that 'without the foundation laid during the Nanjing Decade, China could not have won victory in the eight year-long war of resistance against Japan. Therefore, it was a decade that should not be forgotten'.

Some Chinese scholars have suggested that the Republican economy was actually more successful than the PRC economy in certain sectors. Qin Hui (2011) claims that industrial growth prior to 1937 was certainly no slower than industrial growth during the entire Mao era and was significantly faster than in the 20 year period from the Anti-Rightist Campaign to the end of the Cultural Revolution (1957–1976). It was during the Republican era, Qin argues, that China's industrial development and economic growth surpassed that of India, although the large-scale destructive wars that started in 1937 set China back again. Whilst the post-Mao reform era has seen rapid economic expansion, some commentators have attributed this to the undoing of Maoist practices and a resumption of pre-1949 practices. According to Yuan Weishi (2010b), 'what has been achieved in the last 30 years has been nothing more than returning to history'.

The implication from the above is that the Mao era held China back economically and this is certainly the position of Fu Guoying (2009) during an interview he gave to Southern People Weekly about Chinese entrepreneurial traditions. Fu praised the 'exemplary good traditions' created by late Qing and Republican era businesspeople and lamented that, during the 'socialist reform' in the 1950s, 'the whole entrepreneurial class was uprooted, the chain of history was cut off and everything was reset to zero'.

Yan Changhai (2011b) openly commended Chiang Kai-shek's record in modernising China, whilst accusing the CCP of constraining China. In a 2011 blog that was circulated so widely it attracted the attention of then Taiwan President Ma Yingjiu, Yan argued that 'Chiang's defeat was not just his personal failure, but can also be seen as a major setback in the modernisation of China'. In a separate blog directly attacking the CCP, Yan (2011c) insisted that:

> The violent rise of communism was a backward step in the trend towards China's modernisation, which sacrificed large numbers of elite members in both the KMT and the CCP, starved tens of millions of innocent people to death and set back Chinese society by decades. In the end, the mainland had no choice but to abandon Stalinist communism and begin the reform and opening-up process, starting all over again from scratch after wasting several decades.

A REPUBLICAN NATIONAL IDENTITY

Another notable aspect of Republican fever has been the assertion of a Republican national identity, often as an alternative to the PRC's own national identity. The most daring espousal of this was made by a group of netizens called the Union of Chinese Nationalists (UOCN) established in August 2004, but now banned in the PRC (YZZK 2008). The group identified itself with Sun Yat-sen's Three Principles of the People (nationalism, democracy and people's livelihood) and described its supporters as 'spiritual members of the KMT', claiming to have more than 2000 online registered members. The UOCN's nationalist stance was manifested mainly in its opposition to Taiwanese independence which is why the group was also known as the China Pan-Blue Alliance and pledged to 'work with the KMT for national reunification'. The group organised specific events that commemorated the KMT's war effort during the Second Sino-Japanese War and publicly exhibited Republic and KMT flags in cities such as Wuhan and Chongqing.

In addition to its nationalist activities, the UOCN openly advocated a representative form of multiparty democracy and respect for human rights. Some members attempted to stand for election to local People's Congresses and participated in the democracy-oriented Rights Defence Movement, offering help to protesting workers at the Chongqing Special Steel Group. The group also voiced its support for the human rights protection of the Falun Gong and other persecuted religious and minority groups. However, in 2007 the CCP shut down the UOCN, describing it as an 'illegal organisation' (ZXS 2007) following which it is believed that many of UOCN members were jailed.

Despite this crackdown on the UOCN, a Republican identity narrative continues to be propagated online as popular interest in the Republican era has increased and as social networking and microblogging websites have enabled netizens to express themselves more easily. Supporters of the Republic are active on social media sites such as Renren.com and on the microblogging platform Weibo. They often use Republic and KMT flags as their profile pictures and have the KMT emblem as part of their online monikers, all of which is in open defiance of official Chinese web censors.

Proponents of a Republican national identity frequently assert their views on significant dates in China's modern history. The Hong Kong magazine Asia Weekly noted how on 1 October 2011, some people posted images of the Republican flag on the internet and announced that they were boycotting the PRC National Day in preference for the Republic's centennial on 10 October 2011 (YZZK 2011). In 2012, Taibei's China Times newspaper reported that Republican fans in the PRC had celebrated the Republic's National Day by posting the Republican flag on Weibo and disseminating the official national day address of Ma Yingjiu. An unnamed mainland netizen was quoted in jest as saying, 'when I logged onto Weibo, my computer screen was filled with images of a Blue Sky with a White Sun [the KMT emblem], which almost made me think the mainland had been recovered [by the Republic] overnight!' (ZDB 2012).

Backlash Against Republican Fever

Of course, not everyone in China is convinced by the claims made by advocates of Republican fever. Qian Liqun, professor of Chinese literature at Beijing University suggested in January 2011 that the Republican era education system had been evaluated far too positively in recent years and that a Republican myth had emerged in Chinese intellectual circles (XJB 2011). The New Express columnist Yu Ge argued that any civil freedoms enjoyed during the Republic were accidental, due more to an absence of governmental control than the successful implementation of the rule of law. Yu insisted that whilst it is historically inaccurate to demonise the Republican era as the CCP has done, it is just as inaccurate to idolise it.

Perhaps unsurprisingly, the growth of Republican fever has caused particular unease within the ranks of the CCP. One of the most outspoken opponents is Major General Xu Yan (2010b), a professor at the PLA National Defence University in Beijing. In an article carried by the People's Daily website in 2010, Xu described Republican fever as a blatant attempt by 'hostile forces' to undermine the credibility of the CCP and negate the ideological foundations of the PRC:

> In the field of history, some people with treacherous intent have mainly adopted the method of using history to satirise the present. It does not look very blatant, and is sometimes even conducted under the guise of 'fair assessment' or the 'restoration of the objective truth'. But in fact they want to 'cut off the root' of new China which was born out of the Chinese revolution.

Similarly, in a 2010 article in the official journal Red Flag Manuscript, Mei Ninghua (2010) criticised what he described as 'the historical nihilism of Republican fever', a tendency to 'rampantly overturn historical verdicts and sing praise for old forces that have been swept away by history under the cloak of restoring history'. Mei continued:

> Some people, under the pretext of rectifying the bias in some historical conclusions made before the reforms and opening-up, are attempting to 'overturn the verdict' of history that has been confirmed by China's historical development, deliberately distorting history and confusing truth with falsehood; some people even use humanism as an excuse to fabricate historical accounts, to wantonly paint over, edit and make up history and to heap praise on those who have been correctly judged by history as traitors and reactionary rulers.

To coincide with the centenary of the 1911 Revolution and the marked intensification of Republican fever, the International Herald Leader, run by the Xinhua News Agency, claimed that talking about the Republican era had become a fashion and that 'in some authors' works, the Republic seems to have become a synonym for "democracy", "freedom", "morality" and "justice"'. However, the article rejected the increasing tendency to be 'positive about everything to do with the Republic' and argued that Republican fever should be 'moderately cooled down' (GXD 2011).

But in a clear indication that the fever had not cooled down, the Chinese language version of the Global Times, published an inflammatory editorial on 11 October 2012 (the day after Taiwan's National Day) entitled 'It is a Brazen Act of Lying to Embellish the KMT Regime of the Past' (HQSB 2012). The editorial noted that some people in the PRC were insisting that the KMT's defeat in 1949 'was purely a historical accident' attributable to 'the Japanese invasion which "helped the CCP"'. This claim was rejected as 'out-and-out historical falsification'. The editorial continued:

> Today's Chinese rulers need to accept criticisms and supervision, but criticising them by embellishing the KMT government of the past and extolling the little regime in contemporary Taiwan is not just senseless, it is also an insult to history.

Another article by the Global Times (2014c) is critical of what it describes as a 'morbid nostalgia' for the Republic, suggesting that a small number of 'fanatics' are 'fixated on beautifying that historical period, claiming that it was a time of "democracy, freedom and respect for wisdom"'. This is rejected as a little more than 'political tool, to challenge mainstream historical and political views in Chinese mainland'. The article concludes pointedly that:

> The Republic of China cannot be compared to present-day China, be it national comprehensive strength, international status, level of livelihood, and social security. We could miss the songs, sceneries or figures of that period, but praising the then state system and its influence is a humiliation to the whole Chinese history.

As well as challenging Republican fever from a historical perspective, the CCP has resorted to coercion against some proponents. We noted earlier the incarceration of UOCN activists after 2007. This approach has continued. On 31 October 2012, a week before the opening of the Eighteenth National Party Congress, Cao Haibo, a 27-year-old internet cafe manager in Kunming, was jailed for eight years on a charge of subverting state power (Reuters 2012). Prior to his arrest, Cao had organized an online discussion group called the Association for the Rejuvenation of China and posted articles promoting Sun Yat-sen's Three Principles. Cao announced that he was forming a new political party called the Chinese Republican Party, naming himself party chief, an act his wife described as nothing more than self-entertainment (RFICS 2012). Then on 26 November 2012, Wang Dengchao, a police officer in Shenzhen, was sentenced to more than 14 years in prison. Wang's formal charge was corruption, but

Hong Kong and overseas media reports claimed that Wang was incarcerated for his pro-democracy activities. According to the reports, Wang was an advocate of Sun's Three Principles and he openly applied online to join the KMT (YSZ 2013). According to the South China Morning Post, during early 2013 Wang was detained for attempting to organise a 3000-strong pro-democracy rally in a local park to commemorate the anniversary of Sun's death (SCMP 2013).

In addition to high-profile cases such as these, activists who sympathise with the Republic are routinely harassed by the authorities. According to Taiwan's United Daily News, the Chongqing activist Han Liang often walked around in public wearing a T-shirt bearing the Republican era flag. Han would also give impromptu public speeches on history and social injustice in the PRC to mark the anniversaries of major historical events during the Republican era such as the founding of the Republic in 1912 and the Second Sino-Japanese War. Initially Han was detained by the local authorities, but once they realised that this did more harm than good because Han could then lecture his prison inmates, the Chongqing police decided to take him away from home to 'go on holiday' somewhere else on these 'sensitive dates' (LHB 2016).

CHALLENGING CCP LEGITIMACY?

We have seen in this article how the CCP has moved to accommodate a more positive public re-evaluation of the Republican era in recent years, primarily in an attempt to bolster both its economic and nationalist legitimacy. The evidence we have presented, however, suggests that the exact reverse is taking place. Without the traditionally stringent controls on discussions of the Republic, some people have responded in a manner that is not just supportive of the Republic and the KMT but critical of the CCP and the PRC. Some of the accusations that have been levelled are very serious indeed. Some thinkers have expressed dismay and frustration at the current lack of academic, media and democratic freedoms by comparison even to the most autocratic periods of the Republic. There is a growing feeling that after a promising start by the KMT, the Chinese economy took a massive step backwards during the ruinous Mao era and is only now recovering. Perhaps most alarmingly of all for the CCP are the allegations that the KMT did more to safeguard China's sovereignty than the CCP and that since 1949 the party has never really defended the nation.

A number of questions flow from our analysis in this chapter and indeed throughout the whole book. For example, what is the wider significance of the dissenting views on nationalism that we have examined? How representative are such views of public opinion in China and how do we begin to measure this? Also, how do we assess whether or not the CCP is taking these views seriously and do such views have any impact on the decisions taken by the party. Our concluding chapter will seek to address these questions.

REFERENCES

BBC. (2015c, September 9). *Zhongguo Xuezhe Mao Yushi Jiaru Kangzhan Lishi Lunzhan Yin Reyi* [Chinese scholar Mao Yushi joins debate on war history sparking heated discussions]. Retrieved from http://www.bbc.com/zhongwen/simp/china/2015/09/150909_wwii_china_history_cpc_kmt.

Bergere, M-C. (1989). *The golden age of the Chinese bourgeoisie 1911–1937*. Cambridge: Cambridge University Press.

Bergere, M.-C. (2000). Civil society and urban change in Republican China. In F. Wakeman & R. Edmonds (Eds.), *Reappraising Republican China*. Oxford: Oxford University Press.

BJRB. (2015, November 12). *Lao Keben Zhe Shinian Renao Guo Chenji Guo* [In the past decade, old textbooks experienced both boom and quiet]. *Beijing Ribao* [Beijing Daily]. Retrieved from http://bjrb.bjd.com.cn/html/2015-11/12/content_327120.htm.

Chen, H. (2011, September 16). *Mao Xiansheng Zhidao Wo Xie Lunwen* [Mr Mao's guidance in the writing of my thesis]. *Minguo Chunqiu* [Spring and Autumn Republic]. Retrieved from http://img.mgl1912.com/news/2011/09/16/5d670bb93259eaf40132705bc933006d.html.

Dikotter, F. (2008). *The age of openness: China before Mao*. Berkeley: University of California Press.

FHW. (2010, February 3). *Daxue Zhidao* [Dao of university education]. *Fenghuang Wang* [Phoenix TV Website]. Retrieved from http://news.ifeng.com/history/special/daxuezhidao.

Fu, G. (2009). *Zhongguo Qiyejia de Bentu Chuantong zai Nali?* [Where are the local traditions of Chinese entrepreneurs?]. *Nanfang Renwu Zhoukan* [Southern People Weekly]. Retrieved from http://news.sina.com.cn/c/sd/2009-04-16/092817621498.shtml.

Fu, G. (2010, November 16). *Xiaoxue Yuwen Keben: Yige Minzu de Wenming Dixian* [Primary School Textbooks: The Civic Minimum Standard of a Nation]. Retrieved from http://blog.sina.com.cn/s/blog_48fe46d90100mya7.html?tj=1.

Global Times. (2014c, October 10). Double ten day fervor humiliates history. *Global Times English Edition*. Retrieved from http://www.globaltimes.cn/content/885475.shtml.

GXD. (2011, November 21). *Minguo Huaijiu Re Xuyao Shidu Liangwen* [Republican nostalgia fever should be moderately cooled down]. *Guoji Xianqu Daobao* [International Herald Leader]. Retrieved from http://news.xinhuanet.com/herald/2011-11/21/c_131252850.htm.

HQSB. (2012, October 11). *Meihua Dangnian Guomindang Zhengquan shi Gongran Sahuang* [It is a brazen act of lying to embellish the KMT regime of the past]. *Huanqiu Shibao* [Global Times]. Retrieved from http://opinion.huanqiu.com/opinion_china/2012-10/3177957.html.

Hsu, T L-h. (1974). *Government control of the press in modern China, 1900–1949*. Cambridge, MA: Harvard University Press.

Hu, D. (2010, March 1). *Women Reng Xuyao Xianzheng Qimeng* [We still need constitutional enlightenment]. *Zhongguo Gaige* [China Reform]. Retrieved from http://magazine.caixin.com/2012-02-29/100361976.html.

Hu, X. (2011, November 13). *Jiang Jieshi shi Zhongguo Xiandai Diyi Weiren* [Chiang Kai-shek was the greatest man in modern China]. Retrieved from http://blog.ifeng.com/article/14671895.html.

Huang, Q. (1994, January 14). *Deng Xiaoping Kaifang Kaifa Sixiang yu Shanghai Pudong Kaifa* [Deng Xiaoping's thought on opening-up and development and the development of Shanghai's Pudong]. *Renmin Ribao* [People's Daily], p. 5.

JHSB. (2010, November 30). *Minguo Lao Jiaocai 70 Nian Hou Turan Zouhong* [Republican era old textbooks suddenly become popular after 70 years]. *Jinghua Shibao* [Beijing Times]. Retrieved from http://epaper.jinghua.cn/html/2010-11/30/content_607739.htm.

JJGB. (2010, August 17). *Yang Tianshi: Zhuiqiu Xinshi he Xinzhi* [Yang Tianshi: Pursuing true history and new knowledge]. *Jingji Guanchabao* [Economic Observer]. Retrieved from http://www.eeo.com.cn/observer/grls/2010/08/16/178319_2.shtml.

Kirby, W. (1997). The internationalization of China: Foreign relations at home and abroad in the Republican era. *China Quarterly, 150*, 375–394.

LHB. (2016, June 1). *Ta Ai Chuan Zhonghua Minguo Guoqi Zhuang, Liusi Qian bei Gong An Dai Chuyou* [He likes wearing the Republic of China flag T-shirt, was taken on holiday by police before 4 June]. *Lianhe Bao* [United Daily News]. Retrieved from http://a.udn.com/focus/2016/06/01/21831/index.html.

Li, S. (2005). *Beiyang Junfa Shiqi Weihe Ye You Minzhu?* [Why was there also democracy during the Beiyang warlord era?]. *Yanhuang Chunqiu* [Yanhuang Annals], 4. Retrieved from http://www.yhcqw.com/html/cqb/2008/416/0841612634HDAJE13763198GIICG1H6913.html.

Li, H. (2013). *Reinventing modern China: Imagination and authenticity in Chinese historical writing.* Honolulu: University of Hawaii Press.

Lu, H. (2002). Nostalgia for the future: The resurgence of an alienated culture in China. *Pacific Affairs, 75*(2), 169–186.

Mackerras, C. (1984). Party consolidation and the attack of spiritual pollution. *Australian Journal of Chinese Affairs, 11,* 175–185.

Mao, Y. (2010, November 1). *Zhongguo Renmin shi Shenme Shihou Zhan Qilai de?* [When did the Chinese people stand up?]. *Zhongguo Gaige Luntan* [China Reform Website]. Retrieved from http://www.yhcqw.com/html/yjy/2011/88/1188112576HJA684673862KAD7E6AK64K.html.

Mei, N. (2010, May 21). *Qizhi Xianming de Fandui Lishi Xuwu Zhuyi: Xinhai Geming Bainian Huimou* [Take a clear-cut stand against historical nihilism: Reviewing the 100 years since the 1911 revolution]. *Hongqi Wengao* [Red Flag Manuscript]. Retrieved from http://www.qstheory.cn/hqwg/2010/201010/201005/t20100521_30690.htm.

NFDB. (2011, October 18). *Minguo Lao Keben: Xiufu Women Ceng You de Zhipu he Youmei* [Republican old textbooks: Restore the simplicity and elegance we once had]. *Nanfang Dushibao* [Southern Metropolis Daily]. Retrieved from http://gcontent.oeeee.com/9/d1/9d15081dc54bcd9d/Blog/c93/1ff07d.html.

Qin, H. (2010). *Zhongguo Lishi de Yanxu yu Duanlie* [The continuity and fracture of Chinese history]. *Chuanzhixing Xueshu Tongxun* [Academic Newsletter of the Transition Institute] 8. Retrieved from http://blog.caijing.com.cn/expert_article-151381-12685-2.shtml.

Qin, H. (2011, November 4). *Minguo Lishi de Di Er Mianxiang: Luanshi zhong de Xiandaihua Bufa* [Various aspects of republican history: Steps towards modernisation in a chaotic world]. *Nanfang Zhoumo* [Southern Weekend]. Retrieved from http://www.infzm.com/content/64459.

Qin, H. (2012a, January 19). *Minzu Zhuyi de Shijian: Zhongguo Zhan Qilai le de Licheng* [The practice of nationalism: The process of China standing up]. *Nanfang Zhoumo* [Southern Weekend]. Retrieved from http://www.infzm.com/content/67757/1.

Qin, H. (2012b, February 23). *Ban Zhimindi Zhuangtai de Zhongjie: Zaitan Zhongguo Zhan Qilai le de Licheng* [The end of semi-colonial status: More on the process of China standing up]. *Nanfang Zhoumo* [Southern Weekend]. Retrieved from http://www.infzm.com/content/71090.

RFICS. (2012, November 2). *Cao Haibo bei Zhongpan Banian, Dalu "Minxian Pai" Huyu Ma Yingjiu Guanzhu* [Cao Haibo receives heavy eight year sentence, mainland 'Republican constitutionalism faction' Calls for Ma Yingjiu to pay attention]. *Radio France International Chinese Service.* Retrieved from http://tinyurl.com/c77nr3x.

Reuters. (2012, November 1). *China dissident gets eight years for subversion ahead of congress.* Retrieved from http://www.reuters.com/article/

us-china-subversion-idUSBRE8A008J20121101?feedType=RSS&feedName
=worldNews&utm_source=feedburner&utm_medium=email&utm_campaig
n=Feed%3A+Reuters%2FworldNews+(Reuters+World+News).

Saich, T. (1984). Party consolidation and spiritual pollution in the People's
Republic of China. *Communist Affairs, 3*(3), 283–289.

Schell, O. (2004). China's hidden democratic legacy. *Foreign Affairs, 83*(4),
116–124.

SCMP. (2013, January 4). Policeman Wang Dengchao jailed for graft after
calling for democracy. *South China Morning Post*. Retrieved from http://
www.scmp.com/news/china/article/1119383/policeman-wang-
dengchao-jailed-graft-after-calling-democracy.

Sun, Y. (2008). *Zai Minguo* [In the Republic]. Zhejiang: Zhejiang Renmin
Chubanshe. Retrieved from http://cul.cn.yahoo.com/ypen/20101222/
135469.html/.

SZTB. (2012, September 24). *"Minguo Re" Yao Fang Meihua Huo Shenhua
Qingxiang* ['Republican fever' Should not be embellished or sanctified].
Shenzhen Tequ Bao [Shenzhen Special Zone Daily]. Retrieved from http://
sztqb.sznews.com/html/2012-09/24/content_2217436.htm.

Tang, X. (2008, May 5). *Toushi Minguo Zhishi Fenzi Shi Re* [The essence of
Republican era intellectual history fever]. *Nanfengchuang Zazhi* [Southern
Window Magazine]. Retrieved from http://www.nfcmag.com/articles/769.

Taylor, J. (2009). Discovering a Nationalist heritage in present-day Taiwan.
China Heritage Quarterly, 17. Retrieved from http://www.chinaheritage-
quarterly.org/articles.php?searchterm=017_taiwan.inc&issue=017.

Unger, J. (Ed.). (1993). *Using the past to serve the present: Historiography and
politics in contemporary China*. New York: M.E. Sharpe.

Wang, J. (1997). *Zhongguo Feichu bu Pingdeng Tiaoyue de Lishi Kaocha*
[A review of the history of China's abolition of the unequal treaties]. *Lishi
Yanjiu* [Historical Research], 5. Retrieved from http://www.cssn.cn/
news/446779.htm.

Wang, C. (2008). Recent research on Republican Chinese history. *Journal of
Modern Chinese History, 2*(1), 89–97.

Wang, Z. (2012). *Never forget national humiliation: Historical memory in
Chinese politics and foreign relations*. New York: Columbia University Press.

Wang, L. (2015, February 25). *Yige Jiazu Shuxie de Jiaoyu Shi* [Educational history
written by a Clan]. *Zhongguo Qingnian Bao* [China Youth Daily]. Retrieved from
http://zqb.cyol.com/html/2015-02/25/nw.D110000zgqnb_20150225_1-12.
htm.

Wright, T. (1993). The spiritual heritage of Chinese capitalism: Recent trends
in the historiography of Chinese enterprise management. In J. Unger (Ed.),
*Using the past to serve the present: Historiography and politics in contemporary
China* (pp. 205–238). New York: M.E. Sharpe.

Wu, X. (2014, May 19). *Minguo Shiqi Baoren Qunxiang Lueying* [A glimpse of Republican era newspaper professionals]. *Jin Chuanmei* [Today's Mass Media]. Retrieved from http://media.people.com.cn/n/2014/0519/c384775-25036281.html.

XGL. (2008, April 29). *Jiefeng Minguo* [Unwrapping the Republic]. *Xianfeng Guojia Lishi* [Xianfeng National History]. Retrieved from http://news.sohu.com/20080429/n256586295_3.shtml.

XHRB. (2013, March 26). *Zuojia Yue Nan Tan Dashi Kuifa: Daoshi Cheng Laoban Nanyi Chengjiu Dashi* [Author Yue Nan discusses the lack of great masters: Supervisors have become bosses, making it hard to develop great masters]. *Xinhua Ribao* [Xinhua Daily]. Retrieved from http://news.xinhuanet.com/book/2013-03/27/c_124507722.htm.

Xie, Z. (2008, January 23). *Ganhuai Minguo Daxue de Dixian* [Thoughts on the minimum standard of Republican universities]. *Xinjing Bao* [Beijing News]. Retrieved from http://epaper.bjnews.com.cn/html/2008-01/23/content_148272.htm?div=-1.

Xie, Y. (2010, September 30). *Chen Danqing vs Xie Yong: Jintian Weishenme Tanlun Minguo?* [Chen Danqing vs Xie Yong: Why discuss the Republic today?]. *Fenghuang Wang* [Phoenix TV Network]. Retrieved from http://book.ifeng.com/yeneizixun/special/lixiangguo2010/pinglun/detail_2010_09/30/2678282_0.shtml.

Xin, L. (2009b, November 2). *Jiemi Minguo Huangjin Shinian* [Revealing the secrets of the golden decade during the republican era]. Retrieved from http://blog.ifeng.com/article/3390095.html.

Xin, Li. (2011a). *Zhonghua Minguo Shi [History of the Republic of China].* Beijing: Zhonghua Shuju.

Xin, L. (2011a, November 2). *Minguo Shiqi de Xinwen Ziyou* [Media freedom in the Republican era]. Retrieved from http://blog.163.com/xin_lijian/blog/static/467715702013048574529/.

Xin, L. (2011b, August 30). *Liang'an Tongyi Jichu: 1946 Xianfa* [The foundation of cross-strait reunification: The 1946 constitution]. Retrieved from http://blog.ifeng.com/article/13251191.html.

XJB. (2011, January 22). *Minguo Re: Xinhai Nian Li Weilu Yuedu* [Republican fever: Fireside reading during the Xinhai year]. *Xinjing Bao* [Beijing News]. Retrieved from http://epaper.bjnews.com.cn/html/2011-01/22/content_194383.htm?div=-1.

XKB. (2011, May 8). *Lishi Jizai Zhong de Jiu Zhongguo: Feiji Dapao Dou Neng Zao* [Old China according to historical records: Even aeroplanes and big cannons were being built]. *Xinkuai Bao* [New Express], B:02.

Xu, Y. (2010b, March 31). *Didui Shili Yulun Gongshi shi Chang Wu Xiaoyan Zhanzheng* [Public opinion and the psychological offensives of the hostile forces are like a war without gun smoke]. *Renmin Wang*

[People's Network]. Retrieved from http://military.people.com.cn/GB/1076/52984/11265783.html.

Xue, L. (2010, February 3). *Minguo Jiaoyu Gei Women de Jiejan* [What we can learn from Republican era education]. *Fenghuang Wang* [Phoenix TV Website]. Retrieved from http://news.ifeng.com/history/special/minguodaxue/201002/0203_9438_1536047.shtml.

XZK. (2010, September 1). *Niandai Ju: Zui Ju Yule Xiaoguo de Dianshiju Leixing* [Period dramas: The most entertaining television genre]. *Xin Zhoukan* [New Weekly]. Retrieved from http://www.neweekly.com.cn/index/newsview.php?id=2853.

XZK. (2012, June 1). *Naxie Beiying, Rang Women Faxian Minzu de Zhengmian - Deng Kangyan he Ta de "Xiansheng Men"* [Those receding figures, let us discover the positive image of the nation - Deng Kangyan and his 'Xiansheng']. *Xin Zhoukan* [New Weekly]. Retrieved from http://www.neweekly.com.cn/newsview.php?id=4243.

Yan, C. (2011a, August 22). *Minguo Zhihou Zhongguo Jiujing Diushi Duoshao Tudi?* [How much land did China lose after the republic?]. *Fenghuang Wang* [Phoenix TV Network]. Retrieved from http://www.21ccom.net/articles/lsjd/lsjj/article_2011012729027.html.

Yan, C. (2011b, April 8). *Ma Yingjiu Cheng Lejian Dalu Gaibian dui Jiang Jieshi Pingjia* [Ma Yingjiu says he is glad to see the mainland changing its assessment of Chiang Kai-shek]. *Zhongguo Pinglun Xinwen Wang* [China Review News]. Retrieved from http://www.chinareviewnews.com/doc/1016/5/3/8/101653801.html?coluid=46&kindid=0&docid=101653801&mdate=0408170131.

Yan, C. (2011c, January 27). *Zhongguo Ren Weishenme Yao Huainian Jiang Jieshi?* [Why do Chinese people miss Chiang Kai-shek?]. *Gongshi Wang* [21.ccom.net]. Retrieved from http://www.21ccom.net/articles/lsjd/lsjj/article_2011012729027.html.

Yan, Q. (2015, January 31). *Chongfan Lishi Xianchang, Minguo Guohui de Xin Renzhi* [Returning to the scene of history: A new understanding of the Republican parliament]. *Xin Jing Bao* [Beijing News]. Retrieved from http://epaper.bjnews.com.cn/html/2015-01/31/content_560140.htm.

Yang, H. (2011, June 17). *Kan Jian Dang Wei Ye de Yidian Ganxiang* [Some Thoughts After Watching the Beginning of the Great Revival]. Retrieved from http://yanghengjunbk.blog.163.com/blog/static/45964193201151710048322/.

Yang, K., Chen, D. et al. (2011, September 13). *Minguo shi Lishi Haishi Xianshi?* [Is the Republic history or reality?]. Retrieved from http://book.ifeng.com/yeneizixun/special/lixiangguo2010/pinglun/detail_2010_09/30/2678282_0.shtml.

Yang, S. (1989). *Jiang Jieshi Zhuan [A Biography of Chiang Kai-shek]*. Beijing: Tuanjie Chubanshe.

Yang, T. (2003). *Guanyu Zhuozhu "Jiangshi Midang yu Jiang Jieshi Zhenxiang" de Yanzheng* [Solemn statement about my book 'Chiang's secret files and the truth about Chiang Kai-shek']. *Huanghuagang* [Huanghuagang Magazine], 4. Retrieved from http://www.huanghuagang.org/hhgMagazine/issue07/big5/22.htm.

Ye, H. (2010, November 1). *Qingchu Jingshen Wuran zhong de Yang Shubiao Shijian* [The Yang Shubiao incident in the campaign against spiritual pollution]. *Shuzhai* [Shuzai Magazine]. Retrieved from http://epaper.gmw.cn/sz/html/2010-11/01/nw.D110000sz_20101101_5-04.htm?div=-1.

Yuan, W. (2010b, November 1). *Mao Yushi Deng: Huishou Xinhai Bainian* [Mao Yushi et al: Reviewing the century since the 1911 revolution]. *Zhongguo Gaige Luntan* [China Reform Website]. Retrieved from http://www.chinareform.org.cn/explore/explore/201011/t20101101_49427.htm.

YSZ. (2013, March 11). *Pushuo Mili de Wang Dengchao An: Fantan Haishi Zhengzhi Pohai?* [The confusing case of Wang Dengchao: Anti-corruption or political persecution?]. *Yangguang Shiwu Zhoukan* [iSun Affairs]. Retrieved from http://www.isunaffairs.com/?p=15175.

YZZK. (2008, May 11). *Jiang Xun, Xunhui Sun Zhongshan: Zhongguo Fanlan Lianmeng Xianxiang Beihou* [Finding Sun Yat-sen: Behind the UOCN phenomenon]. *Yazhou Zhoukan* [Asia Weekly]. Retrieved from http://www.yzzk.com/cfm/Content_Archive.cfm?Channel=ac&Path=3522178462/18ae1a.cfm.

YZZK. (2011, October 16). *Zhongguo Dalu "Minguo Rechao" Beihou* [Behind 'Republican fever' in mainland China]. *Yazhou Zhoukan* [Asia Weekly]. Retrieved from http://www.21ccom.net/articles/sxpl/pl/article_2011100746514.html.

ZDB. (2012, October 11). *"'Guofen'" Qing Shuang Shi, Wo Guoqi Weibo Piaoyang'* ['Republican fans' Celebrate double ten, our national flag waves on Weibo]. *Zhongshi Dianzi Bao* [China Times]. Retrieved from http://news.chinatimes.com/mainland/11050506/112012101100164.html.

Zhang, L. (2010, December 14). *Minguo Sixiangjie de Lishi Gaodu* [The historical height of the Republican era intellectual circle]. *Renmin Wang* [People's Network]. Retrieved from http://history.people.com.cn/GB/205396/13481134.html.

Zhang, L. (2011, January 1). *Dakai Xinmen Zhonghua Minguo shi zai Dalu Jian Cheng Xianxue* [Republican Chinese history gradually becomes a prominent subject in the mainland]. *Zhongyang Tongxunshe* [CNA Newsworld]. Retrieved from http://www.cna.com.tw/Topic/NewsWorld/7-1/201209120007-1.aspx.

Zhang, L. (2011, May 16). *Minguo Xuemai: Bainian Qinghua de Lingyi Daotong* [The Republican legacy: Another intellectual origin of the one hundred year-old Qinghua university]. *Nanfang Renwu Zhoukan* [Southern People Weekly]. Retrieved from http://nf.nfdaily.cn/nfrwzk/content/2011-05/16/content_24145893.htm.

Zhang, M. (2011, January 11). *Minguo Shiqi de Meiti* [The media in the Republican era]. Retrieved from http://zhangmingbk.blog.163.com/blog/static/11195065220110194439563.

Zhang, C. (2014, October 29). *Wei Jin Fenggu he Minguo Baoren* [The Wei-Jin character and Republican era newspaper men]. *Xinwen Aihao Zhe* [Lover of Journalism]. Retrieved from http://media.people.com.cn/n/2014/1029/c390220-25932987.html.

Zhou, W. (2008, January 20). *Minguo Re Zhixia de Weiyan Dayi* [The hidden meaning behind republican fever]. *Nanfang Dushi Bao* [Southern Metropolis Daily]. Retrieved from http://epaper.oeeee.com/C/html/2008-01/20/content_370686.htm.

ZQB. (2007, October 24). *Xuxu Shishi Minguo Re* [Republican fever: Appearance or reality]. *Zhongguo Qingnian Bao* [China Youth Daily]. Retrieved from http://zqb.cyol.com/content/2007-10/24/content_1931011.htm.

ZQB. (2012, September 12). *Xunzhao Xiansheng* [Finding 'Xiansheng;]. *Zhongguo Qingnian Bao* [China Youth Daily]. Retrieved from http://zqb.cyol.com/html/2012-09/12/nw.D110000zgqnb_20120912_1-12.htm.

ZXS. (2007, April 25). *Guotaiban: Suowei Zhongguo Fanlan Lianmeng Zuzhi Bingwei Jing Hefa Dengji* [State council Taiwan affairs office: The so-called Union of Chinese Nationalists Organisation is not legally registered]. *China News Service*. Retrieved from http://www.chinanews.com/tw/dlyw/news/2007/04-25/923552.shtml.

CHAPTER 7

Conclusion

One of the underlying objectives of this book has been to identify the political risks for the CCP that are inherent in relaxing the parameters of permissible debate on subjects of historical sensitivity. Through our four case studies, we have seen how the toleration and sometimes active encouragement of public discussion and engagement on the Yuanmingyuan incident, Japanese imperialism and the legacy of the KMT and the Republic have, at times, elicited strong public criticism of the CCP. Although the content of such criticism is varied, one the most commonplace accusations is the failure of the party to protect Chinese national interests in the modern era. This is ironic because the original purpose behind allowing greater public debate on these topics was to bolster the party's nationalist standing as the founder of a nation that is free from imperialist subjugation and hurtling inexorably towards super-power status.

HISTORY REPEATING ITSELF?

This pattern of political relaxation followed by public censure is not new in the PRC. One of the most infamous precedents was the 1957 Hundred Flowers Campaign which granted unconstrained freedom of speech to Chinese intellectuals (MacFarquhar 1974). Prior to this, intellectual expression had been governed by the directives of the 1942 Yanan Conference on Art and Literature (MacDougall 1980) and the Thought Reform Campaign of 1951–1952 which restricted the

© The Author(s) 2017   185
R. Weatherley and Q. Zhang, *History and Nationalist Legitimacy
in Contemporary China*, DOI 10.1057/978-1-137-47947-1_7

articulation of views to those that served the party's socialist aims and objectives. During the Hundred Flowers, these strictures were suspended as scholars from a broad range of disciplines were invited to opine on the successes and failures of the first few years of the PRC. Many of the views enunciated were not directly critical of the CCP, including proposals for institutional reform such as an independent upper chamber of the National People's Congress and amendments to the state constitution that would clarify the hitherto ambiguous legal position of intellectuals. However, some perspectives were deemed wholly unacceptable, particularly the widely held assertion that local party cadres were inept and obstructive in their daily work. As Teiwes (1997, p. 80) has explained, in making this assertion, 'intellectuals were in effect raising the issue of the Party's competence to guide China in the new period of socialist construction'.

As is well-documented, excessive criticism of the party during the Hundred Flowers precipitated the abandonment of the campaign within just six weeks of its launch. This was followed by the implementation of the Anti-Rightist Campaign, a brutal crackdown on over half a million party and non-party intellectuals who had dared to express an opinion. Many were labelled with the ominous tag "rightist" and sent to the countryside for a protracted period of "re-education through manual labour".

Another cycle of political relaxation followed by public criticism and then repression occurred in the late 1970s when Deng Xiaoping was attempting to wrest power from Mao's chosen successor, Hua Guofeng. The lapse in party control that arose during this brief power struggle saw the emergence of a literary genre known scar literature or the literature of the wounded (Barme 1997). The focus of this popular new movement was on the personal suffering and social damage inflicted during the Maoist heyday of political campaigns and mass purges, as characterised by the Cultural Revolution. This served to besmirch the political reputation of Hua Guofeng who remained committed to the ill-fated campaign in the post-Mao era.

The Democracy Wall movement also emerged at around this time, mainly comprising members of China's urban workforce. As the CCP elite gathered for the landmark Third Plenum of the Eleventh Central Committee in December 1978 which eventually established Deng as China's new paramount leader, posters began appearing on walls in central Beijing expressing candid opinions on a number of sensitive political issues. The Cultural Revolution was again the focal point and Mao was criticised in name for masterminding the campaign and for lending his support to the Gang of Four. Other posters derided the redundant policies of Hua's so-called "whateverist" faction, depicting Hua as a puppet controlled by Mao from beyond the grave. Another popular theme was the optimism symbolised by Zhou Enlai's Four Modernisations theory, with several posters endorsing Deng Xiaoping as Zhou's natural successor (Brodsgaard 1981; Goodman 1981).

Yet, in a manner reminiscent of the Hundred Flowers, some Democracy Wall activists went beyond the boundaries of acceptable expression. Having highlighted the traumas of the past, they began to explore contemporary injustices such as continued abuses of human rights and the absence of a system of democracy. A number of unofficial political discussion groups and journals were established, including Exploration edited by the Beijing electrician Wei Jingsheng. Wei advocated a "fifth modernisation"—multiparty democracy—which led to the rapid suppression of Democracy Wall by the ascendant Deng Xiaoping and Wei's arrest and incarceration.

THE LINK TO LEGITIMACY

In terms of encouraging public debate for the purposes of political legitimacy, there is a clear link between the rationale behind the Hundred Flowers and the rationale for initiating some of the discussions on nationalism that we have looked at in this book. Although some scholars argue quite plausibly that the Hundred Flowers was nothing more than a trap by Mao to weed out enemies of the state (Han 1976; Teufel-Dreyer 1996; Lynch 1998), another theory is that Mao launched the campaign because he was genuinely concerned about the waning legitimacy of the CCP (Weatherley 2006). Since early 1956, Mao had been expressing grave concerns that the CCP was drifting away from its revolutionary roots as the party of the people towards a party governing in its own interests, a ruling class rather than a ruling party. This was especially apparent at the local level where party cadres had become complacent about the responsibilities of office and were more concerned with the perks of bureaucratic life. At a decision-making level, Mao identified signs of ideological revisionism as reflected by the increasing reliance on trained technocrats and managers, rather than the views of the ordinary people or the guidance offered by Marxism (so-called "expert" over "red").

Public discontent with the party was manifested by a series of demonstrations that took place during 1956–1957, particularly in Shanghai (Perry 1994). Although some of the unrest was due to food shortages and job insecurity, there was anger at the increasingly bureaucratic workstyle of party cadres and enterprise managers and the reluctance of those in charge to listen to the ideas of others. Events in Eastern Europe during 1956 persuaded Mao that open rebellion was a real possibility in China, with both Poland and Hungary witnessing spontaneous uprisings against inept communist rule. Mao also drew parallels to the situation in the Soviet Union where the ruling party had descended into an unwieldy and unaccountable ruling elite governed by a man (Nikita Khrushchev) who was intent on reforming the economy along market-based lines and aligning Soviet foreign policy with the USA.

The perceived need to haul the party back into line with its original revolutionary principles before it was too late pushed Mao towards the Hundred Flowers. But in typical Maoist fashion, internal reform was not to be carried out "in-house" by designated party work teams with an interest in going easy on the party. If the party was to restore its credibility amongst the population, it had to be rectified in public even if some opinions would be hard to swallow. This is why much of the intellectual input at this time was conducted at officially organised conferences and large public forums. In the end, of course, the Hundred Flowers did not proceed in the way that Mao had anticipated or desired and this forced him to jettison the campaign altogether.

Unlike the Hundred Flowers Campaign, the scar literature and Democracy Wall movements were not actively initiated for the purposes of political legitimation. However, both movements did serve to legitimise Deng in his quest to overthrow Hua Guofeng and certainly Deng was very willing to let this happen until they had exhausted this purpose. As noted already, the subject matter of scar literature, particularly the trauma of the Cultural Revolution, was impliedly critical of Hua who continued to expound the wisdom of the campaign when most of the rest of the country had turned its back on the whole harrowing period. This, in turn, bolstered Deng's image as someone who could bring a new era of economic growth and political stability after decades of turmoil and uncertainty. Democracy Wall was even more critical of Hua as a symbol of discredited past, whilst Deng was heralded as the great hope for the future, at least during the initial stages, prior to his authorised crackdown on the movement.

The CCP's response to dissenting public views on nationalism has been nothing like as punitive as it was in the aftermath of Democracy Wall or the Hundred Flowers. But it would be a mistake to assume that the party does not take such views seriously. We noted in Chap. 5 the outraged official response to allegedly exaggerated media claims about the role of the KMT during the Second Sino-Japanese War. This was accompanied by attempts to assert that the CCP led the charge against Japan and this, in turn, stood them in good stead to defeat the KMT during the civil war. A similarly incensed backlash has emerged against Republican fever, with accusations that proponents of the fever are pedalling historical untruths in an attempt to undermine the authority of the CCP. Moreover, as noted in Chap. 6, UOCN activists have been incarcerated by the CCP and other Republican era sympathisers have been harassed, detained or arrested.

THE DISSENT IN CONTEXT

So what is the wider significance of the dissenting views on nationalism that we have examined in this book? For example, to what extent are these views representative of wider public opinion in China? This is a difficult question to answer because accurately gauging public opinion is not easy in any country, let alone one which is governed under a single-party authoritarian system. But we should at least try to form a perspective to see if we can make sense of these views. Taking a step back for a moment, it seems likely that if a random selection of adults in China were polled about their opinion on, for example, the Yuanmingyuan incident or the legacy of Japanese imperialism, then most of them would probably not default to a condemnation of the party's alleged failure to protect Chinese national interests in the contemporary era. It may not even occur to them to do so. More likely there would be a condemnation of foreign imperialism, which is to be expected given the considerable propaganda efforts expended by the CCP in keeping the Century of Humiliation firmly in China's political consciousness. However, if we were to narrow our survey to those people who have specifically expressed views on Yuanmingyuan and Japan without being asked by pollsters to do so—in other words, the scholars, journalists and politically motivated netizens identified in the introductory chapter—then a significant percentage do indeed take a position that is critical of the CCP's alleged lack of nationalism and failings in other areas such as socio-economic security. This is also true in relation to the Republican era and the legacy of the KMT during that era, including during the Second Sino-Japanese War.

One way that we can usefully identify this preponderance (or at least abundance) of dissenting views is to examine the stream of online comments made in direct response to statements on national issues published in the official Chinese media. For example, we noted in Chap. 4 that many of the responses to the 2016 People's Daily Weibo posting criticising Japanese human rights abuses in China accused the party of committing similar abuses against the Chinese people. Likewise, the 2015 Global Times posting which denunciated Tokyo for brainwashing its people after references to comfort women were deleted from a Japanese history textbook, saw many netizens accuse the CCP of also rewriting much of China's history to suit its own political purposes. One netizen even claimed that the CCP only pretended to care about Japan's whitewashing of history when actually it was much more concerned about safeguarding Sino-Japanese economic ties.

Notwithstanding the above, we should not forget that there is still plenty of public support for the nationalist causes championed by the CCP. Take Yuanmingyuan as an example, from our experience (and that of friends and colleagues to whom we have spoken and academic works we have read (Bickers 2011)), the predominant feeling amongst visitors to Yuanmingyuan is a combination of solemnity at the sight of the ruins, combined with bitterness (not always restrained) towards those responsible for reducing the site to ruins. The same is true of Japan. Thousands have expressed their animosity (often violently) towards this former imperialist power during the numerous state-authorised anti-Japanese public demonstrations that have taken place in China over the last ten years or so. More generally, Anne-Marie Brady (2009) has noted the success with which the CCP orchestrated a very visible nationalistic public support base during the prelude to the Beijing Olympics as part of what she refers to as a 'campaign of mass distraction' away from pressing domestic issues such as environmental degradation, corruption and inequality. This impassioned advocacy of Chinese nationalism was mirrored overseas by the high number of Chinese students who reacted angrily to the pro-Tibetan claims of the seemingly anti-Chinese international media (Nyiri et al. 2010). With all of these in mind, it is certainly not our contention that the party is somehow tottering on the brink of collapse and capitulation amidst a rising critical mass of condemnatory voices over Yuanmingyuan, Japan and the Republic, far from it.

That being said, the CCP is clearly taking the views of its detractors very seriously indeed, which suggests in itself that such views are deemed to be sufficiently widespread to warrant concern. In other words, they are not just the views of a handful of internet trolls, as one delegate suggested during a recent conference that one of the authors attended on Chinese nationalism and religion. Official concern about the party's critics is manifested by the often indignant comments published in the Chinese media in response to such critics. We saw in Chap. 5 the outraged assertion made by Xu Yan of the PLA National Defence University that KMT sympathisers were guilty of over-romanticising the achievements of the KMT during the Second Sino-Japanese War in a flagrant attempt to undermine the legitimacy of the CCP. Similarly, the People's Network website sought to confront public criticism over the ten year incarceration of KMT war hero Wu Dehou by attributing the length of this sentence to his alleged treachery during the civil war. Exponents of Republican fever have also come in for criticism from the media, as we saw in Chap. 6, including accusations of 'historical falsification', 'brazen acts of lying' and 'morbid nostalgia' for the Republican era. In addition, the speed with which anti-Japanese demonstrations are shut down when they threaten to turn against the party shows that there are serious concerns about nationalist-related dissent. We saw this in Chap. 4, particularly regarding the 2010 and 2012 demonstrations that took place across the country.

Another important point to make is that the public discord on issues of national concern is unlikely to subside in light of the growing number of people in China with access to the internet. China's "blogosphere" comprises hundreds of millions of participants and with its increasingly vociferous demands for a more assertive China, the internet is fast becoming what Edward Friedman (2010, p. 25) has described as 'the de facto voice of the people'. Added to this is the increasing sophistication with which the netizens (often using barely decipherable blog names) are employing to side-step the efforts of official online censors (Mackinnon 2008). This is despite the tighter controls being applied by Xi Jinping following his insistence that state-run media outlets 'are propaganda fronts and must have the party as their family name' (Guardian 2016).

We have also seen how some critics of the CCP have not limited themselves to just one issue of national contention examined in this book. For example, the writer Yan Changhai has reproached the party for allegedly whitewashing the history of the Yuanmingyuan incident and further claimed that the KMT and Chiang Kai-shek were more successful at modernising China than the CCP has been. The historian Yuan Weishi has made similar allegations of historical whitewashing over Yuanmingyuan, as well as arguing that the success of the post-Mao PRC economy is little more than a return to the glory days of the Republican-era economy. Another historian Zhang Lifan has rebuked the CCP for its neglect of KMT war veterans (especially from the Burma Expeditionary Force) and praised the Republic for the superiority of its higher education system and the standard of intellectual output, compared to the PRC. The economist Mao Yushi believes the CCP deliberately avoided conflict with the Japanese to save themselves for the civil war and has claimed that it was the KMT that ended the Century of Humiliation in 1945, not the CCP in 1949 so there is plenty of overlap here.

Perhaps the final point to look at in this section is whether or not the dissent that the CCP has faced on issues of national sensitivity is having any impact on how the party behaves or on the decisions that it takes. To a certain extent, we have already answered this question by noting the media backlash against KMT and Republican era sympathisers. The shutting down of anti-Japanese demonstrations that threaten to become anti-party is another example. We also saw in Chap. 3 how the mounting internet opposition to a proposal to invite an Anglo-French delegation to attend the 150th anniversary of the Yuanmingyuan incident forced the Beijing authorities to jettison the idea. Likewise, we noted the online campaign which succeeded in getting a Starbucks café removed from inside the Forbidden City by using, amongst other things, evocative imagery of the Yuanmingyuan ruins to rally support for the cause. So the party is clearly sensitive to dissenting views and is prepared to act in accordance with these views, at least sometimes.

TEXTBOOK LEGITIMACY

By way of some concluding observations on the relationship between history and regime legitimation in the PRC, it is worth noting that the CCP is not limiting its focus to China's recent past as a tool for enhancing its historical legitimacy. The search goes much further back than the late Qing Dynasty and the Republican era. An (as yet) unpublished study of Chinese middle-school history textbooks by Weatherley and Magee

(2017) shows how post-49 sinified concepts of good governance are presented as part of a seamless continuum that goes back over the centuries and beyond. For example, the prioritisation of the people's welfare and material needs which is described as epitomising the rule of Mao, Deng and Jiang Zemin is also described as epitomising the rule of the historically revered sage kings Yao (2357–2256 BC), Shun (2255–2205 BC) and Yu (2200–2100 BC) whom Mencius claimed were the founding fathers of Benevolent Government. Similar traits are accorded to virtuous emperors such as Tang Xuanzong (685–762) known for his contribution to culture, education and economic prosperity (RJC 2013b, p. 12) and Sui Wendi (569–618) who ensured that his subjects were provided with enough food to last for more than 50 years (RJC 2013b, p. 3). The conduct of the CCP as a whole is also portrayed as benevolent, particularly its considerate treatment of "wrongdoers". Examples include generously sparing the life of Chiang Kai-shek following his arrest in December 1936 and allowing former landlords adequate land to subsist in the post-land reform era, notwithstanding their previously exploitative status (RJC 2013d, p. 12).

Other features of Benevolent Government which go back over the centuries but are also characteristic of CCP leaders include self-sacrifice and plain-living. Just as Emperor Han Wendi (202–157 BC) is applauded for refusing to exploit his position of power by showering himself in luxury, declining the opportunity for an expensive burial tomb to be built for him and 'wearing clothes that were rather coarse' (RJC 2013a, p. 67), so Mao is praised for enduring extreme poverty and adversity for the sake of liberating China from imperialism and 'commanding the whole operation [the Long March] from dugout caves' (RJC 2013c, p. 91). Similarly, just as Emperor Tang Taizong (598–649) is acknowledged for refusing to spend money on renovating his palace even though 'it was chilly and damp and was making him unwell' (RJC 2013b, p. 8), so Deng is commended as someone who selflessly forfeited all personal luxury for the good of the people. One chapter in Volume 1 of the Grade 8 history textbook which focuses on modern-era history, contains an anecdote in which Deng repeatedly refused to burden a frail rickshaw driver sent to collect him as he arrived in Nanjing with the Red Army having taken the city from KMT troops in 1945. Instead, Deng helped the old man push the rickshaw until Deng was 'dripping with sweat'(RJC 2013c, p. 97). Even Sun Yat-sen comes in for praise when he is described as preventing an elderly merchant from kowtowing to him in accordance with ancient custom, insisting that 'the president is no more than a servant of the people and must work for all the people of the nation' (RJC 2013c, p. 107).

Intrinsically related to the Mencian theory of Benevolent Government is another Mencian theory known as the People as the Basis of the State. This held that a ruler's legitimacy derived not from coercive laws or strong military control, but from the will of the people. In order to understand the will of the people and obtain their consent, a virtuous ruler listened to their wishes and governed accordingly. These traits are attributed to Han, Sui and the two Tangs mentioned above in the pre-modern-era history textbooks, but were glaringly absent from the tyrannical rule of Emperor Jin Huidi (259–307) who is criticised for ignoring the needs of his people, asking glibly 'if the people have no rice to eat, why not let them eat porridge?' (RJC 2013a, p. 108).

Mao is depicted as continuing with the practise of the people as the basis of the state following his decision to attend peace talks with Chiang Kai-shek in 1945, despite the likelihood that the talks were a trap. This decision is praised as representing the wishes of the citizens of Chongqing where the talks took place (RJC 2013c, p. 89). We are also told how the people 'urgently sought land reform', an aspiration to which the CCP were receptive and duly implemented (RJC 2013d, p. 12). CCP leaders are presented as striving hard for closer relations with Hong Kong (Deng) and Taiwan (Jiang), which was 'the fervent wish of all Chinese people' (RJC 2013d, p. 69). These issues are presented in a highly subjective and emotive manner by using expressions such as 'the pain of being separated from one's own flesh and blood' and featuring pictures of heartfelt reunions between relatives from the PRC and Hong Kong or Taiwan (RJC 2013c, p. 67).

In September 2015, Politburo Standing Committee member Wang Qishan broke a long-standing taboo by openly discussing the question of CCP legitimacy at a high-profile international conference in Beijing. During his speech Wang insisted that the source of party legitimacy derived from history (Epoch Times 2015). Since then, there have been increasing suggestions that the CCP is preparing a white paper on Chinese models of good governance along similar lines to its white papers on Chinese human rights, socialist democracy and law. From what we have seen in this book it seems likely that such a concept will be firmly rooted in China's past.

REFERENCES

Barme, G. (1997). History for the masses. In J. Unger (Ed.), *Using the past to serve the present: Historiography and politics in contemporary China*. New York: M. E. Sharpe.

Bickers, R. (2011). China's age of fragility. *History Today*. Retrieved from http://www.historytoday.com/robert-bickers/chinas-age-fragility.

Brady, A.-M. (2009). The Beijing Olympics as a campaign of mass distraction. *China Quarterly, 197*, 1–24.

Brodsgaard, K. (1981). The democracy movement in China, 1978–79: Opposition movements, wall poster campaigns and underground journals. *Asian Survey, 21*(7), 747–774.

Epoch Times. (2015, September 14). *Why is the Chinese communist party discussing its legitimacy?* Retrieved from http://www.theepochtimes.com/n3/1751948-why-is-the-chinese-communist-party-discussing-its-legitimacy/.

Friedman, T. (2010, September 15). Power to the (Blogging) people. *New York Times*, 25.

Goodman, D. (1981). *Beijing street voices: The poetry and politics of China's democracy movement*. London: Marion Boyars.

Guardian. (2016, February 19). *Xi Jinping asks for 'Absolute loyalty' from Chinese state media*. Retrieved from https://www.theguardian.com/world/2016/feb/19/xi-jinping-tours-chinas-top-state-media-outlets-to-boost-loyalty.

Han, S. (1976). *The wind in the tower: Mao Tse-Tung and the Chinese revolution, 1949–1976*. London: Cape.

Lynch, M. (1998). *The People's Republic of China since 1949*. London: Hodder and Stoughton.

MacDougall, B. (1980). *Mao Zedong's talks at the Yanan conference on literature and art: A translation of the 1943 text with commentary*. Ann Arbor: University of Michigan Press.

MacFarquhar, R. (1974). *The hundred flowers campaign and the Chinese intellectuals*. London: Octagon Press.

MacKinnon, R. (2008). Flatter world and thicker walls? Blogs, censorship and civic discourse in China. *Public Choice, 134*(1–2), 31–46.

Nyiri, P., Zhang, J., & Varrall, M. (2010). China's cosmopolitan nationalists: 'Heroes and traitors' of the 2008 Olympics. *China Journal, 63*, 25–55.

Perry, E. (1994). Shanghai's strike wave of 1957. *China Quarterly, 137*, 1–27.

RJC. (2013a). *Zhongguo Lishi Qinianji Shangce* (Chinese History, Grade 7, Vol. 1). Beijing: Renmin Jiaoyu Chubanshe.

RJC. (2013b). *Zhongguo Lishi Qinianji Xiace* (Chinese history, Grade 7, Vol. 2). Beijing: Renmin Jiaoyu Chubanshe.

RJC. (2013c). *Zhongguo Lishi Banianji Shangce* (Chinese History, Grade 8, Vol. 1). Beijing: Renmin Jiaoyu Chubanshe.

RJC. (2013d). *Zhongguo Lishi Banianji Xiace* (Chinese History, Grade 8, Vol. 2). Beijing: Renmin Jiaoyu Chubanshe.

Teiwes, F. (1997). The establishment and consolidation of the new regime: 1949–57. In R. MacFarquhar (Ed.), *The politics of China: The eras of Mao and Deng*. Cambridge: Cambridge University Press.

Teufel-Dreyer, J. (1996). *China's political system: Modernization and Tradition*. London: Macmillan.

Weatherley, R. (2006). *Politics in China since 1949: Legitimizing authoritarian regimes*. London: Routledge.

Weatherley, R., & Magee, C. (2017). *Using the past to legitimise the present: The portrayal of good governance in Chinese history textbooks* (Unpublished paper).

INDEX

© The Editor(s) (if applicable) and The Author(s) 2017
R. Weatherley and Q. Zhang, *History and Nationalist Legitimacy in Contemporary China*, DOI 10.1057/978-1-137-47947-1